THE
MOVIE
LOVER'S
GUIDE
TO
HOLLYWOOD

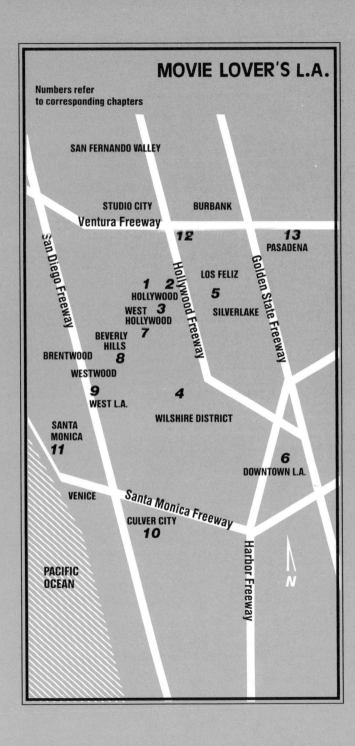

THE
MOVIE
LOVER'S
GUIDE
TO
HOLLYWOOD

RICHARD ALLEMAN

HARPER COLOPHON BOOKS

Harper & Row, Publishers
New York, Cambridge, Philadelphia, San Francisco
London, Mexico City, São Paulo, Singapore, Sydney

*For my mother, Kaye Alleman,
who first took me to the movies—
and my father, R. B. Alleman,
who first took me to California*

Photo credits start on page 327.

FIRST EDITION

*Designer: Abigail Sturges
Maps: Stanley Moss*

Library of Congress Cataloging in Publication Data

Alleman, Richard.
    The movie lover's guide to Hollywood.

    (Harper colophon books; CN/1262)
    Includes index.
    1. Moving-picture industry—California—Hollywood—
Miscellanea. I. Title.
PN1993.85.A44   1985   384'.8'0979494   84-48574
ISBN 0-06-091262-6 (pbk.)

85 86 87 88 89 MPC 10 9 8 7 6 5 4 3 2 1

CONTENTS

In Search of Hollywood / *vi*

1 Hollywood: Birth of a Boulevard / *1*

2 Hollywood: Beyond the Boulevard / *41*

3 Hollywood: The Factory Town / *63*

4 The Wilshire District:
Main Street, L.A. / *83*

5 Los Feliz/Silverlake/Echo Park:
The Original "Hollywood" / *107*

6 Downtown Los Angeles:
The Source / *129*

7 West Hollywood: Border Town / *157*

8 Beverly Hills:
Hollywood's Golden Ghetto / *183*
Star Houses / *201*

9 The Fashionable Westside:
Between Beverly Hills and Santa
Monica / *211*

10 Culver City: "The Heart of
Screenland" / *229*

11 Venice/Santa Monica/Malibu:
Hollywood by the Sea / *243*

12 San Fernando Valley:
The Big Spread / *267*

13 Pasadena/Glendale:
Another Country / *293*

Index / *307*

IN SEARCH OF HOLLYWOOD

Hollywood. Just the name brings to mind magical images. Images of wealth, fame, power, and, above all, the capacity to dream. But many people who travel to Los Angeles looking for the Hollywood of their fantasies go home disappointed. A couple of hours spent on the Universal Studios tour, a few minutes checking out the footprints in front of the Chinese Theater on Hollywood Boulevard, perhaps a swing through Beverly Hills to glimpse some movie-star mansions—that, for most visitors, is Hollywood. So much for dreams.

Nevertheless, extraordinary things happened here. In this very real town, some of the screen's greatest movies were made and its greatest stars lived, often in splendor. The legacy of those films, those stars, those *days* has played a major and undeniable role in the history of Los Angeles. In this book, I have attempted to track down that legacy—not just within the boundaries of Hollywood proper, but in all of the many communities that together make up the city of L.A. When I began this project, people constantly told me that there was nothing left, that everything had been torn down. At times, they were right—a great deal *is* gone. But one of the most pleasant surprises was discovering just how many landmarks and historic sites still exist. Equally encouraging was the number of individuals and groups I encountered in Los Angeles who are committed to preservation and who are willing to do battle with the mightiest developers to save a cherished piece of their city's past: monuments to the magical decades when the motion picture industry first arrived, then flourished in Los Angeles.

The vestiges of L.A.'s movie past are not always easy to find nor instantly recognizable. They're there, though: historic studios of the silent-picture era, lavish 1920s movie palaces, secret locations of some of the world's most famous films. The trick is knowing where to look—and knowing what to look for. I hope that *The Movie Lover's Guide to Hollywood* can help uncover the hidden Hollywood that's lurking between today's parking lots and high rises.

Since Los Angeles is so vast and encompasses so many communities, I have organized *The Movie Lover's Guide to Hollywood* into specific L.A. geographic areas. I have begun with the city of Hollywood—not because this was where the first films were made, but because it is the community that the world associates with the movies and with television; it is also where most people wish to start sightseeing. Surprisingly, Hollywood proper is covered in just three chapters, which points out that the "real Hollywood" was—and is—all of Los Angeles, including many neighborhoods that most visitors to Southern California have never heard of, much less thought of visiting.

To help orient sightseers, a numbered site map precedes each chapter. Not necessarily drawn to scale, these maps are included to show landmarks and sites as conveniently as possible. It is therefore recommended that serious sightseers consult an additional map—such as Rand McNally's Los Angeles—especially when setting out for some of the more distant areas covered in this book. Let me also stress that many of the places described here are private property. Needless to say, the privacy of the owners and tenants in all such instances should be respected. A final note: Since a car is a necessity for almost all sightseeing in Los Angeles, why not travel in one of those glamorous vintage models that can be rented only in L.A.? Lights, camera, action— and drive carefully!

━━━━━━━━

There are many people to thank: my editor Larry Ashmead for his faith in me and in this project; my agent Paula Diamond for making it happen; Roy Barnitt for sharing his knowledge and his library; many mentors from Lois McClarin Revi to Leo Lerman, Despina Messinesi, Kathleen Madden, Lorraine Davis, and Amy Gross; researchers James Ursini, Marvin Brown, and Mark Decker in Los Angeles, Martin Walsh and David Parsons in New York; plus all of the people who gave me their time, their stories, their help—J. Evan Miller, Richard Mouck, Mark Wanamaker, Richard Adkins, Brian Moore, Christy Johnson McAvoy, Jim Heimann, Tony Duquette, Eleanore Phillips Colt, Paul Henreid, Billy Wilder, Maude Chasen, Eleanor Boardman, Buddy Rogers, Jean Howard, Blanche Sweet, Buleah Roth, Leonard Spigelgass, Carroll Carroll, Hutton Wilkinson, Sister Anne Marie, Ronald Haver, David Shephard, Robert Gitt, Forrest J. Ackerman, Walter O'Conner, Frank McCarthy, Tom Glover Sr., Monique Moss, Patricia Yoemans, George Solt, Banks Montgomery, George Montgomery, Walter Scott, Joseph D'Amore, Geri Jean Wilson, Richard Ware, Rhea Smith, Catherine Sawelson, Ruthann Leher, Mitch Tuchman, Evelyn Letizia, Bill Campbell, Alice Allen, Fran Offenhauser, Planeria Price, Barbara Boyd, Paul Lindenschmid, Herb Steinberg, Nickolai Ursin, Fritz Hawkes, Brian Harper, Dick Mason, Debbie Westerlund, Neil Hartley, Karen Huston, Robert Rubin, M. E. Rich, and Al LaValley.

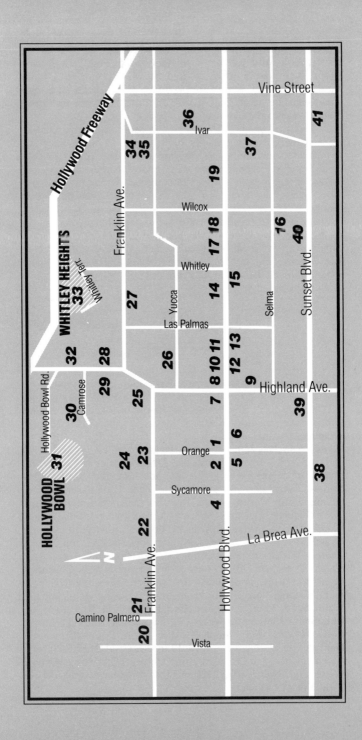

HOLLYWOOD: BIRTH OF A BOULEVARD

Hollywood Boulevard—
from Vista to Vine

Marilyn Monroe in
The Seven Year Itch;
*the gown is on view
at the Hollywood Museum
on Hollywood Boulevard*

A HUNDRED years ago, there were ranches, bean fields, orange and lemon groves. It was a peaceful, pastoral place—a far cry from the big city called Los Angeles that was growing up just five miles to the east. Staunchly conservative, early Hollywood was populated mostly with transplanted Midwesterners. One of these, a prohibitionist from Kansas named Harvey Wilcox, had some 120 acres that his wife had christened "Hollywood" because, so the story goes, she had met a woman on a train who had spoken in glowing terms of her summer home back East called Hollywood. When the Wilcoxes subdivided their property in 1887, the name that Mrs. Wilcox had so fancied was printed on the map advertising the lots the couple was selling for $150 an acre. Hollywood—like so many communities in Southern California—was officially launched as a real-estate development.

The little community grew steadily, if not dramatically. By 1897, Hollywood had its own post office—and in 1903, the citizens (the population was now close to 700) voted to be incorporated as a city. One of the first things that the officials of this new little "sixth-class" city did was to enact a number of ordinances. Ranging from limiting the hours that billiard and pool rooms could be open to banning the sale of alcoholic beverages, Hollywood's laws reflected the essential conservatism of its citizens. When this same citizenry voted in 1910 to have Hollywood annexed by the city of Los Angeles, it wasn't out of any particular fondness for their worldly metropolitan neighbor; it was simply because they needed L.A.'s water and its sewer system.

Needless to say, when the first movie folk came to town in 1911, these Eastern outsiders of questionable moral character were not exactly welcomed with open arms by Hollywood's straight-laced locals. Indeed, in many ways, this Midwestern town that happened to be in Southern California was, except for the weather, an unlikely candidate to become the movie capital of the world.

Ironically, it was Hollywood's conservatism that was indirectly responsible for its first movie studio. For when the Nestor Film Corporation of Bayonne, New Jersey, arrived in California in 1911, they found a perfect setup for moviemaking in a former Hollywood tavern that had fallen on hard times owing to the town's tough liquor laws. Besides its main building, the tavern property offered a barn and corral that would facilitate the shooting of Westerns, a group of small outbuildings that could be used as dressing rooms, and a bungalow for additional office space. Within a matter of days, the Nestor company was turning out three films a week.

Universal's founder, Carl Laemmle, was next on the Hollywood scene. Arriving in 1912, Laemmle set up his first West Coast base of operations on the southwest corner of Gower and Sunset, just across the street from the Nestor company. A year later, a trio made up of Cecil B. DeMille, Jesse Lasky, and Samuel

Hollywood Boulevard, ca. 1930

Goldfish (later Goldwyn) also settled in Hollywood and shot the town's first feature-length film, *The Squaw Man,* based in a barn at the corner of Vine and Selma. As more and more movie people came, the locals who had at first looked down on the film business suddenly found themselves either directly in its employ or involved in businesses—from rooming houses to restaurants—that were making money thanks to motion pictures. In a word, Hollywood was booming—and the little Midwestern town in Southern California would never be the same again. By 1920, Hollywood's population had grown to 36,000. By the end of the twenties it would swell to over 150,000.

As Hollywood made the transition from village to metropolis, a great boulevard kept pace with the new city's growth and came to be the center of its wealth, power, and glory. Edged with movie palaces, stately hotels, glamorous restaurants and apartment buildings, Hollywood Boulevard was, in its heyday, one of the most dazzling thoroughfares in the country. Today, after several decades of decline, this once great main street has lost much of its luster and parts of it are home to punks, prostitutes, and panhandlers. Recently, however, things have started looking up. There's a new spirit in Hollywood these days—one that recognizes the importance of preserving the past. Nowhere is that spirit more evident than along Hollywood Boulevard, where various restoration projects are bringing back some of the street's long-gone splendor and where preservationists have been fighting to get it declared a National Historic Register District.

Surprisingly, owing to the Boulevard's long period of decline in the sixties and seventies, many of its architecturally distinguished buildings and theaters have not been torn down, as they have been in more thriving areas of Los Angeles. The result? Hollywood Boulevard remains a remarkably intact, if somewhat down-at-heels, monument to the city that will always be considered the motion picture capital of the world. In some instances, it takes a bit of looking—among the fast-food places, the tattoo parlors, and the t-shirt shops—to find the history that's lurking here; but it's here just the same. And since so much of this history is connected with the film industry and its larger-than-life personalities, Hollywood Boulevard and its surrounding streets is a logical first stop in the movie lover's Los Angeles odyssey. Here, a look at Hollywood's main street and its fabulous sights—plus trips to some fascinating places beyond the Boulevard—from the legendary barn where *The Squaw Man* was shot back in 1913 to a secret enclave of Mediterranean houses where silent films stars once lived. Welcome to Hollywood—as it is now . . . and as it was then.

NOTE: *For convenient sightseeing, this first chapter covers Hollywood Boulevard and vicinity from Vista to Vine Street. The best way to tour the Boulevard proper is on foot. To reach some of the places mentioned on Franklin Avenue and in the hills behind the Boulevard, a car is suggested.*

1. CHINESE THEATER
6925 Hollywood Boulevard

Built by Hollywood developer C. R. Toberman for theater magnate Sid Grauman in 1927, the Chinese is the most famous movie house in the world. Reason? No other picture palace has ever come up with a publicity stunt as clever or successful as Grauman's hallowed ritual of having movie stars leave their footprints, handprints, and autographs in the cement of the theater's forecourt.

There are all sorts of stories as to how the custom began. The one most widely told is that silent screen star Norma

Grauman's Chinese Theater, ca. 1930

Talmadge stopped by to tour the construction site and accidently stepped into some wet cement as she was getting out of her car. A more likely version has Sid Grauman clumping into the cement himself—which prompted him to call Douglas Fairbanks, Mary Pickford, and Norma Talmadge to come celebrate the construction of his new theater with their much more glamorous prints and signatures. As these proved too faint upon drying, Grauman invited the same three stars as well as a few reporters back for an "official" ceremony. It made good copy—and the rest is history.

Since that time, close to 170 persons have cemented their fame in the forecourt of what is now Mann's Chinese Theater. (Mann Theaters took over the Chinese in 1972.) Not all of the celebs have left just hand- and footprints: silent film star Harold Lloyd's trademark glasses have been immortalized in cement here—as have Sonja Henie's iceskates, John Wayne's fist, Harpo Marx's harp, Jimmy Durante's nose, and one of Betty Grable's "million-dollar" gams. Besides real-live people, Edgar Bergen's dummy Charlie McCarthy has signed in at the Chinese; Roy Rogers' horse Trigger and Gene Autry's Champion have left hoofprints; *Star Wars* robots Artoo-Detoo and See-Threepio have rolled over the cement into immortality; and in 1984 Donald Duck marked his fiftieth birthday at the Chinese with two giant webbed-foot prints.

While movie lovers might question the credibility of some of the "legends" represented in the forecourt of the Chinese, few star presences have ever been publicly protested. A notable exception was Ali MacGraw's December 1972 appearance at the theater, which was met by a small band of chanting and placard-carrying demonstrators who felt Ms. MacGraw's lackluster four-film (at the time) career did not merit the full concrete treatment. (So far, though, Ms. MacGraw's prints are still in place and have not wound up in the basement of the theater—the fate, according to insiders, that a number of the prints of lesser legends is said to have met. According to these same sources, the basement of the Chinese is literally loaded with concrete slabs of long-forgotten stars.)

There is more to the mystique of the Chinese Theater than footprints. Throughout its history, the theater has been one of Hollywood's premier premiere places—ever since Cecil B. De-Mille's *King of Kings* opened the Chinese on May 27, 1927. Besides premieres, the theater hosted the Academy Awards in 1944, 1945, and 1946. The Chinese is also a treasure of movie theater architecture and interior design—and happily, this 1920s movie palace has retained almost all of its original splendor. Outside, the theater's façade is a wonderful fantasy of a Chinese temple—complete with huge stone guard dogs at either side of the entrance and a sky-soaring pagoda roof. Inside, the lavish lobby and auditorium have marvelous murals, columns, Oriental vases, furniture, and carpets. It's the kind of theater they just don't build anymore—and simply being here makes up for anything that might be up on the screen.

NOTE: *Anyone planning on seeing a film at the Chinese should make sure the film they want to see is playing at the original theater and not at one of its two modern "companion" theaters that were added next door in 1979.*

2.   GARDEN COURT APARTMENTS SITE
7021 Hollywood Boulevard

When it opened in 1919, a red carpet was stretched all the way from its grand portico to what was then a very dusty Hollywood Boulevard—and society and movie people arrived in limousines to gaze at the most opulent apartment building Hollywood had ever seen. Suites came furnished with Oriental carpets, baby grand pianos, oil paintings—and early tenants included Louis B. Mayer, Lillian Gish, Mae Murray, Wallace Beery, John Gilbert, John Barrymore.

When they started to tear it down in early 1984, the Garden Court was a nightmare popularly known as "Hotel Hell," a frightening fenced-in wreck inhabited by vagrants and punk squatters. Toward the end, the Garden Court was constantly in the news and in many ways became a symbol of the dilemma faced by a resurgent Hollywood. On one side, there were the developers who believed that the best way to revitalize Hollywood was to tear down dilapidated buildings like the Garden Court to make way for lucrative high-rise office towers. On the other side were the preservationists who had tried desperately to save the Garden Court and who felt that Hollywood's future was best served by preserving what was left of its past.

As court battles raged, there was a brief hopeful moment when it looked as though a more enlightened developer might

Garden Court Apartments, 1931

buy the Garden Court with the idea of incorporating its stately Beaux-Arts façade into the design of a larger office/entertainment complex in much the same way as New York City's landmark Villiard mansions were integrated into the design of the Helmsley Palace Hotel a few years ago. But that never happened and the wrecking crews arrived in early 1984. Instead of making quick work of yet another monument of Hollywood's history, they ripped off the building's ornamental façade—then, suddenly, all work stopped and the building stood in limbo for another year until it was totally demolished in early 1985. The encouraging sign in all of this is that the Garden Court went down fighting. Ten years ago, there would have been no fight at all.

3. THE WALK OF FAME

If Grauman's Chinese Theater could achieve world renown through its sidewalk—why not all of Hollywood? At least, that's what a group of local business people thought in the late 1950s when they concocted a scheme to turn the sidewalks of a deteriorating Hollywood Boulevard into a vast star-studded terrazzo commemorating the legends of the film, radio, television, and recording industries. Shop and property owners along the proposed walkway were asked to contribute $85 per front foot and $1,250,000 was raised to begin the project which initially immortalized 1550 personalities and continues to do so at the rate of about fifteen stars a year. (There are now close to 1800.)

In 1983, theater was added as a fifth Walk of Fame category and Mickey Rooney, then starring in *Sugar Babies* at Hollywood's Pantages Theater, became the first "two-star" celebrity when he was given his second star for his recent theatrical success. To make the Walk of Fame, new stars must be sponsored—by their agents, their producers, their fan clubs, or a local business—for the honor. A special committee of the Hollywood Chamber of

Marguerite De La Motte's
Walk of Fame star

Commerce then votes on the candidate's acceptability, taking into consideration professional as well as humanitarian achievements. If the candidate fulfills the requirements, the sponsor pays approximately $3000 to cover the cost of the star as well as the ceremony that goes along with it.

The Walk of Fame extends for some three and a half miles from Sycamore to Gower along both sides of Hollywood Boulevard and from Sunset to Yucca along Vine Street. It is the only sidewalk in Los Angeles that is cleaned six times a week.

NOTE: *Dedication ceremonies for the Walk of Fame are usually held at noon on the third Thursday of each month. Check with the Hollywood Chamber of Commerce for exact times and locations. Phone: 469-8311.*

4. THE HOLLYWOOD MUSEUM
7051 Hollywood Boulevard

Opened in May of 1984, this is a gem. The collection—assembled from the studios, the Western Costume Company, as well as from important private collectors—has been thoughtfully curated and displayed and includes rare costumes, props, set pieces, lobby cards, posters, stills, and studio portraits. Classic movie themes provide background music as visitors can check out treasures such as Kim Novak's working-girl sweater dress from *Vertigo,* Marilyn Monroe's super-seductive *Seven Year Itch* gown, Judy Garland's blue-checked *Wizard of Oz* pinafore, Tallulah Bankhead's *Royal Scandal* regalia, headdresses and hats worn by Carmen Miranda, and Joan Crawford's 35-pound basic black-beaded dress, designed by Adrian, from *The Bride Wore Red.*

Top props are a chandelier from Rick's Cafe in *Casablanca,* the time machine from *Time After Time,* the coffin from *Love At First Bite,* a chariot from DeMille's 1957 *The Ten Commandments,* a throne from Liz Taylor's *Cleopatra,* an alien head from *Close Encounters of the Third Kind,* and a hand belonging to *The Creature from the Black Lagoon.* Also of interest to the film buff is the museum's historic movie memorabilia: an original stock certificate from D. W. Griffith's *The Birth of a Nation,* a storyboard for *The Incredible Shrinking Man,* photos from Mary Pickford's private collection, a fascinating questionnaire once filled out by Alfred Hitchcock in which the great director was asked to answer questions ranging from his favorite self-directed film (*Shadow of a Doubt*) to the most difficult directorial job of his career ("*Lifeboat* . . . for obvious reasons").

NOTE: *Since the Hollywood Museum's building—a distinctive columned structure that was originally a bank and has since been everything from a smorgasbord restaurant to an Arabian nightclub—is small and its collection large, exhibits will be changed frequently. Also, since this is a relatively new project, one can only*

hope that it will still be around upon the publication of this book.
The museum is currently open from 10 to 9, every day. Admission:
$4.50 for adults, $2.50 for children, and $3.00 for seniors. Call
465-3773 for further information.

5. HOLLYWOOD ROOSEVELT HOTEL
7000 Hollywood Boulevard

A 1927 newspaper ad touted its grand opening as "the
dominant social occasion of the year." "Don't wait," it went on.
"You will see the greatest number of stage and screen stars ever
assembled. Included among those invited are: Mary Pickford,
Douglas Fairbanks, Norma Talmadge, Constance Talmadge, Pola
Negri, Richard Barthelmess, John Gilbert, Harold Lloyd, Greta
Garbo, Gloria Swanson, Rod La Rocque, Janet Gaynor, Will
Rogers, Clara Bow, Sid Chaplin, Sid Grauman, Wallace Beery,
Charles Chaplin . . . and scores of others." And most of them
came—not only because, at twelve stories and 400 rooms, this
was the most impressive hotel ever to be built in Hollywood, but
also because the syndicate that built it included such movieland
notables as Douglas Fairbanks, Mary Pickford, Joseph Schenck,
Louis B. Mayer, and Marcus Loew.

Throughout its history, the Hollywood Roosevelt has had a
strong connection with the motion picture industry. In fact, the
Academy of Motion Picture Arts and Sciences had its first "Merit
Awards" dinner in the Roosevelt's Blossom Room on May 16,
1929. Marking the second anniversary of the founding of the
Academy, this was the first time the Academy Awards were
publically presented.

The Roosevelt has also been a radio and television studio.

The Hollywood Roosevelt
Hotel, 1947

In the 1930s, Russ Columbo broadcast a national radio show from the Roosevelt's Cinegrill—and in the 1950s and 1960s TV's "This Is Your Life" came live from the hotel. By the mid-1960s, however, the "Home of the Stars" was beginning to lose a lot of its former luster. Remodelings had buried many of its handsome Spanish Colonial architectural and decorative details—and minimal maintenance further tarnished the Roosevelt's image. In 1984, however, new owners began a $12 million restoration program aimed at making the hotel as splendid as it was in the 1920s. The reborn Hollywood Roosevelt is scheduled to debut in late 1985.

6. PARAMOUNT THEATER
6834–6838 Hollywood Boulevard

In 1926, a year before the debut of Grauman's Chinese Theater, a lavish legitimate theater opened on Hollywood Boulevard across the street from the Grauman's construction site. Called the El Capitan, the theater featured an opulent East Indian interior—the creation of famous theater designer/architect G. Albert Lansburgh—and was housed in a magnificent building with an intricately carved façade decorated with characters from literature and drama. The first production at the El Capitan was a British revue starring Bea Lillie, Gertrude Lawrence, and Jack Buchanan.

In 1942, the El Capitan was converted to a movie house and its name was changed to the Paramount. The first film shown at the new Paramount was Cecil B. DeMille's answer to *Gone with the Wind,* a southern epic called *Reap the Wild Wind.* Over the years, uninspired remodelings turned the once grand theater into a very ordinary Hollywood Boulevard movie house. The good news now is that new owners—convinced that Hollywood is on the upswing—plan to change the Paramount's name back to the El Capitan, spruce up the interior, and install a 1980s version of the original 1920s marquee.

In addition, the same syndicate plans to renovate the landmark building that houses the Paramount—and also hopes to revive the landmark Masonic Hall next door. Both buildings are conceived as entertainment complexes of theaters, restaurants, stores, and museums of Hollywood memorabilia. Said one of the wheels behind this major undertaking: "We intend to restore Hollywood's heyday."

7. SITE OF HOLLYWOOD HOTEL
Northwest corner of Hollywood Boulevard and Highland Avenue

It was built in 1903—to accommodate the growing number of visitors from back East who found Hollywood with its pepper trees, its orange groves, and its mild climate an ideal place for a winter vacation. About ten years later, another—and very different—group of Easterners discovered Hollywood ... the moviemakers. And suddenly the once staid Hollywood Hotel became the place where many of the early stars and directors stayed and played. Rudolph Valentino was the most famous of the regulars and often tangoed at the hotel's Thursday tea dances. He also spent, by all accounts, a perfectly dreadful honeymoon at the Hollywood Hotel in 1919 with his first wife, Jean Acker, who had a suite there. One story about their wedding night has an overzealous desk clerk refusing to allow Valentino into his new wife's suite until the great screen lover dramatically produced his marriage license. Another story has Jean Acker refusing to allow Rudy into her suite. Seems Jean wanted to keep things platonic. No matter what happened, the marriage was over a month later.

The hotel achieved its greatest fame through legendary gossip columnist Louella Parsons who broadcast a popular radio program called "Hollywood Hotel" from the premises in the 1930s. Inspired by Parsons' successful show, Warner Brothers made a musical in 1938 that was based loosely on the Hollywood Hotel. Directed by Busby Berkeley, *Hollywood Hotel* was a forgettable film that starred Dick Powell and featured a rather awkward Louella Parsons playing herself. Also in the cast was a good-looking young sportscaster turned actor named Ronald Reagan. What did turn out to be memorable about the film was the Richard Whiting–Johnny Mercer song it unleashed upon the world—a little ditty that would go on to become the classic musical embodiment of Hollywood. The song? "Hooray for Hollywood." The hotel—demolished in 1956 to make way for a parking lot and the Federal Savings and Loan high rise—is gone, but the melody lingers on.

The Hollywood Hotel

Security Pacific Bank Building

8. SECURITY PACIFIC BANK BUILDING
6777 Hollywood Boulevard

Originally the home of the Los Angeles First National Bank, this impressive Hollywood Boulevard landmark—with its distinctive neo-Gothic tower—was designed by the firm of Meyer and Holler in 1927. At the time, this was the second-tallest building in Los Angeles. But Meyer and Holler would be far better remembered—especially by movie lovers—for two low-rise Hollywood Boulevard buildings that they designed, Grauman's Egyptian (1922) and Grauman's Chinese (1927) theaters.

9. MAX FACTOR BUILDING AND BEAUTY MUSEUM
1666–1668 North Highland Avenue

It is impossible to imagine Hollywood without makeup—and makeup without Max Factor. Born in Czarist Russia, this cosmetics pioneer began his career as a makeup artist with the Russian Royal Ballet. He emigrated to the United States in 1904 and by 1909 had set up shop in downtown Los Angeles. Among his many contributions to the film industry was his 1914 invention of the first motion picture makeup to be packaged in a sanitary collapsible tube; he also developed panchromatic makeup to be used with the new panchromatic film of the late 1920s that replaced the orthochromatic film of earlier years. Factor received a special Academy Award for this achievement in 1929.

It was also in the late 1920s that Max Factor moved his base of operations from downtown Los Angeles to Hollywood. And

Max Factor Building

when continued prosperity necessitated major renovations of his Hollywood offices, Factor commissioned the famed designer of motion picture palaces, S. Charles Lee, to create the Regency-moderne jewel of a makeup salon building that still glitters on Highland Avenue. Inside, white-marble stairs led to an oval-shaped showroom where cosmetics were (and still are) sold and to sumptuous consultation rooms designed to duplicate the most splendid of movie-star dressing rooms of the thirties. The building's "premiere" took place on November 26, 1935—a star-studded, kleig-light-lit evening to which 3500 were invited and 8000 showed up!

NOTE: *In the summer of 1984, the Max Factor Salon—with its four-story pilasters and green marble base—staged another premiere with the opening of the Max Factor Beauty Museum on the premises. On display here are some eighty years worth of makeup memorabilia, a collection of historic Max Factor print ads that feature Hollywood personalities endorsing Factor products, and Max Factor's "Scroll of Fame," considered one of the most extensive collections of movie-star autographs in the world. There are also lots of fascinating vintage Hollywood photographs, many never before seen by the public. The Max Factor Beauty Museum is open from 9 to 5, Monday through Friday.*

10. HOLLYWOOD WAX MUSEUM
6767 Hollywood Boulevard

Madame Toussaud's of London, it's not. Raquel looks like Farrah Fawcett wearing a wig borrowed from Mae West; Marilyn, her white dress billowing in the air from the infamous *Seven Year Itch* scene that may have cost her her marriage to Joe DiMaggio, resembles a great big Barbie Doll; and Ronald Reagan really could be a double for Howdy Doody. This is Hollywood Boulevard at its tackiest—and may be worth a visit for that reason alone. Besides movie stars, the "museum" also has a Hall of Presidents, a Chamber of Horrors (shades of Vincent Price and Carolyn Jones in Warners' 1954 3-D-er *House of Wax*), and a "faithful life-size recreation" in wax of Leonardo da Vinci's "The Last Supper." If all this isn't enough, a short film on the history of the Academy Awards—featuring vintage footage of Oscar-winning films and performances—runs continuously in the museum's "Academy Awards Movie Theater."

The Spanish Colonial Revival building housing the Hollywood Wax Museum was built in 1928. In the 1930s, its second story was taken over by the Embassy Club—a private dining club for celebrities who wanted to avoid the crowds at the very popular Montmartre Cafe next door. A "secret" passageway connected the two glamour spots.

NOTE: *The Hollywood Wax Museum is open from 10 to midnight, Sunday to Thursday; 10 to 2 a.m., Friday and Saturday.*

11. MONTMARTRE CAFE SITE
6763 Hollywood Boulevard

Designed in the style of an Italian Renaissance palazzo, this Boulevard building originally housed a bank on its ground floor and one of early Hollywood's most glamorous nightspots— Montmartre Cafe—on its second story. The Montmartre opened in 1923 and quickly became *the* place to go for a wild night on the town in the Roaring Twenties. When the Charleston was the rage, Joan Crawford was the star who danced it best. Tango honors went to Rudolph Valentino.

Looking back at the Montmartre, Buddy Rogers remembers white-tie evenings and violins. Vogue editor Eleanore Phillips

Montmartre Cafe, 1930

recalls the Montmartre's maitre d'—"tanned and handsome and always in a white-linen suit." He became Bruce Cabot, the star of *King Kong.* Open at lunch as well as dinner, the Montmartre was a favorite haunt of Louella Parsons who, in the early days of her career, often went table-hopping asking anyone and everyone the question: "Any news, dear?" In 1930, the Montmartre was one of the first clubs to book a young crooner who had recently left the Paul Whiteman orchestra. The singer was Bing Crosby and it was also at the Montmartre where he wooed his first wife, Dixie Lee.

12. HOLLYWOOD THEATER
6764 Hollywood Boulevard

This is the oldest extant movie theater in Hollywood—a former nickelodeon that may date back to as far as 1911. Although many renovations have changed the look of the theater over the years, the Hollywood is still of interest to movie theater historians because of its 1930s neon marquee. A sign of changing times, the marquee was one of the first to be designed with large side panels that were angled to catch the eyes—not of pedestrians—but of passing motorists.

13. UA HOLLYWOOD EGYPTIAN THEATER
6712 Hollywood Boulevard

Another Sid Grauman extravaganza, the Egyptian opened in 1922 with the gala premiere of *Robin Hood* starring Douglas Fairbanks. The Egyptian was the first real movie palace to be erected in Hollywood and its architects—Meyer and Holler—

Hollywood Theater marquee

were the same that Grauman would use for his Chinese Theater five years later. Like the Chinese, the Egyptian is characterized by a large forecourt which in its heyday was edged by Middle Eastern shops and by guards in ancient Egyptian costumes. No wonder Cecil B. DeMille premiered his original *The Ten Commandments* here in 1923. Inside the theater, hierogylphic murals, a sunburst ceiling, and a giant scarab above the proscenium continued the Egyptian theme—especially popular in the early 1920s when major archaeological finds were being made in Egypt—culminating in Howard Carter's discovery of King Tut's tomb in 1922.

Alas, the Egyptian appears not to have fared as well as its younger sibling, the Chinese. Remodelings rather than restorations have taken their toll on the original interior and done away with much of the theater's former fantasy splendor. But the long jungly courtyard and many of the murals remain—and the exterior is still painted a sandy beige color that seems appropriate. Ironically, the best view of the building is not from the front but from the side that edges McCadden Place and looks like the great wall of an ancient temple.

14. MUSSO & FRANK GRILL
6667 Hollywood Boulevard

Opened in 1919, it claims to be the oldest restaurant in Hollywood. And at first everybody—Gloria Swanson, Mary Pickford, Douglas Fairbanks, Jesse Lasky, C. B. DeMille, Barbara La Marr, John Barrymore—came because there weren't too many other places to go to at the time. Sixty years later, celebrities and industry people still come—from as far away as Malibu and

Grauman's Egyptian Theater

Musso and Frank Grill, 1936

Santa Monica—not for the glamour, but for the experience of dining in an old-fashioned, uncomplicated American restaurant. If restaurants were movies, Musso's would be a 1930s MGM musical.

Remodeled in 1937, the restaurant—with its two large dining rooms, beamed ceilings, long counter, red banquettes, wooden booths with coat racks—has changed little since those days in the late 1930s and early 1940s when F. Scott Fitzgerald, Robert Benchley, and William Faulkner were regulars. Possibly they were drawn to Musso's because the place reminded them more of the East than of the West Coast where they never felt at home. Also, it was next door to Stanley Rose's bookshop—an important hangout of the Hollywood intelligentsia at the time.

Musso's menu has also changed little over the years—with no-nonsense entrees like chicken pot pie, beef goulash, steaks, and chops seeming strangely anachronistic in today's *nouvelle* Los Angeles. But Musso & Frank will probably still be around long after the chic places—the Spagos, the Trumps, the Michaels of the moment—have closed their kitchens. Portions are enormous, prices moderate.

NOTE: *Phone for reservations: 467-7788.*

15. LARRY EDMUNDS BOOKSHOP, INC.
6658 Hollywood Boulevard

This is where The Library of Congress paid $12,500 for Bernard Herrmann's original score for the 1941 film *Citizen Kane;* it's also where French filmmaker François Truffaut headed first whenever he was in L.A. It is Hollywood's best-known source for film books, scripts, stills, posters, lobby cards, magazines, and memorabilia. Its catalogue is so vast that it encompasses three volumes; its collection of motion picture still photos—over one million—is said to be one of the largest in the world.

NOTE: *Hours are 10 to 6, Monday to Saturday. Phone: 463-3273.*

16. HOLLYWOOD WILCOX HOTEL
Wilcox Avenue at Selma

An example of humble beginnings, this unprepossessing hotel across from the Post Office was the first Hollywood address of an eighteen-year-old MGM contract player named Ava Gardner, who shared a small flat here with her sister Beatrice in the early 1940s. Recalling those early Hollywood days, Ava had this to say recently: "I was getting $35 a week—I thought I'd be making $50. Bappy (Beatrice) and I stayed at the Wilcox—a little bed, a little kitchen. For the first three weeks we were there, I didn't get paid at all—so Bappy got a job at I. Magnin selling bags. I had to take two busses to get to the studio." Today, Miss Gardner lives in London's posh Knightsbridge neighborhood and her former Hollywood home is now owned by the Church of Scientology Celebrity Center International.

17. JANES HOUSE
6541 Hollywood Boulevard

This odd little "Queen Anne" Victorian house set back from the bustle of 1980s Hollywood Boulevard is typical of the houses that edged the thoroughfare at the beginning of the twentieth century. Built in 1903 when Hollywood Boulevard was a dusty byway called Prospect Avenue, the Janes house was the family residence of three sisters who ran a school on the premises between 1911 and 1926. During those years, the Janes ladies taught the progeny of C. B. DeMille, Charlie Chaplin, Douglas Fairbanks, Carl Laemmle, and Thomas Ince. The last surviving sister lived in the house until 1982 before being moved to a nursing home where she died the following year. After narrowly escaping demolition, the house—the first single-family Victorian dwelling on Hollywood Boulevard—is scheduled to be restored as part of a small office complex.

P.S.: Rumor has it that Henry Farrell, the author of the novel on which the famous 1962 film *Whatever Happened to Baby Jane?* was based, got the idea for the characters in his story from the Janes sisters. Those who remember the film will recall that the former child star portrayed by Bette Davis was called *Jane Hudson.* The Janes house looks across Hollywood Boulevard to Hudson Street. Author Farrell, however, denies any connection.

Janes house

18. HILLVIEW APARTMENTS
6531–6535 Hollywood Boulevard

An early (1917) apartment building typical of those where silent film folk—who bounced back and forth between the East and West Coasts much as actors do today—stayed when in Hollywood. Mae Busch—a veteran of many a Laurel and Hardy film—is said to have lived at the Hillview. The building once boasted a large Mediterranean courtyard—but it has long since been "filled in" with shops.

19. PACIFIC HOLLYWOOD THEATER
6433 Hollywood Boulevard

When it opened in 1927 with the premiere of *Glorious Betsy,* starring Conrad Nagle and Dolores Costello, it was called the Warner Brothers Theater and it was the largest movie house ever built in Hollywood. Today, its original marquee and its name have been changed—and its opulent Moorish interior has fallen victim to a late-twentieth-century engineering technique/economic necessity known as "tri-plexing." In other words, this once grand theater has been sliced up into three smaller theaters. A surprise is that many of the original interior details—such as the sculpted white walls and wood-beamed ceiling of the lobby—were retained in the process.

In the late 1940s, the Warner employed a young Hollywood High student as an usherette. A child of alcoholic parents, the

Warner Brothers Theater, late 1920s

young woman lived with her grandmother up the street from the theater at the Mayfair Apartments at 1760 Wilcox Avenue. A quarter of a century later, the same woman would live in a huge house in Beverly Hills and she would be honored with her own star along the Walk of Fame in front of the movie theater where she once worked. The woman? Carol Burnett.

20. ANITA STEWART HOUSE
7425 Franklin Avenue

In the teens, she was one of the biggest names at Vitagraph Studios. Enter Louis B. Mayer and his newly created Louis B. Mayer Pictures in 1917. In need of a big star to add class and clout to his new company, Mayer went after, and got, Miss Stewart. Not only would he match the $3000 a week that she was getting at Vitagraph, he would even throw in a unique perk for the period: an automobile! The only hitch to the whole deal was the fact that Miss Stewart's Vitagraph contract had not yet run its term. The result? Vitagraph sued and won a landmark breach of contract case that proved, for the moment at least, that movie studios were stronger than movie stars. The suit is said to have cost Mayer some $123,000. After it all died down, Miss Stewart went on to make a number of successful pictures with Mayer—but the Brooklyn-born actress was smart enough to exit the picture business just as talkies were coming in. This massive Franklin Avenue mansion with the ten columns and two balustrades was Anita Stewart's one-time Hollywood home.

Ozzie and Harriet house

21. THE OZZIE AND HARRIET HOUSE
1822 Camino Palmero Drive

This is where Ozzie, Harriet, David, and Ricky Nelson lived while they were portraying the ideal American family in their popular 1950s television series. A pleasant upper-middle-class dwelling, it fit the Nelsons' screen image so well that their television house was modeled after it—and occasionally the real house would be used for exterior long shots. When the Nelsons went to work in the morning, they didn't have far to go since the Hollywood General Studios where "The Ozzie and Harriet Show" was shot were just five minutes away on Las Palmas. Ozzie and Harriet Nelson were still based in their Camino Palmero home when Ozzie died in 1975. Harriet sold the house and moved out several years later.

22. HIGHLAND GARDENS HOTEL
7047 Franklin Avenue

On October 4, 1970, rock star Janis Joplin was found dead of a drug overdose in this Hollywood hostelry. Known as the Landmark Motel at the time, it is now called the Highland Gardens and still caters to music people. Famed for drinking Southern Comfort on stage and for espousing the virtues of getting and staying "stoned," Janis was a child of the 1960s who just barely made it into the seventies. Her greatest moment professionally was her gut-wrenching performance of "Love Is Like a Ball and Chain" at the 1967 Monterey Rock Festival—a performance which was immortalized in the film *Monterey Pop.* Later, Joplin would again be remembered on screen—in the film *The Rose,* which starred Bette Midler in a role patterned after Joplin. Often questioned by the press about her wanton life and singing style, Janis Joplin once answered: "Maybe I won't last as

The Magic Castle

long as other singers ... but I think you can destroy your *now* worrying about tomorrow." Her death in Hollywood at age twenty-seven came less than three weeks after fellow rock star Jimi Hendrix, also twenty-seven, O.D.'d in London.

23. THE MAGIC CASTLE
7001 Franklin Avenue

This splendid Gothic mansion on Franklin Avenue was erected in 1909 as the family home of a banker named Rollin S. Lane. Later, in the early 1930s, it was home to actress Janet Gaynor and her then husband, attorney Lydell Peck.

Since 1963, however, the mansion has been the clubhouse of what is said to be "the only club in the world devoted to magicians and lovers of magic." Frequently used as a location by TV news shows doing Halloween features, the beautifully restored "castle" is made up of bars, dining rooms, theaters, and secret chambers. In the Houdini Seance Room, the ghost of master magician Harry Houdini returns twice nightly. In the Invisible Irma Room, a phantom pianist named Irma plays requests. Fittingly, this private club keeps its membership list top secret. But the following famous part-time magicians are rumored to be members: Johnny Carson, Orson Welles, Mohammed Ali, Cary Grant, Steve Martin, Tony Curtis, and Bill Bixby.

24. YAMASHIRO
1999 North Sycamore Avenue

Called Yamashiro ("mountain palace"), this is one of Hollywood's most delightful sights—an authentic replica of a Japanese Palace perched almost 300 feet above Hollywood Boulevard. Surprisingly, this architectural treasure of teak and cedar with gold-lacquered rafters was not the fantasy home of an early film

Bernheimer Residence, now Yamashiro

star but was built between 1908 and 1912 by two brothers named Bernheimer who were dealers in Oriental antiques. Yamashiro's connection with the movie business began in 1923 when the mansion became the clubhouse for the Club of the Hollywood Four Hundred. This organization of the Hollywood film elite was formed partially as a response to the cool reception motion picture people received at many of Los Angeles' old-monied and very restrictive private clubs. The prejudice against movie people went back to the days when they first arrived in Hollywood. At the time (1911), Hollywood was basically a small Midwestern town that happened to be in California. Nicknamed "movies," early film people were discriminated against to such an extent that it was common to see signs in the windows of rooming houses that said "Dogs And Motion Picture Actors Not Allowed Inside."

As times changed and Hollywood film stars were elevated to the status of royalty, there was less and less a need for the Club of the Hollywood Four Hundred and it was eventually disbanded. Yamashiro then passed through various hands until Tom Glover, Sr., bought it in 1949 and restored it. Often used as an instant Oriental location for films and television shows, Yamashiro "appeared" as the American Officers Club in *Sayonara,* the 1958 film starring Marlon Brando, Miiko Taka, Red Buttons, and Miyoshi Umeki. Allegedly, during the shooting of the film (in which newcomer James Garner played an officer) some of Yamashiro's bonsai trees mysteriously disappeared. Whether the trees turned up in later scenes of the film or in somebody's backyard no one knows for sure.

Since 1960, Yamashiro has provided what is probably the western world's most glorious setting for a Japanese restaurant. By day, visitors can stroll 8 acres of grounds that include Japanese gardens (often used as backdrops for television commercials), a

600-year-old pagoda, an authentic Japanese teahouse, and a small hotel. At night, the romantic view of the lights of Hollywood looks like the one James Mason showed Judy Garland during the first reel of *A Star Is Born*.

NOTE: *For lunch and dinner reservations, phone HO 6-5125.*

25. FIRST UNITED METHODIST CHURCH OF HOLLYWOOD
6817 Franklin Avenue

This handsome house of worship at the busy corner of Franklin and Highland Avenues features a clean neo-Gothic exterior and a wood-beamed ceiling that's a scaled-down replica of the one in Westminster Abbey. Dedicated in 1929, the church has appeared in a number of famous Hollywood films. In David O. Selznick's 1932 *What Price Hollywood?*—directed by George Cukor—Constance Bennett plays a Hollywood hopeful who finds that success in tinseltown does not bring happiness. Her mid-picture marriage to a polo-playing socialite takes place at the First Methodist Church. In 1941, Warners' Academy Award-nominated *One Foot in Heaven* featured Fredric March, Martha Scott, Beulah Bondi, Gene Lockhart—and the First Methodist Church as, of all things, a Methodist church! Science-fiction fans may also remember the First Methodist Church as one of the places where the terrified inhabitants of Los Angeles sought shelter during the invasion of their city by Martian spaceships during the climactic ending of the 1952 classic, *The War of the Worlds.*

First United Methodist Church

Besides its importance as a location, the First United Methodist Church of Hollywood has had a number of famous members through the years. Among them: Robert Taylor, Busby Berkeley, Barbara Britton, and Bob Barker.

26. KFAC RADIO
6735 Yucca Street

Now headquarters for KFAC AM and FM radio, this Hollywood-Elizabethan bungalow once upon a time was an Italian restaurant called the Villa Capri. Run by the D'Amore family, the Villa Capri had a friendly family atmosphere—which is perhaps the reason it became "home" to James Dean. First introduced to the place by Pier Angeli (the actress who broke Jimmy's heart when, at her Italian Catholic family's insistence, she married Vic Damone), Dean continued coming to the Villa Capri restaurant even after the breakup of their romance. In fact, he was so at home here that he entered through the kitchen— and even rented a house from one of the Villa's maitre d's.

On the evening of September 29, 1955, Hollywood columnist James Bacon remembers seeing Dean "doing 80 miles an hour" up McCadden Place and screeching to a halt in front of the Villa Capri. As Dean got out of his his brand-new special-model Porsche Spyder, Bacon admonished the young actor, saying: "Jimmy, that's a good way to keep from growing old." Replied Jimmy: "Who wants to grow old?" The next day saw Dean die at the wheel of the same Porsche.

After Dean's death, the Villa Capri became a shrine to his legend. Fans would arrive, try to sit at their hero's table, order his favorite dishes. The restaurant closed in 1982 and became the offices for the KFAC radio station in 1983.

27. THE MONTECITO APARTMENTS
6650 Franklin Avenue

Built in the early 1930s, this Franklin Avenue classic is reported to have been Ronald Reagan's first Hollywood home. According to legend, young Reagan, upon his arrival in tinseltown, hot-footed to the Montecito because he wanted to live in the same building where his idol Jimmy Cagney had lived. Particularly popular with the New York crowd in the 1950s and early 1960s, the Montecito was a place where, according to a former resident, "No one ever bought their beer by the six-pack—since no one ever knew how long they'd be staying."

For Raymond Chandler fans, the Montecito was the prototype for the Chateau Bercy apartment building in Chandler's Philip Marlowe detective novel *The Little Sister*. Today, the Montecito sits boarded up. Present owners are supposedly planning a major refurbishing—but so far, little seems to be happening.

28. THE ROMAN GARDENS
2000 North Highland Avenue

Practically invisible from the street, this landmark courtyard apartment building has come to be known as "Villa Valentino"—because, so the story goes, the famed screen lover of the 1920s carried on various amorous adventures within its lush interior. Yet another example of the power of the myths surrounding the movie idol, this story would appear to have little basis in reality since Valentino died the year the Roman Gardens was completed: 1926. Unless, of course, he was as active off-screen as he was on—which, according to another set of stories, was definitely *not* the case.

Valentino's sex life aside, the Roman Gardens—with its sensual Moorish courtyards and fountains, its shaded patios and arcaded walkways—has an important place in the history of Los Angeles architecture and ranks among the city's best designed courtyard apartment buildings. It was the work of the brothers Walter S. and F. Pierpont Davis, who also designed the equally beautiful (and currently in a much happier state) Villa d'Este apartments in West Hollywood.

29. THE AMERICAN LEGION
2035 North Highland Avenue

Guess who's post this is? Or at least *was* until 1982 when he transferred his membership over to Pacific Palisades where he owned a house at the time. But even though Hollywood Post 43 lost Ronald Reagan, it can still count among its current ranks the legendary celluloid cowboy Gene Autry. Other famous mem-

Hollywood American Legion Post 43

bers of this post have been Clark Gable, Conrad Nagle, old-time cowboy star Art Acord, and Adolphe Menjou—one of Hollywood's most notorious "squealers" during the McCarthy witch hunt of the early 1950s. The American Legion building—a dazzling neo-Mesopotamian temple designed in 1929 by architect Eugene Weston, Jr.—ranks with the best of Hollywood's fantasy architecture.

30. THE HIGH TOWER
End of Hightower Drive

Are you in Hollywood—or Bologna? One of Hollywood's most enchanting architectural oddities, this Italian-looking tower actually conceals a working elevator that services the houses on the top of the hill. Built in the 1920s as part of a development known as the Hollywood Heights, the area and its "High Tower" were used extensively as locations in United Artists' *The Long Goodbye* (1973) starring Elliott Gould and Nina van Pallandt. Directed by Robert Altman, the film was based on the Raymond Chandler novel of the same title.

NOTE: *High Tower Drive is off Camrose Drive, which lies just west of Highland Avenue not far from the Hollywood Bowl.*

31. HOLLYWOOD BOWL
2301 North Highland Avenue

The sylvan setting for this world-famous outdoor amphitheater was originally known as Daisy Dell. In early Hollywood, it was often used by silent-film makers as a location for low-budget

Hollywood Bowl

Western movies. Its location days were interrupted in 1919, however, when a Mrs. Christine Witherill Stevenson of the Pittsburgh Paint fortune felt Hollywood needed a little "serious" culture and went about forming a group that purchased Daisy Dell with the idea of presenting religious plays there. Bickering over the cost of a proposed theater structure for the site quickly brought about the dissolution of Mrs. Stevenson's high-minded group and a new organization acquired the Dell and began using it for public concerts as well as for sunrise services on Easter. Today, the Easter services and the concerts continue at what is now known as the Hollywood Bowl.

The dramatic concrete band shell that most people associate with the Bowl was built in 1929; it was preceded by various other structures, two of them designed by Frank Lloyd Wright's architect son, Lloyd Wright. One of the classic symbols of "Hollywood," the Bowl has appeared in a number of films set in the city. In the 1937 version of *A Star Is Born,* Esther Blodgett (Janet Gaynor) meets a very drunk Norman Maine (Fredric March) at a Bowl concert toward the beginning of the film. In *Anchors Aweigh,* sailors Gene Kelly and Frank Sinatra come across Jose Iturbi practicing before a Bowl concert.

NOTE: *A museum celebrating the architectural and musical history of this famed concert hall has been installed in the former teahouse near the entrance to the Bowl. Days and hours of opening vary with the season. For information, call 850-2058. Admission is free.*

32. HOLLYWOOD STUDIO MUSEUM
2300 North Highland Avenue

In 1913, a New York film company decided to make a feature-length cowboy movie "on location." The site chosen for the production was Flagstaff, Arizona—but upon arriving there, the film's director was said to have found the territory a little too realistic, what with warring cattlemen and sheep ranchers taking potshots at one another. Instead of returning East, the intrepid director continued westward and wound up in Hollywood, California. There, he set up headquarters in a horse barn that he rented from a local named Jacob Stern. The director from the East went on to become a legend in the motion picture business— he was Cecil B. DeMille. His partners in the project did pretty well, too. One was Jesse Lasky and the other was Samuel Goldfish (later Goldwyn). And their western, *The Squaw Man*—the film that DeMille directed while using a horse barn as a studio—is considered to be the first feature ever shot within the borders of the town of Hollywood.

Jacob Stern's barn might have gone the way of most of the makeshift "studios" used in Hollywood's early silent days were it not for the foresight of DeMille and Lasky who, in 1927, had it

DeMille barn today

moved to the back lot of Paramount Studios. At Paramount, the barn's exterior was often used for Western films—and its interior became the studio gym where stars like Fred MacMurray, Gary Cooper, Cornel Wilde, Burt Lancaster, and Kirk Douglas stayed in Paramount-perfect shape.

As long as DeMille or Lasky were at Paramount, the barn was safe. But after they were gone, then what? DeMille, realizing how quickly Hollywood forgets, managed to have the barn declared a California Historic Landmark in 1956—a designation that would make it difficult for later generations to tear it down. In 1979, however, Paramount decided that, historic landmark or no, the barn had no place in the renovations it was planning for the studio. So it gave the barn to a division of the Hollywood Chamber of Commerce known as the Historic Hollywood Trust which moved it to a parking lot on Vine Street until someone could come up with something more interesting to do with it. To the rescue came a vital organization—dedicated to preserving the landmarks of Hollywood's past—called Hollywood Heritage. Through a great amount of effort, this enthusiastic group of private citizens found a permanent home for the barn on Highland Avenue across from the Hollywood Bowl. Today, Hollywood's oldest extant movie studio has been beautifully restored and is the town's first museum dedicated to the history of silent motion pictures. Hooray for Hollywood!

NOTE: *For information on museum hours, call 874-BARN.*

33. WHITLEY HEIGHTS

For a feeling of what Hollywood was really like in the 1920s, perhaps no other neighborhood expresses it better than this little-known hilltop enclave of Mediterranean houses just north of Hollywood Boulevard and east of Highland Avenue. Built by an

Street scene, Whitley Heights

important Los Angeles developer of the early twentieth century named H. J. Whitley, Whitley Heights was to be his dream development, the final achievement of his career. Here, smack in the middle of Hollywood, he would create an authentic Italian hilltown—and, in order to get it just right, he sent his chief architect to Italy to study the age-old secrets of hillside construction and landscaping. Ground was broken for the project in 1918 and the building of Whitley Heights continued feverishly for the next six to eight years.

Immediately popular with the silent set, Whitley Heights became Hollywood's first "Beverly Hills," if by that we mean an unusually heavy concentration of celebrities living in one area. In fact, screenland's first movie-star house tours started bringing sightseers up to Whitley Heights in the early 1920s. Among the many stars who lived here at the time, the biggest of them all was Rudolph Valentino who, at the height of his career between 1922 and 1925, resided at 6770 Wedgewood Place with his second wife, Natacha Rambova. The house was torn down in 1947 to make way for the Hollywood Freeway.

It is not what is gone but what remains in Whitley Heights that makes the neighborhood so fascinating. Awarded National Historic Register status in 1982, Whitley Heights preserves beautiful tile-roofed Mediterranean houses that were home to everybody from Richard Barthelmess, whom Lillian Gish described as "the most beautiful man who ever went before a camera," to Barbara La Marr who was known as "the girl who was too beautiful" and who died of "nervous exhaustion" at the age of twenty-nine. The Barthelmess house—where Norma Talmadge was a frequent visitor, even though she was married to powerful producer Joe Schenck at the time—sits above Whitley Terrace fronted by a balustrade topped with pineapple-shaped finials. (Whitley Heights residents are very concerned with security and, for that reason, no house numbers are included here.)

Former Whitley
Heights mansion of
Robert Vignola

Next door to where Barthelmess lived is a large villa that was once owned by director Robert Vignola. William Randolph Hearst is said to have handpicked Vignola to direct many of the films made by Marion Davies in the 1920s since Hearst knew that Vignola was a homosexual and could therefore be trusted with la Davies. Hearst is also rumored to have built the Vignola house as a hideaway for himself and Miss Davies.

The Barbara La Marr house—suspended above the hillside near where Whitley Terrace meets Grace Avenue—is said to have had a "secret" passageway between the chauffeur's quarters and Miss La Marr's boudoir. Further along Whitley Terrace, an odd but attractive house that resembles a fat round tower was home to, at various times, character actor Joseph Schildkraut, *Lost Horizon* author James Hilton, Rosalind Russell, and, last and longest, Beulah Bondi, who resided there from 1941 until her death in 1981. Continuing along Whitley Terrace, the pretty house with terraced gardens and various balconies was—according to local lore—used as a location in Bette Davis' forties film classic *Now Voyager.* (Bette was also a former Whitley Heights resident— her house, however, was torn down in 1962 to make room for a Hollywood Museum that was never built.)

Still further along Whitley Terrace, steep Whitley Avenue may seem familiar to many filmgoers since it often doubles for a San Francisco street in movies as well as in television shows. The street where Burgess Meredith sold his miracle medicine in *The*

Day of the Locust was Whitley Avenue. Beyond the intersection of Whitley Terrace and Whitley Avenue, the house with the massive fortresslike garage was once Jean Harlow's.

On the other side of the Heights, Janet Gaynor and costume designer Adrian (her husband at the time) lived at the end of Watsonia Terrace in the beautiful three-story villa that looks as though it should be in Venice. Called "Villa Vallambrosa," it was built in 1922 by socialite Eleanor De Witt—who leased it over the years to Dame Judith Anderson, Danny Thomas, and Leonard Bernstein. A few houses away—near the junction of Watsonia Terrace and Milner Road—there's another villa with an impressive rental history: William Faulkner, in Hollywood to write screenplays for Columbia, lived here—as did Gloria Swanson, who took the place in 1949–1950 and resided here with her mother while making her great screen comeback in *Sunset Boulevard*.

At the highest point of the hill upon which Whitley Heights is built, a group of tall Royal Palm trees was once part of a posh estate called "Topside." The place boasted silent screen idol Francis X. Bushman as a former tenant and it was also here that Hollywood's first swimming pool supposedly was built. Later, the well-known lecturer and producer of early travelogues, Burton Holmes, resided at Topside until his death in 1957. Another victim of "progress," Topside was torn down in the late 1970s by a developer who wanted to build condominiums on the historic site. It was this action that finally made the residents of Whitley Heights realize that the only way to preserve their precious past was to get their neighborhood declared an historical district. Through a great deal of hard work, they eventually succeeded in saving a very important part of early Hollywood history.

NOTE: *The best way to see Whitley Heights is on an organized walking tour of the area. These are given several times a year by the Whitley Heights Civic Association. Not only do the docents*

Villa Vallambrosa, former home of Janet Gaynor and Adrian

Rudolph Valentino and wife Natasha Rambova outside their Whitley Heights manse

tell exactly who lived where, they also let tour members go inside a number of historic houses. For information on when tours are given, write: Whitley Heights Heritage Tours, P.O. Box 1008, Hollywood, CA 90078.

For those who want to explore the area on their own, the easiest way to reach Whitley Heights is to head up Whitley Avenue from Hollywood Boulevard or to go north on Highland Avenue and turn right onto Milner Road. For the moment, Whitley Heights can be seen both by car (minimal parking, however, so a drive around is recommended) or by foot (steep climbs involved). As this book goes to press, there is some talk of trying to close Whitley Heights to the public and to turn it into a private "gated" community. Should this happen, the Whitley Heights Civic Association would offer its official guided walking tours on a more frequent basis.

34. ALTO-NIDO APARTMENTS
1851 North Ivar Avenue

This hill-topping California-Spanish apartment building is where we see unemployed screenwriter Joe Gillis (William Holden) working at his typewriter in the early part of Billy Wilder's classic 1950 film about Hollywood, *Sunset Boulevard*. Gillis, as we all know, soon finds "employment" as writer/gigolo-in-residence with aging silent film star Norma Desmond (Gloria Swanson). The rest is film history.

Alto-Nido Apartments

35. PARVA SED-APTA APARTMENTS
1817 North Ivar Avenue

Author Nathanael West moved into this odd-looking Holly-wood-Tudor apartment building with the equally odd name (it means "small but suitable" in Latin) in 1935. From this base, he got to know the neighborhood prostitutes, hung out at nearby Musso & Frank Grill on Hollywood Boulevard, wrote screenplays, and made notes for what would be one of the greatest novels ever written about Hollywood: *The Day of the Locust.* Ironically, the book was not a commercial success at the time of its publication in 1939. West died a year later in a car crash that also killed his wife, Eileen McKenney, sister of the author of *My Sister Eileen.* At the time, more was made of her death than of his and it was another ten years before Nathanael West was "discovered" by the literary establishment. The film version of *The Day of the Locust,* directed by John Schlesinger in 1974, met with as little initial success as the novel that inspired it. Whether it, too, will come to be accepted as an important work of art remains to be seen.

36. HOLLYWOOD KNICKERBOCKER HOTEL
1714 North Ivar Avenue

By the 1920s, the flourishing film industry was turning small-town Hollywood into a city that would have a population of over 150,000 at the end of the decade. To meet the needs of these

Hollywood Knickerbocker Hotel

boom years, a number of big hotels like the eleven-story Knickerbocker were built in downtown Hollywood. The Knickerbocker opened in 1925 and was popular with celebrities between coasts, between marriages, between studios. Early guests included Rudy Vallee, Gloria Swanson, Dick Powell, Bette Davis. When Errol Flynn arrived in Hollywood, he made the Knickerbocker his first base. Later, Frank Sinatra and Elvis Presley would also stay here early in their careers.

The hotel has been the scene of a number of Hollywood's more bizarre happenings. In 1936, the widow of escape artist Harry Houdini held a well-publicized séance on the Knickerbocker's roof, at which she tried to contact her dead husband. Then, in 1943, the hotel found itself in the news when police broke into the room of low-on-her-luck "Paramount Pretty" Frances Farmer. Claiming she had failed to report to her parole officer for an earlier drunk driving/disorderly conduct conviction, the police dragged the unfortunate Frances half-nude and screaming obscenities across the Knickerbocker lobby.

In 1962, the hotel again was part of lurid headlines when famous MGM costume designer Irene (*Gaslight, State of the Union, Easter Parade*) registered at the Knickerbocker in the morning, tried unsuccessfully to slash her wrists later in the day, and then leapt to her death from the eleventh floor. Newspapers attributed her suicide to depression over business problems as well as over the recent death of her husband. Two days before, she had displayed her latest collection at a fashion show in Beverly Hills.

Another tragic event connected with the hotel took place in July of 1948 when pioneer silent film director and producer D. W. Griffith suffered a fatal cerebral hemorrhage in his rooms at the Knickerbocker where he lived alone. Griffith, seventy-three years old at the time, had not made a film since 1931 and was ignored by the industry he helped found. Ironically, his funeral service at the Hollywood Masonic Temple a few days later brought out some 300 film industry celebrities. In his eulogy, Charles Brackett, a producer and then Vice President of the Academy of Motion Picture Arts and Sciences, said: "It was the fate of David Wark Griffith to have a success unknown in the entertainment world until his day, and to suffer the agonies which only a success of that magnitude can engender when it is past. There was no solution for Griffith but a kind of frenzied beating on the barred doors. Fortunately, when he is dead, a man's career has but one tense. The laurels are fresh on the triumphant brow. He lies here, the embittered years forgotten."

Today the Hollywood Knickerbocker is a retirement hotel.

37. THE HOLLYWOOD USO
1641 North Ivar Avenue

Better known as the "Bob Hope USO Club," this building—with a caricature of Hope smiling from its façade—was officially dedicated in 1973 with a ceremony that brought out Hope, Edgar Bergen, Charlie McCarthy, and Martha Raye. Bob Hope's connection with the Hollywood USO goes back to 1941—the year he first put together a Christmas show for U.S. servicemen at the March Air Force Base east of Los Angeles. The following Christmas saw Hope and his troupe entertaining the troops in Alaska—and in 1943, he went overseas for the first time. From then on his USO shows became legends of the entertainment industry and starred almost every major movie sex goddess from Betty Grable to Marilyn Monroe to Raquel Welch.

What many thought would be Bob Hope's last overseas USO show was his final visit to Vietnam in 1972—but in 1983, at age eighty, he once again revived the tradition of entertaining outside of the United States by taking Ann Jillian, Cathy Lee Crosby, Vic Damone, George Kirby, Julie Hayek (Miss U.S.A.), and Brooke Shields to the Eastern Mediterranean where the performers did a number of shipboard shows for U.S. forces involved in the Lebanon conflict.

38. COLLECTORS BOOKSTORE
7014 Sunset Boulevard

Inside this spacious former bank building across from Hollywood High, movie lovers will find what is perhaps Hollywood's largest collection of movie stills—plus an extremely impressive selection of fan magazines, film scripts, and autographed photos of the stars. The store also specializes in comic books and science-fiction magazines.

39. HOLLYWOOD HIGH SCHOOL
1521 North Highland Avenue

When it opened in 1904, it was bounded by bean fields and a lemon grove—and there were students who arrived on horseback.

It is one of the oldest high schools in Los Angeles and it counts among its distinguished graduates Norman Chandler, publisher of the *Los Angeles Times;* Nobel Prize winner (chemistry) William Schockley; and 1960s activist Episcopal Bishop James J. Pike. Not to mention all of the show-biz people who have been part of Hollywood High's student body through the years. Among them: Nanette Fabray, Marie Windsor, Marge Champion, Jason Robards, Alexis Smith, Ruta Lee, Sally Kellerman, Linda Evans, Ricky and David Nelson, Carol Burnett, Yvette Mimieux, Stephanie Powers, Mike Farrell, James Garner, Joel McCrea, and Lana Turner (who was not discovered at Schwab's Drugstore but at the Top Hat Malt Shop across the street from Hollywood High on the southwest corner of Sunset and Highland; the site is now a service station).

Today, Hollywood High has 2400 students 70 percent of whom belong to some ethnic minority. The school's most famous recent graduate, however, is American-as-apple-pie John Ritter, a member of the Class of 1966.

40. BERWIN ENTERTAINMENT COMPLEX
6525 Sunset Boulevard

Today, Island Records (the recording company of pop stars Grace Jones, Peter Tosh, King Sunny Ade) is one of the many show-biz tenants of this beautifully restored office/entertainment complex. But for movie lovers, the ultimate appeal of this graceful 1924 Spanish-style structure—built by Meyer and Holler, the same firm that did Grauman's Chinese and Egyptian theaters— is the fact that it began its life as the Hollywood Athletic Club.

In the 1920s and 1930s, every major male star in town was a member of this ultra-exclusive swim-and-gym organization. Johnny "Tarzan" Weissmuller and Buster Crabbe did laps in the

Hollywood Athletic Club, 1930

Cinerama Dome Theater

club's huge pool, John Wayne tossed billiard balls from the roof at passing cars on Sunset, and Walt Disney, after a nervous breakdown, worked out in the club's gym at the suggestion of his doctor.

Among the many stars who stayed here at one time or another were Charlie Chaplin, Rudolph Valentino, Bela Lugosi, Bud Abbott, and Lou Costello. The Club's grandest "digs" were the five rooms that made up its penthouse suite. These were often leased (under assumed names) by Hollywood's early playboys— and although women were not allowed in the penthouse tower, security guards were rumored to be somewhat lax when it came to enforcing this rule.

In 1949, the Athletic Club was used for the first televised Emmy Awards broadcast. From the mid-fifties until the late seventies, the building was taken over by a religious school and uninspired remodelings did away with much of its original splendor. In 1978, however, local entrepreneur Gary Berwin took over this Hollywood landmark and began a long and expensive restoration process. Today, the Berwin Entertainment Complex/ Hollywood Athletic Club is a triumph of preservation.

41. CINERAMA DOME THEATER
6360 Sunset Boulevard

Four decades after the era of Hollywood's great movie palaces—characterized by Grauman's Egyptian (1921), Grauman's Chinese (1927), the Warner (1927), and the Pantages (1930)— along comes the Cinerama Dome. The year was 1963 and the Dome's premier attraction, *It's a Mad Mad Mad Mad World,* seemed an appropriate offering to introduce this bizarre bit of 1960s theater architecture. Built in a decade when America was mesmerized more by technology than by motion pictures, the Dome boasted not only a futuristic geodesic shell but a state-of-the-art Cinerama screen and stereo sound system. Today, the theater is one of the best places in Los Angeles to see spectacle films such as *Raiders of the Lost Ark* where a big screen and blaring Dolby soundtrack make the special effects extra-special.

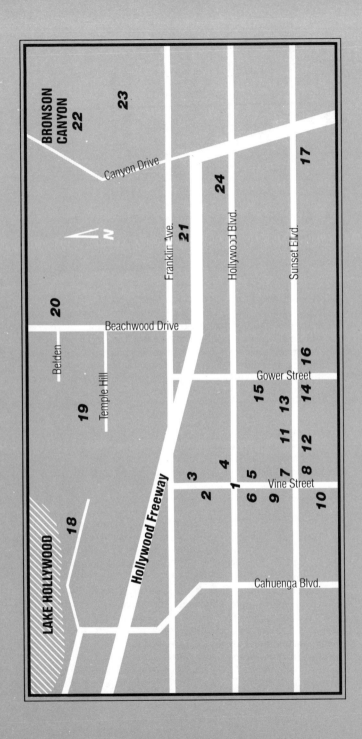

HOLLYWOOD: BEYOND THE BOULEVARD

Central Hollywood—
between Vine and Western

The most famous intersection on earth: Hollywood and Vine

STARTING with Vine Street and heading east, most of Hollywood's major sights are no longer on Hollywood Boulevard. Instead, they turn up on Sunset Boulevard, Franklin Avenue, and on Vine Street itself. (The great exception to this generalization is the spectacular Pantages Theater, which is on Hollywood Boulevard just east of Vine.)

On Sunset Boulevard, the attractions range from historic motion picture studios to fabulous 1940s nightclubs to the vestiges of Hollywood's once great radio industry. Franklin Avenue—the main street that is north of both Sunset and Hollywood boulevards—is more residential. Of particular interest to movie lovers are Franklin Avenue's spectacular chateau apartment houses that were built in the 1920s to accommodate the many motion picture people who commuted between New York and Hollywood. Although some of these imposing structures are in a sad state of repair today, their essential splendor can still be appreciated, as can their juicy histories. Other attractions in the area include the exclusive housing development that the famous Hollywood sign was built to promote . . . secret spots used as locations in classic Hollywood films . . . a landmark house created for a silent superstar who met a tragic end in the 1960s . . . a "James Dean stayed-here" hotel . . . an early residence of Charlie Chaplin . . . and, last but not least, one of Hollywood's greatest unsolved mysteries.

NOTE: *The first seventeen sites listed in this chapter can be seen on a walking tour. The last group are best visited by car.*

1. "HOLLYWOOD AND VINE"
Intersection of Hollywood Boulevard and Vine Street

It may be the most disappointing intersection on earth—and an ongoing debate among local history buffs centers around how it came to symbolize "Hollywood" at its most glamorous. The most plausible theory attributes Hollywood and Vine's notoriety to the fact that many of Hollywood's important radio studios were located on and around Vine Street in the 1930s. Historians go on to argue that since "brought to you from Hollywood and Vine" was a familiar opening to many an early broadcast, the intersection came to be thought of as glamorous because it *sounded* glamorous—especially to the millions of radio listeners who had never actually seen it.

2. THE PALACE
1735 North Vine Street

With its handsome Spanish-baroque façade and its gleaming Art Deco lobby, it came on the Hollywood scene back in 1927 as a legitimate theater called the Hollywood Playhouse. Then came the Depression and the Works Project Administration took over the place and continued to use it for plays and shows until

*Bob Cummings and
Marsha Hunt crossing
Hollywood and Vine, 1936*

1939. After that, the Hollywood Playhouse was occasionally used as a radio studio (CBS's "Baby Snooks," starring Fanny Brice originated from here) until 1942 when a new owner changed the theater's name to the El Capitan and Ken Murray came along with his famous *Blackouts* revue. When it closed in 1949, *Ken Murray's Blackouts* had become the longest running show in U.S. entertainment history—playing 3844 performances at the El Capitan.

Next came television: "The Bob Hope Chesterfield Specials," "This Is Your Life," "The Jerry Lewis Show" are among the shows telecast from the El Capitan. Then, in 1964, ABC changed the theater's name to the Palace and began beaming the "Hollywood Palace" variety show from the renamed theater. Bing Crosby was often a host of this very successful series and an unknown beauty named Raquel Welch was a card-carrying "Hollywood Palace" showgirl. After the series ended in 1970, the Palace continued to be used for television productions, the most famous being "The Merv Griffin Show" which was based here for four years. By the mid-1970s, the theater stood abandoned and was a prime candidate for demolition. It was saved by a couple of Hollywood-booster businessmen—Dennis Lidke and Paul Hendison—who wound up spending four years and $7 million on its restoration. Today, the theater is used for television specials, video production, premiere parties, and as a nightclub. The Palace also has offices, two restaurants, and recording studios. It was featured in the 1984 film *Against All Odds* as Jake's Palace.

3. CAPITOL RECORDS TOWER
1750 North Vine Street

Used to "establish" the fact that we are in Hollywood in countless films and television shows, the Capitol Records Tower is a symbol not just of Hollywood but of the city's powerful role in the recording industry. Rising thirteen stories and standing 150 feet tall, the Capitol Records Tower was (on account of a 1905 Los Angeles building-height-limit law that had more to do with aesthetics than with earthquakes) as high as any building in Los Angeles could be back in 1955. Some people have attributed the building's whimsical, stack-of-records shape to the fantasies of Capitol superstar Nat King Cole and Capitol songwriter/co-founder Johnny Mercer. The architect of this Hollywood landmark was Welton Becket who, a decade later, would build another local landmark—the Music Center complex in downtown Los Angeles.

4. PANTAGES THEATER
6233 Hollywood Boulevard

One of the most splendid Art Deco theaters in the world, the Pantages opened in 1930 with MGM's *The Floradora Girl* starring Marion Davies. In addition to the film, the "mixed bill" included an edition of Movietone News, a Walt Disney cartoon, a stage piece, and Slim Martin conducting the Greater Pantages Orchestra. The real star attraction, however, was the theater itself—with its lavish auditorium, lounges, lobbies, staircases, and rest rooms. A theater where the comfort of the moviegoer came before economics, the Pantages gave over 40 percent of its interior

Capitol Records Building

Pantages Theater lobby, 1930

space to public areas; and every detail—from the tiled water fountains to the stylized exit lights—was a work of art.

Originally built by the great theater-circuit mogul Alexander Pantages, the Pantages actually opened as a Fox theater since Pantages was serving a jail sentence at the time for a rape conviction that was later overturned. In 1949, the theater was acquired by Howard Hughes who changed its name to the RKO Pantages. It was during its RKO era that the Pantages was the site of the Academy Awards presentations (1949 to 1959). Pacific Theaters bought the Pantages in 1967 and a decade later joined forces with the Nederlander theater organization to turn it into a legitimate house for road companies of Broadway musicals. Major refurbishing and renovations brought the building back to its original dazzle in the early 1980s and today it is one of the most spectacular theaters on earth. A must!

NOTE: *To find out what's on at the Pantages, the telephone number to call is 410-1062.*

5. BROWN DERBY
1628 North Vine Street

When Hollywood lunched in the 1930s and 1940s, the Brown Derby was the place to go to see and to be seen. In those days, crowds would jam the Derby's entrance waiting to be seated at what was Hollywood's most famous restaurant—and head waiter Bill Chilios would just let them stand until all of the regulars were seated. Chilios took good care of the regulars. Occasionally he went too far. Once, for example, when Groucho Marx arrived at the Derby in the company of the wife of radio producer Carroll Carroll, Chilios refused to seat them until he was sure everything was on the up and up. For the Brown Derby was a very public place—a place where news was made (Clark Gable proposed "officially" to Carole Lombard in Booth 54), photographs taken, interviews given, and the more times you were paged and had a telephone brought to your table, the better it looked. You didn't do any serious business at the Derby—you confirmed (or tried to) your status as an important member of the Hollywood establishment.

Although the Vine Street Brown Derby called itself the "original" Brown Derby, it was actually the second of what was ultimately a chain of four restaurants started by a former husband of Gloria Swanson (and father of her daughter Gloria), Herbert Somborn. His first venture, a lunch counter on Wilshire, opened in 1926; this was the Brown Derby in the shape of the hat. The Vine Street branch opened in 1929 and was followed by a Beverly Hills operation in 1931 and a little known Los Feliz branch in 1941. While the Derbys are often confused, it is the Vine Street Brown Derby that became the most famous because of its proximity to the movie and radio studios.

The Brown Derby, along with many businesses in central Hollywood, started to decline in the 1960s, and by 1975 the place was on the verge of closing. At the last minute, however, it was bought by Walter and Elizabeth Scharfe, who totally renovated the aging landmark. Sad news: In April of 1985 the Vine Street Brown Derby abruptly closed, supposedly owing to problems with its lease. By the time this book is published, the historic restaurant may have wound up a parking lot. Meanwhile, it is reported that the Brown Derby's owner may try to open a new Brown Derby in another part of Hollywood.

6. PLAZA HOTEL
1637 North Vine Street

One of many 1920s Hollywood hotels turned old-age home, the Hollywood Plaza was, in its day, especially popular with radio

Vine Street Brown Derby, 1937

people since most of the broadcast studios were either on, or just off, Vine Street.

In 1937, silent films' hottest Jazz Baby, Clara (the "It Girl") Bow, her film career long over, opened a nightclub adjacent to the Plaza and called it, appropriately, The It Cafe. Alas, the "It" was a short-lived affair—yet another of Miss Bow's comeback tries that didn't pan out. One of the main reasons for the demise of Miss Bow's film career was a major Hollywood scandal of 1930 that forever shattered her reputation—and her peace of mind. Miss Bow's troubles started when a secretary whom she had fired got back at her by selling the "secrets" of her former employer's love life to a sleazy New York tabloid. Of all the revelations that sprang from this newsmaking affair, the most spectacular was one that had Miss Bow "entertaining" the entire starting lineup of the University of Southern California football team—including a tackle named Marion Morrison who would later achieve screen fame as John Wayne. Even though Clara took her secretary to court and won, the story of Clara Bow and the USC Trojans remains one of Hollywood's most enduring myths.

7. HOME SAVINGS AND LOAN ASSOCIATION
1500 North Vine Street

This massive bank building—a 1970s American version of Mussolini-moderne architecture—celebrates Hollywood's past with the names of hundreds of movie stars inscribed on its white-marble façade. Accompanying the names are colorful mosaic images of legends like Garbo, Valentino, Pickford, Fairbanks, Chaplin, Davis, Cooper—even Nanook of the North! Inside, the

Home Savings and Loan
Association Building,
Mary Pickford mosaic

Hollywood theme goes on—with huge murals depicting scenes from Cecil B. DeMille's 1913 film *The Squaw Man.*

The first feature-length motion picture ever made in Hollywood, *The Squaw Man* was shot a block away, near the corner of Vine and Selma. With the film's success, Jesse Lasky, one of its producers, was able to expand his studio to include the present-day location of the Home Savings and Loan. Ultimately, Lasky's Feature Players Company occupied the entire block between Sunset and Selma from 1914 to 1926. (A plaque marks the spot—incorrectly—at the northeast corner of Vine and Selma.)

Lasky's was the studio that became Paramount, and it was on this site that Mary Pickford made some her first Hollywood films and Rudolph Valentino made many of his. After Paramount moved to Melrose Avenue in 1926, the Sunset/Vine studios became everything from a rental lot to a miniature golf course. Then, in 1938, NBC Radio leveled the works to build its massive moderne Radio City—which was a Hollywood landmark until it was torn down in 1964.

8. LOS ANGELES FEDERAL SAVINGS AND LOAN BUILDING
6290 Sunset Boulevard

Standing twenty stories tall, this is Hollywood's loftiest structure. Built in 1963, when improved construction techniques allowed earthquake-prone Los Angeles to reach heights it never dreamed possible, the L.A. Federal Savings and Loan Building was nonetheless one of the skyscrapers that almost bit the dust in the 1974 Universal film *Earthquake.* Today, among the building's tenants is the Hollywood Chamber of Commerce. Their office is on the fifth floor—and will provide visitors with Hollywood information, maps, and brochures.

9. HUNTINGTON HARTFORD THEATER
1615 North Vine Street

A theater with a checkered past, the Huntington Hartford started out in 1927 as a legitimate house called the Vine Street Theater. By the mid-1930s, after several incarnations and renamings, it was taken over by Hollywood's burgeoning radio industry and became the CBS Playhouse Theater. It was from here that the famous "Lux Radio Theater"—hosted by C. B. DeMille and featuring major stars in radio versions of current movies—emanated. (DeMille would bow out of the series in 1945 after a widely publicized dispute with AFRA, the radio performing artists' union.) In 1954, the theater once again went "legit" and was named the Huntington Hartford, after the millionaire A&P heir who bankrolled its renaissance. The opening attraction: *What Every Woman Knows,* starring Helen Hayes. Today, the Huntington Hartford often hosts road companies of Broadway plays.

10. McDONALD'S
1411 North Vine Street

"You must remember this, a kiss is still a kiss . . ." And a Big Mac is still a Big Mac—even though Hollywood's Vine Street McDonald's serves them in one of the most whimsical settings on earth. A veritable shrine to the film *Casablanca,* this fast-food parlor is all done up with wicker chairs and stools, louvered panels, potted palms, mock Moorish columns, and, of course, ceiling fans. If that isn't enough, there's even a duplicate of the famous neon "Rick's Café Americain" sign that hung outside Humphrey Bogart's fabled club in the 1943 Warner Brothers classic. There are also numerous *Casablanca* stills on the walls. For the movie lover and McDonald's, "this could be the beginning of a beautiful friendship!"

11. HOLLYWOOD PALLADIUM
6215 Sunset Boulevard

During the big-band days of the 1940s, this was where they all played and where all of L.A. came to listen and to dance. Originally built by *L.A. Times* publisher Norman Chandler, the Palladium opened in 1940 with Tommy Dorsey who was featuring, at the time, a skinny young vocalist from New Jersey named Frank Sinatra. Among the many stars who were regulars at the Palladium, two lovely ladies—Alice Faye and Betty Grable— wound up marrying boys in the band (Phil Harris and Harry James, respectively).

By the 1950s, the big bands played less frequently and the Palladium started doing more private parties and banquets. But Lawrence Welk changed the Palladium picture at the beginning of the 1960s when he began broadcasting his immensely popular television show from here. Besides "The Lawrence Welk Show," the Palladium has also been used for numerous Emmy, Grammy, and Golden Globe awards telecasts. The famous club has had an extensive movie career, too—and has appeared in everything from *The Day of the Locust* to *F.I.S.T.* to a clinker called *Skatetown, U.S.A.* in which its vast dance floor was turned into a roller-skating rink. Today, rock groups and stars—from the Rolling Stones to Billy Idol—are frequently booked into the Palladium and it is still used for television specials as well as for big Hollywood bashes.

12. AQUARIUS THEATER
6230 Sunset Boulevard

When it opened in 1938 as the Earl Carroll Theater, *le tout Hollywood*—Gable, Lombard, Dietrich, Flynn, Power, et al.— showed up at the glittering first night of what was the largest (it seated 1000 people), if not the poshest, supper club L.A. had ever known. The man behind the magic was impresario Earl Carroll who came to the West Coast after over a decade of producing the very successful (and often raided) *Vanities* revues in New York. Among the Hollywood stars who leapt to screen careers from Earl Carroll's stage were Yvonne De Carlo, Marie "The Body" MacDonald, and Sheree North. But the fun all came to an end in 1948 when Earl Carroll and his headliner/girlfriend Beryl Wallace were killed in a plane crash.

In 1953, the club was given a new lease on life when it reopened as the Moulin Rouge and featured big-name entertainers. Fifties' TV fans may also remember the Moulin Rouge as the scene of the melodramatic "Queen for a Day" show which gave housewives the chance to beat the blahs through winning one wonderful day in Hollywood. The Moulin Rouge closed its doors permanently in 1960—when Las Vegas had pretty much cornered the supperclub market.

The same space had yet another life in the following decade as the Aquarius Theater, and it was here that the rock-musical *Hair* had a long West Coast run in the late 1960s. Today, the Aquarius is used for special events and theatrical productions.

13. KNX COLUMBIA SQUARE
6121 Sunset Boulevard

When the Nestor Film Company of Bayonne, New Jersey, came to Hollywood in 1911, they found an old roadhouse called the Blondeau Tavern on the northwest corner of Sunset and Gower Street. A victim of a recent prohibition ordinance passed by the ultra-conservative residents of early Hollywood, the tavern proved to be a suitable—and available—place for the Nestor Company to set up their operations. The Eastern filmmakers wasted no time and within a matter of days started churning out the first films ever produced in the town of Hollywood. Mostly one-reel Westerns and comedies, these early films were directed by a man named Al Christie, who, with his brother Charles, continued to produce "Christie Comedies" at the corner of Sunset and Gower up until the beginning of the 1930s. After that time, their studio became a rental lot.

CBS entered the picture in 1936 when it razed the old Nestor/Christie studios and broke ground for its Columbia Square

CBS Columbia Square today

radio complex. Among the many famous radio broadcasts that originated from these CBS studios were "Burns and Allen," "Beulah," "Edgar Bergen and Charlie McCarthy," "The Saint," "Our Miss Brooks," and "The Lucky Strike Hit Parade." Still standing in the same spot, the CBS building, despite renovations, is an architectural classic—designed with the clean bold lines and great simplicity that exemplified an offshoot of Art Deco known as the "International Style." Today, Columbia Square is home to the CBS-owned news radio station KNX.

14. GOWER GULCH
Corner of Sunset Boulevard and Gower Street

In the 1920s, there were so many small store-front movie studios along Gower Street that the area came to be known as "Poverty Row." At the same time, the corner of Gower and Sunset got the nickname "Gower Gulch" because of the large numbers of celluloid cowboys and Indians who hung out here—often in costume—waiting for bit parts or extra work in the low-budget one- and two-reel Westerns that many of the Poverty Row studios produced. Today a small shopping center occupies a corner of what once was Gower Gulch. Built in 1976, a time when Hollywood was starting to take its own history seriously, the Gower Gulch Shopping Plaza resembles a back-lot Western street with boardwalks and frontier-town façades. In its own way, this little mall pays hommage to the past whereas so many other shopping centers and parking lots built over historic Hollywood sites have not.

15. GOWER PLAZA HOTEL
1607 North Gower Street

This little hotel north of Hollywood Boulevard is believed to be where the late James Dean resided briefly while working as a

Gower Gulch in the 1930s

parking-lot attendant at the CBS Columbia Square Radio complex down the street. The year was 1951 and Jimmy would have been barely twenty years old. In September of the same year, Dean took off for New York—the first stop in the brief odyssey that would see him have it all/lose it all in a mere four years. Dean died on the night of September 30, 1955, when his silver Porsche Spyder went out of control on a road near Paso Robles, California. This was just four days after he had completed filming the final scenes for *Giant*. It was his third and last starring part in a motion picture. Rumor has it that actor Nick Adams was called in to loop some of the dialogue we hear Dean speak in the finished version of *Giant*.

16. SUNSET-GOWER STUDIOS
1438 North Gower Street

Television addicts will be interested in knowing that this studio complex has recently been the home of "General Hospital," "Days of Our Lives," and numerous other California-taped soap operas. But for film buffs, the Sunset-Gower Studios are noteworthy because from 1926 until 1972 they were the headquarters of the Columbia Pictures Corporation. Columbia started out as a small independent studio in the early 1920s when the Cohn brothers— Harry and Jack—and a third partner named Joe Brandt began making short comedies under the banner of the CBC Film Sales Company. By the time they took over the California Studios at 1438 North Gower in 1927, they had changed their company's name to the classier-sounding Columbia. Gower Street at the time was known as "Poverty Row" since it was the center of numerous small and often fly-by-night studios. Columbia, however, turned out to be Poverty Row's only real success story and the studio quickly increased in size through taking over a number of failing Poverty Row operations.

During the 1930s, Columbia came to fame largely through director Frank Capra's string of successful comedies that often used stars borrowed from other studios. The first and still one of the most famous of these Capra classics was *It Happened One Night* (1934) with Clark Gable (on loan from MGM) and Claudette Colbert (on loan from Paramount). The picture won Columbia its first Academy Award.

By the time the 1940s rolled around, Columbia had manu- factured its own great star. When she was discovered in the late 1930s, this young castoff from Fox had a widow's peak, a weight problem, and an ethnic last name (Cansino)—and she seemed hardly a candidate for the superstar status she would attain. But Columbia boss Harry Cohn played his hunches and ordered the studio to put the young woman under contract, on a diet, and to fix her hairline as well as her name—and thus Rita Hayworth was born. In the mid-1950s, she handed over the title of resident glamour goddess to another Columbia beauty and Cohn creation:

Kim Novak. In 1958, Harry Cohn—one of the last of the old-time studio bosses—died and an era ended. He was buried a few blocks away at Hollywood Memorial Cemetery in a plot that he had specially selected so that he could still keep an eye on his studio.

In 1972, Columbia moved across the Hollywood Hills to the Burbank Studios, whose facilities it now shares with Warner Brothers. The years 1977–1978 saw Columbia weather one of the greatest scandals in the history of the entertainment industry. The problems began when it came out that David Begelman—the president of Columbia who had turned the company around with films like *Funny Lady* and *Close Encounters of the Third Kind*—had forged some $75,000 worth of checks. To make matters worse, it was alleged that a number of other studio bosses had attempted to cover up the incident. Perhaps if Columbia had remained on the Hollywood side of the hills, within sight of Cohn's ever-watchful eye, the whole messy Begelman affair might never have been allowed to happen.

In 1982, Columbia was bought by the Coca-Cola Corporation and today is a wholly owned subsidiary of that conglomerate.

17. KTLA
5858 Sunset Boulevard

Now headquarters for cowboy star Gene Autry's Golden West Broadcasters, this handsome neo-Colonial building was erected in 1918 by a quartet of movie-mogul brothers named Warner. It was here that Warner Brothers perfected a technique that would change the course of motion picture history—namely synchronized sound. Contrary to popular belief, Warners' 1927 *The Jazz Singer* was not the first commercial sound film. That honor goes to Warners' 1926 *Don Juan* which featured a synchronized track of musical accompaniment by the New York Philharmonic Orchestra. Then came *The Jazz Singer* in 1927 with synchronized songs and some synchronized dialogue. The first true "all-talking" picture, *The Lights of New York,* was released by Warner Brothers a year later.

Former Warner Brothers Studios as bowling center in the 1940s

Barbara Stanwyck's house in Double Indemnity

In 1929, Warner Brothers took over the former First National Studios in Burbank and made them its main base of operations. The Sunset Boulevard facilities were subsequently used for the production of Warners' animated cartoons—Porky Pig, Bugs Bunny, and Daffy Duck. In 1942, Warners' Sunset studios were acquired by Paramount; after that, they were converted into one of the world's largest bowling centers—with fifty-two lanes. Gene Autry bought the property in 1964 and today his television station KTLA and radio station KMPC are based here.

18. "DOUBLE INDEMNITY" HOUSE
6301 Quebec Street

"It was one of those California Spanish houses everyone was nuts about ten or fifteen years ago—this one must have cost somebody about thirty thousand bucks." So speaks Fred Mac-Murray as insurance investigator Walter Neff at the opening of Billy Wilder's classic 1944 film, *Double Indemnity.* And as soon as MacMurray utters the line, the audience in the revival cinema breaks into gales of laughter because the house up there on screen would easily cost ten times that much in the inflated real-estate market of today's Los Angeles.

In the film, the house belongs to Barbara Stanwyck and to the husband she and MacMurray plot to kill. It appears in many scenes, the most memorable being the one in which Stanwyck helps her husband—he's on crutches owing to an unforeseen accident—down the front steps to the garage where MacMurray is hiding in the back seat of the LaSalle ready to strangle him to death.

Surprisingly, this house that seems such an ideal representative of the Big Spanish mansions that characterize East Hollywood's Los Feliz neighborhood isn't in Los Feliz at all. Instead, the *Double Indemnity* house sits on a quiet corner up in the Hollywood Hills.

NOTE: *The house is not easy to find. Serious movie lovers should consult a good map to get to Quebec Street—and take care not to disturb the occupants.*

Postcard view of Charlie Chaplin's Hollywood (not Beverly) Hills home in the early 1920s

19. CHARLIE CHAPLIN HOUSE
6147 Temple Hill Drive

According to a 1923 postcard, this enchanting little castle was once the home of Charlie Chaplin. The house is not in Beverly Hills, however, as the postcard says. It is in the lower Hollywood Hills on Temple Hill Drive north of Franklin Avenue and west of Beachwood Drive. Mary Astor is another movie person who is said to have lived here.

NOTE: *Temple Hill Drive is a marvelous pocket of early Hollywood fantasy architecture; a quick spin around it will reveal a number of other exotic villas, castles, and tiny Arabian palaces.*

20. HOLLYWOODLAND AND THE HOLLYWOOD SIGN
Beachwood Drive at Westshire Drive

High in the Hollywood Hills and visible from almost anywhere in the Hollywood "flats," the Hollywood sign has come to symbolize the city of Hollywood in much the same way as do Grauman's Chinese Theater, the intersection of Hollywood and Vine, and the Marathon Avenue Gate of Paramount Pictures. Unlike these other Hollywood landmarks, however, the sign has no connection with the entertainment industry. Instead, it originally represented the one Hollywood business that is—and always has been—even bigger than show-biz: real estate.

When the Hollywood sign was erected in 1923, it didn't even spell out Hollywood—but rather "Hollywoodland" which was the name of the urban utopia that *L.A. Times* publisher Harry Chandler and two other local big-businessmen were developing in the Hollywood Hills. Their dream development (where silent movie producer Mack Sennett had his lot all picked out but never built) boasted architectural styles that included Norman castles, Elizabethan cottages, Moorish mansions, and Spanish haciendas.

All were advertised as being "above the traffic congestion, smoke, fog, and poisonous gas fumes of the Lowlands." (It would seem that air pollution was a Los Angeles problem even in the idyllic 1920s; it would be christened "smog" some two decades later.)

While perhaps not the utopia promised by its developers, the Hollywoodland/Beechwood Canyon area remains one of Hollywood's loveliest neighborhoods. It is approached by driving north on Beachwood Drive and continuing through the handsome Hollywoodland Gates at Westshire Drive. The storybook cottage to the right is the original—and still functioning—office of the Hollywoodland Realty Company. To the left, the intersection of Beachwood and Belden was immortalized in the original *Invasion of the Body Snatchers* as the center of the small California town whose zombielike populace Kevin McCarthy and Dana Wynter tried to escape until the end of the movie. A large still of this scene from the 1956 Allied Artists film hangs above the meat counter of the Beachwood Market at 2701 Belden Drive.

A drive up Beachwood will reveal the intriguing architectural diversity of the area, an area that remains much as it was in the 1920s and 1930s and one that has been traditionally favored by screenwriters as a quiet place to live and to write.

Looming over this beautiful fantasyland, the famous sign has had a life of its own quite separate from the real-estate development it was built to advertise. The most famous event associated with the sign was the suicide jump of Peg Entwistle, a young actress who tried to parlay her success on the Broadway stage into a Hollywood film career. Unfortunately things didn't work out "just like in the movies" and in September of 1932, Miss Entwistle climbed to the top of the "H" and jumped to her death 50 feet below.

Despite this tragic event, life went on in Hollywoodland. But as the development prospered, its huge emblem was allowed to deteriorate until all maintenance of the sign was discontinued in 1939. Finally, the dilapidated structure was deeded to the Hollywood Chamber of Commerce which removed the "LAND" portion in 1945 in an attempt to make the sign represent the

The new Hollywood sign

whole city of Hollywood. In subsequent years, the sign has been restored several times, the most recent restoration being that of 1978 when a major "Save the Sign" campaign succeeded in raising enough money to create a brand-new, super-reinforced version of the famous sheet-metal landmark that's 45 feet tall, 450 feet long, and weighs 480,000 pounds.

21. CHATEAU ELYSEE
5930 Franklin Avenue

Of all the "chateau" apartment buildings erected in Hollywood during the booming 1920s, none was more impressive than the Chateau Elysee. Built in 1928 by the widow of the famous early movie producer Thomas Ince, the Chateau Elysee—sometimes known as "Chateau Ince," but usually just as "the Chateau"— was designed by prominent architect Arthur E. Harvey as a luxury hotel in the form of a gigantic seven-story Norman castle. So solid were its foundations that the Chateau has never needed to be upgraded to meet the more stringent earthquake regulations of subsequent decades.

Originally this grand hotel had seventy-seven apartments and the celebrities who resided here, both short- and long-term, included some of the most famous names of the 1930s. Cary Grant was a former tenant and in recent years he returned to the Chateau to show his old apartment to his new wife, Barbara Harris. According to Chateau records, Gable and Lombard also lived here in the 1930s and hid away (they weren't yet married) in apartment #604; George Burns and Gracie Allen spent some of their early Hollywood days in #609; Ginger Rogers shared #705 with her mother Lela; and Lily Pons had an opulent multilevel suite (#416) that had three bedrooms and three baths but no kitchen. No need for that, as a dazzling "European" dining room served meals and also provided room service.

The center of the film world's "chateau life" in the 1930s, the Elysee was often the scene of glamorous parties and saw frequent visits by Hollywood nobility dwelling in nearby "castles." Humphrey Bogart, for example, is said to have once lived a few blocks away in the Hollywood Tower (6200 Franklin Avenue) and often came over to the Chateau to play tennis. Another neighbor was Gloria Swanson—who is rumored to have shared luxurious secret quarters at Castle Argyle (1919 Argyle) with her mentor/lover Joseph Kennedy.

Like all fairy stories, there was a dark side to some of the glamour at the Chateau Elysee. For there was always talk that the hotel may have concealed one of Hollywood's greatest unsolved mysteries. The secret of the Chateau was that it was not Mrs. Ince's money that built the castle but rather that of newspaper heavyweight William Randolph Hearst. The basis for this story goes back to the mysterious sudden death of Thomas Ince while on a weekend outing aboard Hearst's yacht *Oneida* in 1924. The

Chateau Elysee today

official version of *l'affaire Ince,* as it came to be known, was that Ince suffered an acute attack of gastritis aboard the boat and was quickly taken to his home in Beverly Hills where he died. A far juicier account of the incident purports that Ince was shot aboard Hearst's yacht and suggests that the person who pulled the trigger was none other than William Randolph Hearst! The reason for the supposed shooting is even more bizarre. It seems that Hearst suspected his movie-star girlfriend, Marion Davies, of having a fling with Charlie Chaplin. Both Chaplin and Davies were aboard the *Oneida* and when Hearst found Davies alone in a cabin with a man he thought to be Chaplin, he fired. The man, however, was not Chaplin but Ince. Everyone on board was then sworn to secrecy, including a young Hearst columnist named Louella Parsons whose career supposedly started to soar once *l'affaire Ince* blew over.

Meanwhile, poor Mrs. Ince was out a mate and many people have speculated that Hearst financed "Chateau Ince" because of his great guilt over having killed the woman's husband by mistake. It is also speculated that Hearst built the Villa Carlotta across the street from the Chateau at 5959 Franklin Avenue for the same reason. (Louella Parsons was an early Villa Carlotta resident.) So the story goes . . . and goes. If nothing else, it's a pretty good story!

In 1952, the Chateau Elysee was turned into a luxury retirement hotel called Fifield Manor. In 1973, the building was acquired by the Church of Scientology of California and today its movie-star apartments are used for Scientology training sessions. Slowly, the Scientology organization has also been trying to restore the building to at least some of its former splendor—and visitors are welcome to take a quick peek inside. Even in its current condition, with a bit of imagination, one can imagine the magical goings-on at this grandest of Hollywood's chateaux.

22. BRONSON CANYON
Griffith Park and Canyon Drive

Before it became fashionable—and feasible—to shoot films on location all over the world, movie studios stayed as close to home as possible. After all, what were all those soundstages and back lots for, anyway? There's an old Hollywood story about a young director who told producer Sam Goldwyn that he needed an out-of-town location for the picture he was working on. Replied Goldwyn: "A rock's a rock, and a tree's a tree. Shoot it in Griffith Park!" And with some 4000 acres of pastoral scenery, Griffith Park was not only the largest municipal park in the country, it was a Godsend to early moviemakers as a location.

A prime Griffith Park location has always been Bronson Canyon, which to this day looks like everyone's fantasy of the Wild West. Besides the hundreds of low-budget silent Westerns—most of them now lost—shot around Bronson Canyon, the area has furnished backgrounds for numerous episodes of "Gunsmoke," "High Chapparal," and "Bonanza," to name but a few television series. Equally popular as a setting for science-fiction films were the nearby Bronson Caves. Batman stored his Batmobile in one of these caverns; Kevin McCarthy and Dana Wynter hid out in another at the end of *The Invasion of the Body Snatchers;* and all manner of extraterrestrial creatures and monsters have lived and died in the Bronson Caves in films such as *Night of the Bloodbeast* and *It Conquered the Earth.*

NOTE: *To reach the Bronson Canyon, drive north on Bronson Avenue until it turns into Canyon Drive. Continue north on Canyon until you enter Griffith Park. The caves are a short hike to the east.*

23. RAMON NOVARRO HOUSE
5699 Valley Oak Drive

Looking like an exotic pre-Columbian temple, this magnificent concrete-and-copper mansion is one of many dramatic Hollywood homes designed by Lloyd Wright, an architect whose significant accomplishments are often overlooked because of the greater fame of his father, Frank Lloyd Wright. Built in 1928, this particular Lloyd Wright landmark once belonged to silent screen superstar Ramon (*Ben Hur*) Novarro. Not content with any ordinary interior for his extraordinary residence, Novarro supposedly had MGM set designer Cedric Gibbons do up the place in black fur and silver. And when Novarro entertained in this marvelous maison, he sometimes insisted that his dinner guests dress for the decor and wear no colors other than black, silver, or white.

Novarro's movie career and his days of living lavishly were all part of the distant past at the time of his death in the late 1960s. By then, the life-long bachelor was living—surrounded by the mementos of his glory years—in a ranch-style house on the San Fernando Valley side of Laurel Canyon. On Halloween night of 1968, Novarro picked up a pair of male hustlers on Hollywood Boulevard and brought them back to the house. The ensuing events are among Hollywood's most horrible: the two young thugs totally destroyed the sixty-nine-year-old former actor's home and savagely beat him to death in the process. Later, actor-turned-novelist Tom Tryon would loosely base the "Willie" story in his bestseller, *Crowned Heads,* on this grisly event.

24. FLORENTINE GARDENS
5951 Hollywood Boulevard

Never one of Hollywood's most glamorous nightspots, this 1940s club featured Italian food and a tacky, often risqué floor show. It was the kind of place where working people went for a night on the town. And when sixteen-year-old Norma Jean Baker married twenty-two-year-old factory-worker Jim Dougherty in June of 1942, the wedding party celebrated the event at Florentine Gardens. The couple never had a honeymoon and the marriage ended four years later as Norma Jean Baker Dougherty was starting a new life with a new name . . . Marilyn Monroe.

After numerous owners and lives (one of which featured stripper Lili St. Cyr as the headliner and another saw the building used as a Salvation Army post), Florentine Gardens was recently a rock club.

Former home of Ramon Novarro—designed by Lloyd Wright

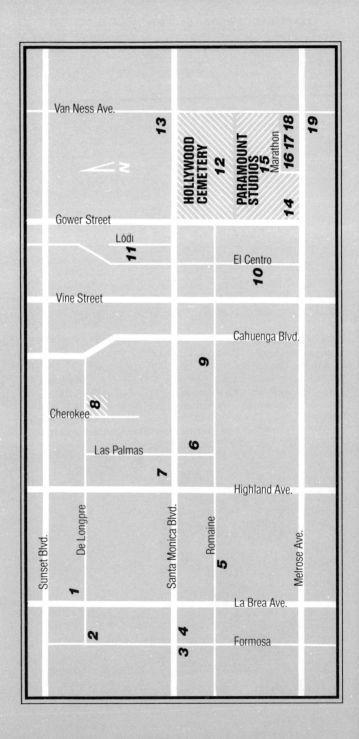

HOLLYWOOD: THE FACTORY TOWN

Central Hollywood—
south of Sunset Boulevard

3

Captains of industry:
Mary Pickford and Douglas Fairbanks
inaugurate their Hollywood studio in 1922

PICKFORD-FAIRBANKS
STUDIOS

SOUTH of Sunset Boulevard lies a great flat section of Hollywood where massive moviemaking installations share space with tiny streets of Spanish bungalows and craftsmen-style cottages fronted by neatly tended lawns and gardens. This is the center of Hollywood, the factory town—but from the look of things, this is a factory town straight out of the movies. It's all surprisingly attractive, especially on the side streets where the feeling is often one of a small Southern California town. It's all a little strange too, since the great studios and film processing plants that cover the area seem to have almost no architectural relationship to their environment. The studios, the dream factories, are simply there—alien, private worlds that appear to be outside the scheme of things. Yet, they are the heart of things.

Today, little has changed in this part of Hollywood. The little streets with their bungalows and cottages are still here, many now housing Hispanic and Oriental families. The movie plants are still here as well. In fact, the area continues to have one of the world's greatest concentrations of movie-related industries; and even though many historic early movie lots have changed owners and names a number of times over the years, the lots themselves continue to flourish, turning out not only films, but television shows, commercials, and music videos. Indeed, Hollywood the Factory Town is alive and well south of Sunset.

Of all the studios in this part of Hollywood, the most famous still in operation is Paramount—which has been in exactly the same spot since 1926. But for the movie buff, much of the fun involved with discovering this neck of the Hollywood woods will no doubt have to do with seeing what's become of vanished studios like RKO, Charlie Chaplin, and United Artists. Another of the treats in store for the movie lover south of Sunset is the Hollywood Memorial Cemetery. Built smack in the middle of studioland, this famous and rarely visited cemetery is where some of the greatest names in the motion picture industry have been laid to rest amidst an exotic setting of palms, obelisks, and temples worthy of a Cecil B. DeMille epic. No wonder Mr. DeMille himself chose to be buried here!

NOTE: *This chapter covers a lot of ground and the sites mentioned here should be seen by car. The last six sites, however, are all within an area of a few blocks around Paramount Studios and will be best appreciated on foot.*

1. A & M RECORDS
1416 North La Brea Avenue

A row of fairy-tale Tudor cottages forms the façade of this important record company's headquarters. The cottages were originally built by Charlie Chaplin as part of the independent studio he founded in 1918 and which eventually occupied the entire block between De Longpre Avenue and Sunset Boulevard.

Chaplin Studios, 1929

For a while, Chaplin lived at the studio in a large Tudor mansion off Sunset that had a tennis court and stables. Today, a Safeway supermarket stands where the house once was but inside the A & M Records complex many of the original Chaplin Studios' buildings remain, notably the main soundstage (Chaplin's "duck-walk" footprints are embedded in the cement in front of this structure)—plus dressing rooms, carpentry shop, and stables. Chaplin had the studio until the early 1950s and made most of his classics here. Among them: *A Dog's Life* (1918), *The Kid* with Jackie Coogan (1920), *The Gold Rush* (1925), *City Lights* (1931), *Modern Times* (1936), and *The Great Dictator* (1940).

After Chaplin sold the studio, it passed hands numerous times. Subsequent owners included American International, Red Skelton, and CBS. From 1952 to 1957, many episodes of the popular TV series "Superman," starring the late George Reeves, were filmed on this lot. "Perry Mason" was also done here, and Raymond Burr (taking a cue from Chaplin?) is said to have had his own apartment on the property. Finally, in 1966, A & M Records, headed by Herb Alpert and Jerry Moss, took over the premises, restored them, and made them its headquarters. Today, some of Hollywood's most advanced recording studios are housed here and Charlie Chaplin's original soundstage is often used for the taping of rock-music videos (Police's "Every Breath You Take," Ray Parker, Jr.'s "Ghostbusters," and the Stevie Wonder sequences of "Ebony and Ivory," among them) as well as for filming commercials and TV specials.

2. COURTYARD APARTMENTS
1328–1330 North Formosa Avenue

There are so many stories associated with this little cluster of "Hansel and Gretel" cottages that we may never know the truth about them. Some people say the buildings were constructed by Charlie Chaplin as a movie set; others say that Chaplin built them as stables; still others insist that Chaplin used them as dressing rooms and guest quarters. Given the proximity of Chaplin's studios, a Chaplin connection would seem plausible—although neither building permits nor assessor's records make any mention of the man.

More Hollywood stories center on the famous people who have lived in the cottages over the years. Naturally, Valentino heads the list (he did get around!), followed by the Munchkins who supposedly stayed here during the filming of *The Wizard of Oz*. (In truth, these little folk were put up at a full-sized hotel over in Culver City near the MGM Studios where the movie was filmed.) Marilyn Monroe is another name one hears in connection with this location—and the stories go on and on. No matter who lived here, the buildings are historic from an architectural point of view—since the original building permits list the name Zwebell as the architect. Zwebell was actually the last name of a husband and wife (Arthur and Nina) architect team who later were responsible for a number of notable Los Angeles courtyard apartment buildings, the most famous being the Andalusia (1926) in West Hollywood. Built in 1923, the Formosa Avenue Zwebell apartments would appear to be one of the couple's earliest works.

3. WARNER HOLLYWOOD STUDIOS
1041 North Formosa Avenue

Warner Brothers took over the former Samuel Goldwyn Studios in 1980—and it is here where the current king of television, Aaron Spelling, has his offices and controls his dynasty of popular series. Both "Dynasty" and "The Love Boat" are among the Spelling series shot on the Warner Hollywood lot.

The Warner Hollywood lot is one of the town's most historic and dates back to 1918 when producer Jesse D. Hampton turned

Mary Pickford and Douglas Fairbanks open their studio in 1922

out pictures here starring a well-known silent actor named W. B. Warner. Then in 1922, Mary Pickford and Douglas Fairbanks, who in 1919 along with Charlie Chaplin and D. W. Griffith had formed United Artists in order to free themselves of studio contracts and constraints, took over the Hampton lot and renamed it the Pickford-Fairbanks Studios. This is where Fairbanks turned out such swashbuckling classics as *Robin Hood* and *The Thief of Bagdad* and Pickford did *Tess of the Storm Country* and *Rosita.* Photos from the period show the mammoth sets of many of these early epics towering above Santa Monica Boulevard.

In 1928, with the addition of Samuel Goldwyn to the United Artists team, the Pickford-Fairbanks facility was renamed United Artists Studios and Goldwyn made the lot his permanent base. By 1936, the studio came to bear Goldwyn's name although Mary Pickford retained principal ownership. Among the Goldwyn productions of this era were *Roman Scandals* (1933), *Nana* (1934), *Barbary Coast* (1935), *Dodsworth* (1936), *Stella Dallas* (1937), *Wuthering Heights* (1939), *The Little Foxes* (1941), *The Best Years of Our Lives* (1946), *Hans Christian Andersen* (1952), and *Guys and Dolls* (1955). Goldwyn bought out Pickford in the mid-1950s and headed the studio until his death in 1974. The property was sold to Warner Brothers in 1980; and today the Samuel Goldwyn Company—headed by Sam Goldwyn, Jr.—has moved to another location on Santa Monica Boulevard and is involved in the production of original films as well as the distribution of foreign films and Goldwyn classics. Meanwhile, television reigns at the old studio where once Douglas Fairbanks cavorted as Robin Hood and Mary Pickford languished as Tess.

4. FORMOSA CAFE
7156 Santa Monica Boulevard

Since 1945, this little Chinese/American restaurant has served as unofficial commissary for the various movie studios in the area. The closest of these studios was Samuel Goldwyn (now Warner-Hollywood) which was literally a stone's throw away across Formosa Street. Inside the long dinerlike building of the Formosa Cafe, practically every inch of wallspace is taken up with photos of the many stars who have dined here at one time or another. Most of the photos are signed with best wishes to the restaurant's owner, Lem Quon. A legend of the Formosa Cafe is that Elvis Presley once gave a Formosa waitress named Dora a white Cadillac Eldorado convertible. The car sat for many years on Dora's lawn on Melrose Avenue at El Centro.

5. FORMER HOWARD HUGHES HEADQUARTERS
7000 Romaine Street

A massive Babylonian-moderne fortress was the long-time Hollywood headquarters of eccentric millionaire Howard Hughes.

Former Howard Hughes headquarters

It was from here that Hughes controlled a vast empire that, at various times, encompassed film studios, movie theaters, aircraft factories, and Trans World Airlines. (He sold his stock in the latter for a cool $546 million in 1966.)

Hughes moved into 7000 Romaine Street in 1927. At the time he was involved with his Caddo Pictures company, which produced *Hells Angels* (the 1930 film that unleashed Jean Harlow) as well as the original *Scarface* (1932), starring Paul Muni. Both films were edited on Romaine Street as was Hughes' controversial Jane Russell film, *The Outlaw,* which was completed in 1943 but not released until 1946. The reason for the long interval between the picture's completion and its release was partially because of the censors and partially owing to Hughes' perverse personality: He would make the public want to see his film by withholding it from them as long as possible!

Hughes's legendary eccentricities were also responsible for the special film printing room at Romaine Street that had a series of doors in order to keep any dust from contaminating his precious film. Anyone entering the room was under boss's orders to vacuum their clothing ahead of time. There's another story about Hughes that had him experimenting with carrier pigeons at Romaine Street—and it is said that the cagelike structure still attached to the building was used during Hughes's pigeon period. Hughes died in 1976. Today, his former fortress is just another Hollywood office building.

6. HOLLYWOOD CENTER STUDIOS
1040 North Las Palmas Avenue

Producer/director/screenwriter Francis Ford Coppola was the last big name to head this studio. Coppola had a dream: He wanted to create in the New Hollywood of independent producers and production companies a studio that would be run along the lines of the great Old Hollywood studios of the 1930s. For his

Zoetrope Studios, Coppola would have a stable of contract players (Teri Garr and Raul Julia were among the actors he signed), writers, directors, technicians. Zoetrope would be a place where creative people would find a hospitable filmmaking environment rarely found in Hollywood. It would be a breeding ground for new talent as well as a place where veterans like writer/director Michael (*The Red Shoes*) Powell would have a chance to pick up their careers.

It was all a lovely idea—but, alas, Zoetrope's Hollywood studio was a financial disaster. Aside from *Hammett, One from the Heart,* and *Escape Artist,* the studio produced little in the way of motion pictures and even less in the way of profits. By 1983, money problems forced Coppola to sell the studio and return to the commercial realities of tinseltown.

The studio where Coppola indulged his dream was founded in 1919 as a rental lot called Jasper Studios. In the mid-1920s, when comic Harold Lloyd split from producer/director Hal Roach, Lloyd made this lot his headquarters for his own production company. In 1929, Howard Hughes produced and directed *Hells Angels* here and detonated blonde bombshell Jean Harlow in her first major role. Another important independent who used the same studio was Alexander Korda, who lensed *That Hamilton Woman* here with Laurence Olivier and Vivien Leigh in the early forties.

By the time the 1950s rolled around, the Las Palmas lot was known as Hollywood General Studios and it became an important center of television production. Hollywood General (later known as General Service Studios) was the home of "The Ozzie and Harriet Show," "Love That Bob," and "The Burns and Allen Show" (George Burns still has an office on the property). The

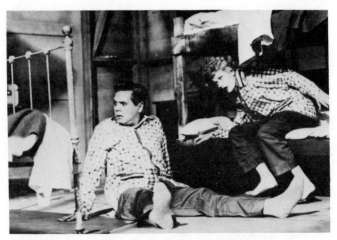

"I Love Lucy," long-time tenant of Hollywood General Studios

Bust of Rudolph Valentino in DeLongpre Park

studio also saw a lot of the most famous TV series in history, "I Love Lucy," which shot at Hollywood General for most of its lifetime from 1951 to 1957. Today, it is once again a rental lot and is often used for commercials.

7. CALIFORNIA STATE BUREAU OF EMPLOYMENT SECURITY
6725 Santa Monica Boulevard

In show business, there's one great leveler: unemployment. Even big stars often go for lengthy spells "between engagements." Therefore, at any given time, large numbers of Hollywood's acting community can be found standing in line inside this unprepossessing low-rise government building. Some of those waiting in line may have left their Mercedes convertible or Rolls Royce outside. Never mind—every little bit helps. Even in Hollywood!

8. DELONGPRE PARK
Cherokee Avenue at DeLongpre Avenue

Strange bedfellows: In the middle of a little municipal park, Hispanic and Oriental preschoolers play and shout, an occasional burned-out hippie relaxes on a park bench, and movie lovers will find a memorial to Hollywood's greatest screen lover—Rudolph Valentino. Erected in 1930 (four years after Valentino's death) by "friends and admirers from every walk of life, in all parts of the world, in appreciation of the happiness brought to them by his cinema portrayals," the memorial statue—entitled "Aspiration"—is of a nude male with head thrust back and looking up to the sky. Next to this statue, a bronze bust of Valentino completes the picture.

Hollywood Television Center, former Technicolor Building

9. HOLLYWOOD TELEVISION CENTER
6311 Romaine Street

From 1930 to 1975, this impressive Art Deco building housed the offices and laboratories of Technicolor, Inc., the company that made color a permanent part of the Hollywood picture in the early 1930s. The original Technicolor process was developed between 1914 and 1922 by Dr. Herbert Thomas Kalmus and some of his fellow alumni of the Massachusetts Institute of Technology. The name "Technicolor," it turns out, is in honor of MIT!

At first the process was used mostly for short subjects and for color sequences within otherwise black-and-white feature films. With Dr. Kalmus heading up Technicolor, Inc., his wife Natalie became the company's "Color Director" and was responsible for showing producers renting Technicolor equipment how to use it correctly. (Film buffs will remember that Mrs. Kalmus's name appears on the credits of all Technicolor films up until 1949, the year the patent ran out.)

The original Technicolor process was far from perfect. Using two negatives, it resulted in blurred images and in a color range limited to greens and oranges; pure blues and pure yellows were impossible to achieve. By 1931, however, Dr. Kalmus had developed a three-negative Technicolor process that resulted in colors that were practically flawless. The first producer to use the new process was Walt Disney, who began photographing his "Silly Symphonies" cartoons in advanced Technicolor in 1932. The first three-strip Technicolor feature film debuted in 1935. The film was *Becky Sharp*, starred Miriam Hopkins, and was produced by two wealthy socialite cousins, John Hay ("Jock") Whitney and Cornelius Vanderbilt ("Sonny") Whitney. The same two gentlemen producers also bought 15 percent of Technicolor, Inc., and while *Becky Sharp* was not a great artistic or commercial success, Technicolor was. In fact, at its peak in the early 1950s, the Romaine Street headquarters had some 2500 employees working round-the-clock—and it was here that some of Hollywood's most famous Technicolor films were processed and color-corrected.

In 1975, Technicolor moved to North Hollywood and recently its former headquarters have been shared by Walter Lantz Productions (of "Woody Woodpecker" cartoon fame) and by the film archives of the University of California at Los Angeles (UCLA). Ironically, a recent UCLA project here involved the restoration of the original *Becky Sharp*—the film that started it all.

10. HOLLYGROVE
815 North El Centro Avenue

Formerly known as the Los Angeles Orphans Home Society, this institution dates back to 1880 and has stood on El Centro Avenue since 1911. Surrounded by movie studios and production facilities (Paramount, RKO, Technicolor, Western Costumes), it was here that ten-year-old Norma Jean Baker (Marilyn Monroe) came to live in 1935 after having been bounced around among several foster homes. Crying "I'm not an orphan" as she was taken inside the main building (no longer standing), Norma Jean would spend close to two years here, playing on its sports field, attending the nearby Vine Street School (955 North Vine), occasionally making excursions to downtown Los Angeles (during which she sometimes wore lipstick), plotting at least one escape attempt, and dreaming, perhaps, of a happier life. In 1980, a former "orphan" at the home during the mid-1930s remembered Marilyn in an interview with Lisa Mitchell that appeared in the July issue of *Westways* magazine: "She was a very generous person who would never say no to you if you asked her for something. I remember her sitting quietly at a piano we had there and playing for us. She always reminded me of a doe. A funny thing: In 1962, I got the feeling that I should write to her. Whether she'd remember me or not, I wanted to let her know she had a friend. I did write the letter and a month later, she passed away."

Today, Hollygrove specializes in providing residential care and treatment for emotionally disturbed boys and girls, ages five through ten.

11. HOLLYWOOD STUDIO CLUB
1215 Lodi Place

The Hollywood Studio Club was established in 1916 when the Y.W.C.A.—Mrs. C. B. DeMille and Mary Pickford also lent their support to the project—saw the need to provide a decent

Hollywood Studio Club Building

place to live for the large numbers of young women who had come to Hollywood to work in the movies. Originally located in a former private home at 6129 Carlos Avenue, the first Studio Club housed Zasu Pitts, Carmel Myers, Mae Busch, Janet Gaynor, Marjorie Daw, as well as writer Ayn Rand. But this facility soon proved too small to accommodate the ever-increasing throngs of young hopefuls constantly arriving in Hollywood—and so, after an extensive fund-raising campaign, a new Studio Club was built at Lodi Place. Designed by woman architect Julia Morgan (her greatest achievement would be William Randolph Hearst's castle, San Simeon), the new building resembled a Renaissance palazzo and featured a trio of graceful arches at the entrance and a beautiful interior courtyard. The Lodi Place Studio Club went on to provide a Hollywood home to everyone from Peg Entwistle (the woman who jumped from the Hollywood sign to her death in 1932) to Kim Novak, Dorothy Malone, Donna Reed, Nancy Kwan, Rita Moreno, Anne B. Davis, Barbara Eden, Sharon Tate, and Sally Struthers. Its most famous former resident, however, was Marilyn Monroe, who lived in room 334 for a short time in 1948 when she was doing walk-ons as a contract player at Twentieth Century-Fox.

In the early 1970s, the club went coed—and by the mid-1970s, it looked as though it was going to close its doors permanently. But in 1977, the Y.W.C.A. turned it into a training center for the Los Angeles Job Corps program; it is still being used for that purpose.

12. HOLLYWOOD MEMORIAL PARK CEMETERY
6000 Santa Monica Boulevard

One of the great cemeteries of the world, Hollywood Memorial Park is a delightfully dramatic fantasy world that could have been conceived by a Cecil B. DeMille or a D. W. Griffith as a background for an epic film. From the outside, the view is of long high walls and tall palm trees. Inside, there are small Greek, Roman, and Egyptian temples; obelisks and urns, beautiful green lawns, and more palm trees. At the same time, Hollywood is everywhere: Paramount Studios—with its water tower soaring into the air—is smack against the cemetery's southern wall. To the north, the Hollywood sign dominates the Hollywood Hills. Yet, despite its location in the middle of Hollywood, the Hollywood Cemetery is a delightfully peaceful place and seems strangely set apart from the sometimes frenetic city on the other side of its walls. All in all, it looks like a pretty good place for some of the most famous names of early Hollywood to have wound up. In fact, it may be one of the most pleasant places in town.

The grandest graves are mostly clustered around a lovely little lake on the eastern side of the park. Here, Cecil B. DeMille is next to his wife, Constance Adam DeMille. A striking double tomb marks the spot. Across the way, Columbia's Harry Cohn has the exact same double marble marker as DeMille—but shares it with no one. Also lakeside are Nelson Eddy, Adolphe Menjou, Tyrone Power, and Marion Davies. Miss Davies is buried in a massive white-marble mausoleum inscribed with her family name, Douras.

The cemetery's biggest star—Rodolfo Guglielmi Valentino (1895–1926)—is inside the Cathedral Mausoleum in crypt number 1205 at the extreme southeast end of the building. Even though the famous "Lady in Black" no longer turns up every year on the anniversary of Valentino's death, the flowers on his crypt are always fresh. Peter Finch is directly across the aisle from Valentino. Barbara La Marr, Peter Lorre, and Eleanor Powell are in other alcoves of the same building. Back outside, a stone staircase leads to Douglas Fairbanks' reflecting pool, monument, and final resting place—reportedly paid for by his ex-wife Mary Pickford.

More Hollywood royals are over at the western end of the

Douglas Fairbanks reflecting pool and tomb, Hollywood Memorial Park

park in the Abbey of Palms Mausoleum. Here, sisters Norma and Constance Talmadge are together in the Sanctuary of Eternal Love, pioneer producer Jesse Lasky is in the Sanctuary of Light, and director Victor Fleming *(The Wizard of Oz* and *Gone with the Wind)* is in crypt 2081 toward the back of the building.

This cemetery is not all big names, however. There are a lot of everyday folk buried here, too. Surprisingly, many of the less famous monuments in the Hollywood Memorial Park Cemetery bear Armenian names and script. These graves are decorated with tiny vases of flowers, clusters of candles, and various Eastern Orthodox icons. A little known fact about today's Hollywood is that it has one of the largest concentrations of Armenian Americans in the United States.

NOTE: *The Hollywood Memorial Park Cemetery is open from 9 to 5, every day. A map indicating who's buried where is available free at the main entrance.*

13. ABANDONED STUDIO
5823 Santa Monica Boulevard

Across the street from the Hollywood Memorial Cemetery, this abandoned hulk of a studio at the corner of Santa Monica Boulevard and Van Ness Street is a relic that dates back to 1916. First called the Pacific Studio and Laboratory, it was used in the late teens by the National Film Corporation to shoot parts of the original *Tarzan of the Apes* and *The Romance of Tarzan* with Elmo Lincoln. Hal Roach used the same lot for a couple of early Harold Lloyd comedies. In 1930, after several changes in ownership, Larry Darmour took over the studio and produced the "Mickey McGuire" series, which starred a very young performer who later became Mickey Rooney. In 1933, Majestic Productions made the classic horror film, *The Vampire Bat,* here; it starred Fay Wray and Melvyn Douglas. After Majestic, Columbia made the studio an annex and lensed their 1940s *The Whistler* and *The Lone Wolf* series—popular Saturday afternoon double-feature fare—on this lot. Today, the great black studio with its old slat-sided stage could provide the setting for a wonderful Hollywood horror story but chances are more likely that it will turn into a shopping center.

14. SITE OF RKO STUDIOS
Corner of Gower Street and Melrose Avenue

RKO stopped making pictures in 1957, but will always be remembered for classics like the original *King Kong* (1933), the Fred Astaire–Ginger Rogers musicals of the 1930s, and Orson Welles' famous *Citizen Kane* (1941). Before every RKO picture, a huge globe with a radio tower on top of it would flash lightning bolts that spelled out "RKO-Radio Pictures." Today, the former RKO studios are part of the Paramount Studio complex but the famous RKO globe, now painted over, can still be distinguished

RKO Studios in the 1930s

atop the corner of the building at Gower and Melrose.

Some movie fans may also remember RKO's connection with two famous American millionaires who dabbled in the motion picture business. The first was Joseph P. Kennedy—patriarch of *the* Kennedy family—who produced pictures via his F.B.O. organization which eventually formed part of RKO. Gloria Swanson was Kennedy's leading lady both on and off screen. The second RKO millionaire exec was Howard Hughes; in 1948, Hughes made news when he bought RKO lock, stock, and barrel.

In 1957, another RKO sale was in the news. This time the company was going out of the movie business and a former RKO starlet was purchasing the RKO lot for $6 million. The buyer was Lucille Ball, who with her husband Desi Arnaz made RKO's Gower Street property part of their Desilu empire. In the midsixties, the lot again changed hands when next-door neighbor Paramount took it over and incorporated it into its facilities. Today, Paramount mostly uses the former RKO soundstages for taping television series. "Happy Days" was done here as were "Laverne and Shirley," "Mork and Mindy," and "Taxi."

NOTE: *For information on how to attend a taping in the old RKO studio building, call Paramount's ticket information number: 468-5575.*

15. PARAMOUNT STUDIOS
5451 Marathon Street

And there it is, the legendary wrought-iron gate at Bronson Avenue and Marathon that divides the real world from the magical and very exclusive realm of the motion picture studio. The most beautiful and most famous of all studio entrances, the Paramount Gate has been immortalized in scores of newsreels and movies about Hollywood. Of all its motion picture appearances, however, none is more memorable than the famous scene in *Sunset Boulevard,* when Gloria Swanson, as aging silent movie queen Norma Desmond, returns to her old studio in her great Isotta-Fraschini automobile driven by Erich von Stroheim. And to this day, it is said that good luck will come to the aspiring performer who hugs the gate and repeats those magic *Sunset Boulevard* words: "I'm ready for my closeup, Mr. DeMille."

Paramount, the studio inside the gate, is the last major studio to be headquartered in Hollywood. Paramount also has the oldest roots of any studio in town—and can trace its origins back to Jesse Lasky, Samuel Goldfish (later Goldwyn), and Cecil B. DeMille, the trio who produced Hollywood's first feature film, *The Squaw Man,* in 1913. Adolph Zukor entered the Paramount picture in 1916 when his Famous Players merged with Lasky's Feature Play Company to form the Famous Players-Lasky Corporation which produced "Paramount" pictures. For over a decade, their studio occupied a hefty chunk of the property formed by Sunset Boulevard, Vine Street, and Selma Avenue. In 1926, Famous Players-Lasky-Paramount made their move to Paramount's present location.

Paramount's great stars of the 1920s included Gloria Swanson, Clara Bow, and Rudolph Valentino. In the early thirties, Claudette Colbert, Miriam Hopkins, Gary Cooper, Maurice Chevalier, and Marlene Dietrich were important names on the Paramount roster—but Mae West was the studio's biggest moneymaker, starring in risqué comedies made from her own screenplays. The late thirties and early forties saw Veronica Lake, Frances Farmer, Fred MacMurray, Ray Milland, Alan Ladd, Betty Hutton, Bing Crosby, Bob Hope, and Dorothy Lamour come to fame in Paramount pictures. The last three are perhaps best remembered for their series of "Road" pictures.

Paramount Studios gate as seen in Sunset Boulevard, *1950*

Cecil B. DeMille was Paramount's most famous director, even though he split from the organization in the mid-twenties to form his own producing organization. After several years operating out of the former Thomas Ince studio in Culver City, DeMille returned to the Paramount lot and made many of his famous epics—*Cleopatra, The Sign of the Cross, Samson and Delilah, The Greatest Show on Earth*—from this base. Other great directors who worked at Paramount were Josef von Sternberg, Ernst Lubitsch, Preston Sturges, and Billy Wilder.

In 1966, the Paramount Pictures Corporation was bought by Gulf & Western and became a wholly owned subsidiary of that huge conglomerate. Two years later, the studio bought its next-door neighbor, Desilu Studios (formerly the RKO lot), increasing the size of Paramount's facilities to some 62 acres. Today, the studio is involved in the production of feature films, as well as filmed and videotaped television series.

NOTE: *Unfortunately, Paramount does not offer a tour of its facilities to the general public. There are two ways, however, to experience the studio. One is to attend the taping of a television show on the Paramount lot. For ticket information (tickets are free), call 468-5575. The other way to see Paramount—and this is the most satisfying short of a private VIP Tour—is simply to walk around the outside of the studio on Melrose Avenue. Through the new main entrance, there's a great view of the Paramount water tower (which used to be the RKO water tower and was built as a fire-prevention measure) and of a huge structure that looks like a drive-in movie screen painted with a blue sky and white clouds. This is the backdrop for the studio's water tank; it's used to create battle scenes with scale-model boats. Beyond the new entrance, a turn onto tiny Marathon Street will lead to the beautiful—and luckily unaltered—original Paramount Studios Gate. Give it a hug, say the magic words, and welcome to Hollywood!*

16. 716 VALENTINO PLACE
Corner of Valentino Place and North Bronson Avenue

Another of many Hollywood sites with a dubious connection to Rudolph Valentino. One story about this little Tudor-style apartment/office complex with the jungly forecourt says that Valentino owned it. Another purports that he kept an apartment here and wooed his first wife Jean Acker on the premises. Still another suggests that Valentino kept offices in the building which he used while making motion pictures at Paramount—this same story goes on to say that Valentino went from lot to office via a secret tunnel so that he wouldn't have to contend with the hordes of fans standing outside the gate waiting for him. Alas, the unromantic truth of the matter is that 716 Valentino Place seems to have been built several years after Valentino's death in 1926. Oh, well.

17. HOLLYWOOD CAFE LEGENDS
723 North Bronson Avenue

Just a few feet from the "Gloria Swanson Gate" of Paramount Studios, this was the site of Oblath's restaurant up until the summer of 1984. Back in the 1920s, the Oblath family, Hungarian Jewish immigrants, ran a lunch wagon at the corner of Vine and Sunset that did a thriving business with the actors and crew people of Famous Players-Lasky (later Paramount) studios which were on the same block. When Famous Players moved to Melrose Avenue in 1925, the Oblaths came with them and their lunch wagon was transformed into a bar/restaurant that remained popular with Paramount people—especially at lunchtime—for half a century.

Today, a much more glamorous restaurant has taken over the legendary Oblath's site. Called Hollywood Cafe Legends, Oblath's successor conjures up Hollywood's magical past with a huge, specially commissioned, black-and-white oil painting of Gloria Swanson dominating the entryway. More stars can be found in the dining room and bar where original charcoal portraits of Dietrich, Crawford, Harlow, Monroe, Valentino, Garland, and Gable—to name a few—grace the salmon-colored walls. With its dining-room sconces moulded at Twentieth Century-Fox and its sign outside fashioned in the prop studios of Paramount, Hollywood Cafe Legends is definitely part of the Hollywood scene and seems to be taking up, indeed going beyond, where Oblath's left off. An attractive place for lunch or a drink while sightseeing in the Paramount area.

NOTE: *Open daily for lunch and dinner; no lunch on Saturday, however, and brunch is served on Sunday. Reservations: 465-1662.*

18. WESTERN COSTUME CO.
5335 Melrose Avenue

Built so close to the Paramount lot that it appears to be part of the studio, Western Costume Co. is the outfit that outfits the movies. It began when a trader named L. L. Burns moved to Los Angeles in 1912 and set up a shop that dealt in American Indian gear. A chance meeting between Burns and cowboy superstar William S. Hart resulted in Burns' commenting to Hart that the costumes worn by the Indians in a recent Hart film were grossly inaccurate. Next thing Burns knew, "Big Bill" had arranged for him to supply all of the Indian garb for future Hart westerns . . . and Western Costume Co. was born.

Later, Burns and several associates bought out an existing theatrical costume house and started supplying all types and periods of costumes for what were becoming increasingly extravagant and lavish films. A case in point was director/actor Erich von Stroheim's 1926 *Wedding March* in which Von Stroheim insisted on authentic Hapsburg court costumes. Not content with made-in-Hollywood versions, Von Stroheim further stipulated that Western's European representative find and buy up actual uniforms, carriages, and military decorations of the Austro-Hungarian Empire. These were then shipped to Los Angeles and not only added to the splendor of *Wedding March* but bolstered Western's impressive inventory.

As the company continued to expand, it changed locations—and owners—several times. By 1932, Western had moved to its present location on Melrose Avenue. Over the years, the establishment also had its share of financial difficulties. When it looked as though Western might go under in 1947, several studios stepped in and helped bail out the company. Today, Western has an inventory of more than one million costumes worth over $20 million—and is considered the largest costuming organization in the world. Supplying clothing and props for motion pictures, television, and professional and amateur theatrical productions, Western Costume Co. can create hats, saddles, boots, and shoes in its workrooms.

19. RALEIGH STUDIOS
650 North Bronson Avenue

With its rustic clapboard office buildings edging Bronson Street, Raleigh looks more like a ranch than a movie studio. Ironically, back in 1914 when Adolph Zukor's Famous Players made *The Girl From Yesterday* with Mary Pickford here, the place actually was a horse farm! After Famous Players exited the premises, L.A. theater owner William H. Clune purchased the property with money he had made as a producer of D. W. Griffith's *The Birth of a Nation.* Clune's first venture was a film version of *Ramona* which Donald Crisp directed.

Rather than produce films, however, Clune mostly rented out his studio to numerous independent production companies—and indeed kept doing so for close to sixty years. One of the most famous early "tenants" of this important rental lot was Douglas Fairbanks Productions—which did *The Mark of Zorro* and *The Three Musketeers* at Clune's studio in the early 1920s. In the early 1930s, Walt Disney is another famous name who did some work at Clune's—which was then called the Tech-Art Studios. The early thirties also saw Harry "Pop" Sherman produce a number of films on this lot, the best remembered being the *Hopalong Cassidy* series which he filmed into the 1950s. Producer Stanley Kramer was also based here in the 1950s.

In the sixties Clune's was renamed Producers Studios and Robert Aldrich lensed *Whatever Happened to Baby Jane?* here in 1961 with Bette Davis and Joan Crawford. It was also in the sixties that Ronald Reagan hosted "Death Valley Days" at Producers Studios. It was his last professional acting job.

Today, Raleigh Studios remains one of Hollywood's most important rental lots.

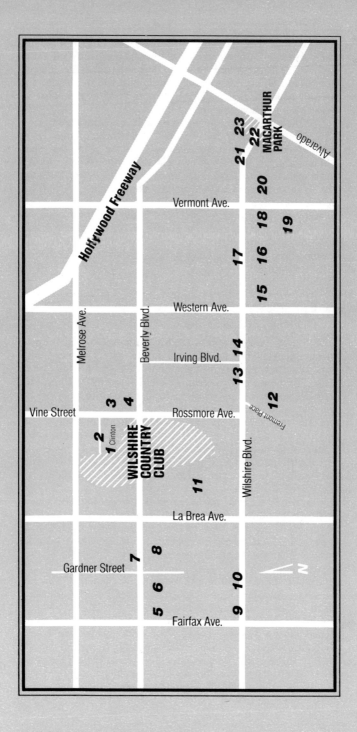

Hollywood Freeway

Vermont Ave.

Melrose Ave.

Beverly Blvd.

Western Ave.

Irving Blvd.

Vine Street

3
4

Rossmore Ave.

2
1 Clinton

WILSHIRE
COUNTRY
CLUB

11

13 14

17

15 16 18

19

20

21 23
22

MACARTHUR
PARK

Alvarado

Fremont Place

12

Wilshire Blvd.

La Brea Ave.

7
8

Gardner Street

N

5 6

9 10

Fairfax Ave.

THE WILSHIRE DISTRICT

Main Street, L.A.

Mae West, long-time Rossmore Avenue resident, with Cary Grant

IF THE great sprawl of communities that makes up metropolitan Los Angeles can be thought of as having one main street, that street would undoubtedly be Wilshire Boulevard. Named for H. Gaylord Wilshire, a nineteenth-century developer who is said to have been both a millionaire and a Marxist (only in L.A.!), Wilshire Boulevard is a serious commercial thoroughfare for most of its sixteen-mile run from the Pacific Ocean at Santa Monica to downtown Los Angeles. The area known as the "Wilshire District" begins roughly at La Cienega Boulevard and encompasses the neighborhoods on either side of the Boulevard for approximately the next five or six miles to the east. The westernmost section of the Wilshire District—the one closest to Beverly Hills— has traditionally had a large middle-class Jewish population. Beginning at about Highland Avenue, the area starts becoming increasingly WASP-y as Wilshire cuts through an old-monied enclave of Los Angeles known as Hancock Park. Finally, closer to downtown, the demographics again change and Hispanics and Asians now form the majority. A "district" in name only, Wilshire encompasses many neighborhoods, ethnic groups, social classes, and lifestyles.

For movie lovers, the Wilshire District and Wilshire Boulevard offer a diverse assortment of sights worth seeing—from the Los Angeles Tennis Club in Hancock Park, one of the few places where the nouveau world of Hollywood rubbed shoulders with the tightly sealed-off society of Old Los Angeles . . . to a group of grand old apartment houses with fascinating histories of movie-star tenants and sometimes movie-star owners . . . to monumental Art Deco department stores that were L.A.'s chicest shopping-spots during the 1930s and 1940s . . . to a landmark hotel that was home to some of the earliest Academy Awards ceremonies as well as to the most glamorous nightclub Los Angeles has ever known.

NOTE: *A car is a must to see all of the places included in this chapter. A walk around Bullocks Wilshire is highly recommended, as are walks around the grounds of both the Ambassador Hotel and the Pan Pacific Auditorium.*

1. "HAPPY DAYS" HOUSE
565 North Cahuenga Avenue

For openers, it's not your typical Southern California house— which is no doubt one of the reasons it was chosen to be used as the Cunningham family home in the long-running TV series "Happy Days." (The series was set in Milwaukee, Wisconsin.) Another reason for using the house was probably its proximity (a matter of blocks) to Paramount Studios on Melrose Avenue where the show was taped before a live audience.

Long before "Happy Days," Mexican-born Hollywood star, Lupe Velez, lived in this same Cahuenga Avenue home in the

"Happy Days" house

1930s. Nearby, at 531 Cahuenga, lived the mother of La Lupe's boyfriend at the time—Gary Cooper. Miss Velez—who wound up with Johnny "Tarzan" Weissmuller for a husband—is less known for her films than for her newsmaking suicide in Beverly Hills in 1944.

2. LOS ANGELES TENNIS CLUB
5851 Clinton Street

Beyond the attractive Spanish Colonial clubhouse lie the seventeen courts of the premier tennis club of Southern California. Founded in 1920, the LATC was quickly discovered by the status-conscious stars of early Hollywood who thought it chic to play on the club's courts and to attend its matches. Once the club initiated its annual Pacific Southwest Championship tournament in 1927, having a box for the event became *the* thing to do every fall for Charlie Chaplin, Harold Lloyd, Frank Capra, Janet Gaynor, William Powell, Gary Cooper, Joan and Constance Bennett, Clark Gable, and Carole Lombard. One year, Marlene Dietrich dazzled the crowds when she showed up for this tournament dressed in a black-satin tuxedo suit; Jean Harlow did likewise in white-satin pajamas; Mae West favored furs. Starlets—emulating their better-known colleagues—frequently turned up at matches in full makeup and glamorous attire to be photographed by studio publicity people.

Hollywood's connection with the LATC went beyond show. Many stars who were members of the club took their tennis seriously. One of the best celebrity players was Errol Flynn, who often entered (and sometimes won) LATC tournaments during the 1930s. Other star members were/are Rudy Vallee, Mickey Rooney, Ozzie Nelson, Charles Farrell, Dinah Shore, and Vincent Van Patten. In addition to movie stars, the LATC has also been home to an impressive number of major tennis stars—Don Budge, Frank Parker, Jack Kramer, Pancho Gonzales, Alex Olmedo, Stan Smith, Louise Brough, Billie Jean King, and Arthur Ashe, to name a few.

3. RAVENSWOOD
570 North Rossmore Avenue

Built in the late 1920s, this Art Deco apartment building was where Mae West lived for the half century (1932–1980) she spent in Hollywood. Edging the very conservative old-monied area of Los Angeles known as Hancock Park, the Ravenswood would seem an odd place for the controversial Miss West to call home. In fact, her early films were so risqué they were one of the reasons that the Catholic Church established its National Legion of Decency censorship board in 1934. It was actually the William Morris Office who found Miss West her Ravenswood apartment. It was convenient—just three blocks from Paramount Studios where she worked. It would be a good first residence before she found something more permanent in Beverly Hills. Mae, however, chose never to move, even though her films were Paramount's

1938 Motion Picture Tournament at Los Angeles Tennis Club:
left to right: *Frank Shields, Gilbert Roland, Gretl Dupont, Mervyn LeRoy, Josephine Cruickshank, Colly Baiano, Errol Flynn, umpire Craufurd Kent*

Ravenswood—Mae West's long-time Hollywood home

most successful of the early 1930s. Deep down, she was a city gal
and apartment living suited her style. "I'm not a little girl from
a little town here to make good in a big town," she told all of
Hollywood on her arrival in tinseltown, "I'm a big girl from a
big town who's come to make good in a little town."

Living in super-stuffy Hancock Park didn't cramp Miss
West's style in the least. The decor of her sprawling sixth-floor
apartment is legendary—a fantasy of white, white, and more
white with a little gold here and there for accent. According to
writer Mitch Tuchman, one of the last journalists to interview
Miss West before her death in 1980, every detail of the apartment
had been carefully planned to show off its star occupant to her
best advantage. At sunset, Miss West's preferred interview time,
a champagne-colored light filtered in through the window of the
main salon, perfectly framing the chair where Madame Mae
held court.

There are many stories that say Mae West owned the
Ravenswood. Although Mae had extensive real-estate holdings in
the L.A. area, its seems, according to various Hollywood old-
timers, that Ravenswood was not one of them. What many
people feel is that in the shaky early thirties, financially flush Mae
might have helped out the owners of the Ravenswood by holding
a mortgage or two on the place, which they paid off when times
got better. Mae may have owned the large apartment building
across the street from her, however. According to writer Leonard
Spigelgass, it seems Mae didn't like the color of the building her
apartment looked out on—so she bought it and immediately had
it painted!

4. EL ROYALE APARTMENTS
450 North Rossmore Avenue

Just up the street from Mae West's Rossmore apartment building, the El Royal was also built in the late 1920s. Among the building's former celebrity tenants are George Raft; Columbia head man Harry Cohn; William Frawley, the actor who played Fred Mertz on "I Love Lucy"; and later President John F. Kennedy—who is said to have stayed here during the Democratic National Convention in Los Angeles in 1960. If the building looks familiar, it is perhaps because it was once the Denver apartment house that sexual switch-hitter Steven Carrington lived in on the television series "Dynasty."

5. CBS TELEVISION CITY
7800 Beverly Boulevard

This sprawling complex at the corner of Fairfax Avenue and Beverly Boulevard is CBS Television's main West Coast base. Built in 1952, it was one of the first studios to be designed solely for television broadcasting—and since that time, news programs, TV series, soaps, and game shows have originated from here. Among them were: Judy Garland's 1963–1964 TV try, "The

El Royale apartments

Pan Pacific Auditorium, 1984

Carol Burnett Show," "All in the Family," "Sonny and Cher," "Alice," "Newhart," and "The $25,000 Pyramid."

NOTE: *Many of the shows taped at CBS are done before live audiences. To get tickets (free), contact the CBS Television City Information Window between 9 and 5 daily—or call 852-2455.*

6. PAN PACIFIC AUDITORIUM
7600 Beverly Boulevard

Does anyone remember *Xanadu,* one of the all-time awful film musicals that any studio ever dared release? *Xanadu* (Universal, 1980) starred Olivia Newton-John, Gene Kelly, Michael Beck, and the Pan Pacific Auditorium. Of the film's four stars, the only truly memorable performance was turned in by the last—a landmark Streamline-Moderne showspace built in 1935 for expositions, auto shows, ice revues, and concerts. (Elvis played the Pan Pacific in 1957 just before he entered the army; the police told him to clean up his act or they'd close it down.)

The concerts and special events had long since ceased by the time Universal lensed *Xanadu.* But in the film, the Pan Pacific—abandoned and in a state of semiruin—is magically transformed (in the same way that Mickey and Judy used to turn old barns into glamorous theaters in their MGM musicals) into a glittering 1980s roller disco. Alas, while cinematic magic managed to work wonders with the Pan Pacific, for a long time preservationists had a lot less luck in their efforts to save the place in real life. After a long period of uncertainty as to the building's future, the Hollywood Happy Ending is that the landmark auditorium is being restored and turned into a multi-use complex with offices, shops, hotel, and the country's first national cinemathèque/video center—all scheduled to open in 1986.

7. A. B. HEINSBERGEN & CO. BUILDING
7421–7415 Beverly Boulevard

Anthony B. Heinsbergen was one of Los Angeles' most important early muralists and decorative artists. During the 1920s, he lent his talents to the design and decoration of the interiors of some of the city's most lavish movie palaces. Today, among the theaters where his craftsmanship and talent can still be appreciated are The Wiltern on Wilshire Boulevard and the Los Angeles Theater in downtown L.A. Heinsbergen's former office building— erected in the mid-1920s—shows what happens when a designer of fantasy interiors has his way with an exterior. The result here is a medieval marvel of brick, stone, and leaded glass that would be much more at home in the old section of Heidelberg or Ghent than on Beverly Boulevard in Los Angeles.

8. EL COYOTE RESTAURANT
7312 Beverly Boulevard

Room after room of outrageous Mexican decor—piñatas, gigantic paper flowers, tin lanterns, bright muraled walls—plus waitresses in flouncy South-of-the-Border costumes make a meal at El Coyote a memorable visual, if not culinary, experience. Over the years, the place has lured film-industry people with its own special brand of restaurant show business. In early August of 1969, a young movie star, her hairdresser, and a couple of friends were reported to have dined at El Coyote before retiring to the star's luxurious home up in the Benedict Canyon section of Beverly Hills for nightcaps. Their Mexican meal may have been their last supper—because later that evening, a crazed group of creatures known as the Manson Family attacked the house and murdered Sharon Tate, her unborn child, and her guests.

9. MAY COMPANY DEPARTMENT STORE
6067 Wilshire Boulevard

Before there was "Rodeo Drive," there was the "Miracle Mile"—a long stretch of Wilshire Boulevard between Beverly Hills and Hancock Park where serious L.A. shoppers went to spend their time and their money. Developed in the 1920s, the Miracle Mile became not only an important shopping mecca, but also a showcase of Art Deco commercial architecture. The May Company—with its distinctive gold-and-black "silo" on the corner of Wilshire Boulevard and Fairfax Avenue—was built in 1940 and is an example of a late deco style that looked to the future rather than to the past.

On January 28, 1966, the May Company was in the news when former superstar Hedy Lamarr was arrested there for allegedly walking off with some $86 worth of May Company

Missing scene from A Star Is Born, *rediscovered by Ron Haver of L.A. County Museum of Art*

merchandise. Eventually acquitted, Miss Lamarr sued the store for $5 million in damages. The suit was later dismissed.

10. LOS ANGELES COUNTY MUSEUM OF ART
5905 Wilshire Boulevard

Besides its extensive collections of Asian, European, and American art, the L.A. County Museum also has one of the city's most vital film programs. Open to the public, screenings of classic films are held Friday and Saturday evenings year round (special programs on Wednesdays as well) in the Leo S. Bing Theater. Often a star speaker—Gregory Peck, Hal Roach, Bette Davis, Olivia De Havilland, Catherine Deneuve have all appeared here—is part of the program. Heading the Museum's Film Department is Ronald Haver, who helped make movie history in 1983 for his role in the discovery and reassembling of the "missing" twenty-six minutes of the 1954 Judy Garland/James Mason *A Star Is Born.*

NOTE: *For information on what's playing at the L.A. County Museum, call: 857-6201, Tuesday–Friday, 10 to 4:30. Saturdays, noon to 4:30.*

11. "WHATEVER HAPPENED TO BABY JANE?" HOUSE
172 South McCadden Place

Welcome to the house where Bette Davis (as former child star Baby Jane Hudson) did all of those horrible things to her invalid sister Blanche (Joan Crawford) in Robert Aldrich's 1962 Hollywood-gothic classic, *Whatever Happened to Baby Jane?*

House shared by Bette Davis and Joan Crawford in Whatever Happened to Baby Jane?

Note, especially, the wrought-iron driveway gate on the left side of the house—of major plot significance—where Jane ran over Blanche in their car many years earlier. Or did she? While the McCadden Place house was used for many exterior scenes, most of the film was shot on the nearby lot at Raleigh (then Producers) Studios.

12. FREMONT PLACE
Fremont Place and Wilshire Boulevard

Behind the heavy gates of this ultra-private Los Angeles community live many of the city's oldest, wealthiest, and WASPiest families. Between 1918 and 1920, Mary Pickford lived here with her mother at 56 Fremont Place. Many years later, black boxer Mohammed Ali moved into a Fremont Place mansion at number 55. Historical footnote: When Nat King Cole bought a home in the nearby Larchmont neighborhood in the late 1940s, property owners banded together and tried to oust the black entertainer. When Mohammed Ali moved into the even more exclusive Fremont Place enclave, no objections were raised.

Lou Rawls and Karen Black have also been Fremont Placers, and in 1977, actor Cliff Robertson was renting a house at number 97 Fremont Place West when he received an IRS form that indicated he had earned $10,000 the previous year from Columbia Pictures. Since Robertson had not worked for the studio in 1976, he looked into the matter further, and ultimately uncovered the massive forgeries of Columbia executive David Begelman. Thus began the "Begelman Affair," one of Hollywood's biggest scandals of recent times.

*Norma Desmond at home
on* Sunset Boulevard, *1950*

13. "SUNSET BOULEVARD" MANSION SITE
Northwest corner, Wilshire and Irving Boulevards

It belonged to a former wife of J. Paul Getty and had not been lived in for several years when Billy Wilder decided to use it as Norma Desmond's mansion in his 1950 film, *Sunset Boulevard.* Actually, the site of the movie mansion was a good six miles from the section of Sunset Boulevard in Beverly Hills where the script said the mansion should be. At the same time, it was a mere ten blocks from Paramount where the film was shot.

It was also, according to Wilder, just the house that he wanted, except for the swimming pool. There wasn't one—and the script, as we all remember, definitely called for one. (The film is narrated by the corpse of William Holden whom we see floating in the swimming pool at the beginning of the film.) The former Mrs. Getty—who had given acting classes on the property—was reportedly pleased at the prospect of having the movie company install a free pool for her. Only thing was, this was a Hollywood pool—which meant that it was for show only and had practically no plumbing. Although it was never used for swimming after the film was shot, the pool that *Sunset Boulevard* built was used in another famous film. The film was *Rebel Without a Cause* and it was in the bottom of the same pool—now empty—where James Dean, Natalie Wood, and Sal Mineo parody their parents in a touching scene toward the end of the film.

A few years after *Rebel* was released (1955), the Irving Boulevard house was demolished, the pool filled in.

NOTE: *Movie lovers who visit the* Sunset Boulevard/Rebel *site should check out the impressive Tudor mansion at nearby 605 South Irving. Another former Getty property, this is now the official residence of the Mayor of Los Angeles.*

14. LOS ALTOS APARTMENTS
4121 Wilshire Boulevard

Many stories say that William Randolph Hearst built this magnificent Moorish apartment palace that dominates the 4000 block of Wilshire Boulevard. According to the building permit, however, the Los Altos was erected by a pair of gentlemen named Luther T. Mayo and Preston S. White. When the place opened in 1925, it made real-estate history as the first "own-your-own-apartment" (i.e., cooperative) apartment building in Los Angeles. According to current residents as well as numerous newspaper accounts, Hearst did buy a large apartment in Los Altos for Marion Davies. One account says the apartment had ten rooms, six baths, and a screening room. Another puts the Davies suite as a duplex with a mere five bedrooms. A long-time resident of the building, however, doubts if either Marion Davies or Hearst ever lived in the apartment and suggests that it was used mainly for business meetings and receptions. The apartment, number 207, has since been broken up—but the main wing still has massive $100,000 (according to one old-timer) carved doors plus marble floors, vaulted ceilings, and three bathrooms.

A number of other Hollywood names are connected with the Los Altos. Silent screen star Jane Novak (one of many former fiancées of William S. Hart, the Western star who made a habit of becoming engaged to his leading ladies but never marrying

Los Altos apartments in the 1940s

them) was a long-time early resident. Clara Bow also lived here, although one resident remembers Miss Bow being in the building in the early thirties and another says she lived on the fifth floor in the late 1940s. Bette Davis is said to have once resided in suite 107; no one is sure just when. By the 1930s, it should be noted, the building was no longer a co-op and had become an apartment hotel that rented suites both on a long- and short-term basis. In the late 1930s, Los Altos is also said to have been June Allyson's first Hollywood address. Later years saw Una Merkel live in the great Wilshire apartment house, as well as Peter Finch.

In recent years, Los Altos has become popular with L.A.'s burgeoning community of artists who are attracted by low rents, large spaces, the building's mystique, as well as its convenient location midway between the galleries of downtown Los Angeles to the east and those of West Hollywood and Beverly Hills to the west. Developers have also been also attracted by the sixty-year-old building's prime Wilshire Boulevard location and for a while it looked as though Los Altos was slated to be torn down. But recently a new owner seemed committed to preserving the building.

15. WILTERN THEATER
3780 Wilshire Boulevard

Designed by G. Albert Lansburgh, the dean of American theater architects (he also did the Warner Theater in Hollywood and the Orpheum in downtown L.A.), the Wiltern ranked with Hollywood's Pantages theater as one of the most impressive Art Deco movie palaces on the West Coast. When the 2300-seat Wiltern (originally called the Wiltern-Warner) made its debut back in 1931, it was to have been the flagship of the Warner Brothers chain and it was quite an opening night. William Powell acted as master of ceremonies and introduced the new theater as well as Warners' new film, *Alexander Hamilton,* starring George Arliss. A special wooden "Bridge of Stars" was erected over Wilshire Boulevard (because the city of L.A. refused to block the street) which made celebrity "entrances" especially glamorous. Speaking of those entrances, Bette Davis once told how Warner Brothers, a studio never known for being extravagant, used to bus contract players to premieres, drop them off around the corner from the theater where the same limousine would then take them in small groups round to the front for their "official" arrival.

Despite its dramatic opening and its extraordinary beauty, the Wiltern was the wrong theater in the wrong place at the wrong time. The Depression was in full swing—even in Hollywood—and the Wiltern was simply too large for the residential neighborhood in which it found itself. Attendance was disappointing and two years after it had opened, Warner Brothers pulled out and the theater went dark. Later, it reopened as the Wiltern—and was moderately successful from the late 1930s to the late

1950s. The 1960s saw the theater decline steadily in both attendance and maintenance—and by the end of that decade, the Wiltern was reduced to showing Kung-Fu flicks and closed-circuit televised sporting events.

By 1980, the wrecking crews had arrived to demolish not only the theater but the magnificent terra cotta-tiled, bronze-trimmed office tower (known as the Pellissier Building) that was built around it. Luckily, the preservationists won this one—when, in the knick of time, enlightened developer Wayne Ratkovitch bought the Wiltern Theater/Pellissier Building and embarked on an extensive restoration program. Today, the tiled façade of this landmark Art Deco complex gleams once again and the Wiltern Theater has been brought back to life as a performing arts center for plays, musicals, dance, and opera.

NOTE: *To find out what's on at the Wiltern, this is the number to call in Los Angeles: 489-3181.*

16. AMBASSADOR HOTEL
3400 Wilshire Boulevard

First came the society people—old Los Angeles—who welcomed this luxurious new hotel so ideally situated between

*The Pellisier Building
and Wiltern Theater*

The Cocoanut Grove today

downtown Los Angeles and their own grand residences in Hancock Park and Fremont Place. For them, the Ambassador—which opened in 1921—was a wonderful new place to dine, entertain, throw debutante parties, weddings. There were even, in the early days, horse shows held on the hotel's vast grounds that attracted all the right people.

The Ambassador also attracted, very quickly, movie people. Many, in fact, lived here in the large comfortable bungalows that are still part of the hotel. Particularly for actors and actresses who commuted between New York and Los Angeles, a bungalow at the Ambassador often made more sense than renting a house in Los Angeles. And besides, there was room service, there was the hotel's great pool with its sand "beach," and, best of all, there was always something to do in the evenings because the Ambassador boasted the most glamorous nightclub in all of Los Angeles: The Cocoanut Grove.

The Grove opened several months after the hotel and was an instant hit. The decor was pure fantasy: a wild interior of palm trees—supposedly left-over set pieces from Rudolph Valentino's film, *The Sheik*—in which stuffed monkey dolls with electrically lit "eyes" watched over the crowds on the dance floor. The stories of the Grove are endless and almost every Angelino has one. There's the time John Barrymore—who lived in an Ambassador bungalow with a pet monkey as a roommate—brought the little beast to the nightclub and let it loose in the palm trees. People still talk, too, about Marion Davies—she and William Randolph Hearst had a wing of the Ambassador for close to a year in the early 1920s—riding a horse through the Ambassador lobby and on into the Grove for a costume party.

The Grove was also where a number of the early Academy Awards ceremonies were held. Years: 1930, 1932, 1934, 1940, and 1943. In those days, the Oscars were more like parties and dinner and cocktails were part of the festivities. The 1937 *A Star Is Born* provides a picture of what the Oscars at the Grove were like in a memorable sequence of that film. In the 1954 *A Star Is Born,* the Cocoanut Grove is again used as a location. Only this time James Mason is looking for a late-night date at the nightclub—but is told by the maitre d' that the woman he is interested in is "Pasadena," i.e., society, i.e., hands-off!

Besides Grove stories, there are lots of stories told about the Ambassador's bungalows and especially about the amorous goings on that took place inside these very private places. Once, a very young Tallulah Bankhead—infatuated with a much older John Barrymore—tried to catch the noted actor's attention in the Ambassador dining room by tripping him. It was Miss Bankhead, however, who wound up falling on the floor. Later the same evening, at the urging of her friends and no doubt after many bourbons, Miss Bankhead sneaked into Barrymore's bungalow and hid under his sheets. When Barrymore returned and discovered Tallulah, all he said was: "Another time, Tallu . . . I'm too drunk and you're too awkward." Howard Hughes also lived in an Ambassador bungalow. This was in the late 1920s when he was working on *Hell's Angels* as well as on quite a few young Hollywood beauties.

Valentino is also associated with the Ambassador. It seems that after he had separated from his second wife, Natacha Rambova, Valentino was seeing Ambassador bungalow resident Pola Negri. This was not long before Valentino's death in New York in 1926. When the grief-stricken Miss Negri left her bungalow for the train that was to take her back East to her lover's funeral, she is said to have "emerged" from the bungalow two times—once for real and a second time so that the photographers could capture every nuance of her "performance."

Another superstar with an Ambassador connection was Marilyn Monroe. In 1947, she was a student of Emmaline Snively's Blue Book Modeling Agency, which was located on the Ambassador premises. Later, when she was a star, she would return to the Ambassador and to the Cocoanut Grove often.

Ambassador Hotel, 1943

Besides all the glamorous goings-on, the Ambassador has had its share of tragic events, too. One that will always be associated with the hotel is the assassination of Democratic presidential primary candidate Robert F. Kennedy at the Ambassador on June 5, 1968. Two years later, the Ambassador would also play a supporting role in another great American tragedy: It was here that the jury for the Manson Family trial was sequestered during the trial for some nine months in 1969–1970 before a verdict was reached on the murders of actress Sharon Tate and her friends.

Today, the Ambassador still functions, although it's used a lot for conventions and for group tours from Japan and South America. A great disappointment is the Cocoanut Grove, which still exists but without palm trees, monkeys, or celebrities. These days the room is mostly the scene of private parties and conventions. Still hinting of the Ambassador's grand old days, however, are its gardens—here, the grass is green, the foliage lush, and those famous bungalows look as though they were built for a movie-star era that knew nothing of package tours.

17. BROWN DERBY
3377 Wilshire Boulevard

The Vine Street branch had the glamour and fame—but this little lunch counter in the shape of a hat was the first of what quickly became L.A.'s most famous chain of eateries. The man behind the Brown Derbys (there were four branches at one time) was Gloria Swanson's second husband, Herbert K. Somborn; he opened up this Derby in 1926, the same year in which his divorce from Miss Swanson became official. There are many tales of how the Derby got its shape. One says the building was inspired by New York Governor Al Smith—a friend of Somborn's—who was wearing a brown derby on a visit to Los Angeles. Another says that Somborn had been challenged by a friend who said: "If you know anything about food, you can sell it out of a hat." Then

Wilshire Boulevard Brown Derby, 1983

there are those who see the derby hat as being a symbol of upper-middle-class social acceptability. According to this you-are-where-you-eat theory, what could be classier than dining inside a derby?

Whatever the real reason for the Derby's design, it quickly became a Los Angeles landmark. In 1980, however, the landmark restaurant had closed and was about to be demolished when a group of concerned citizens intervened and managed to block the demolition. Today, what's left of the grand old hat on Wilshire Boulevard is another *cause célèbre* for preservationists, *bête noire* for developers. As this book goes to press, a compromise appears to have been reached and it is expected that the hat will be restored and incorporated into whatever development is built on the property.

18. THE TALMADGE
3278 Wilshire Boulevard

A portrait of the great silent screen star, Norma Talmadge, hangs above the reception desk—and the current manager tells a lovely story of the building's beginnings. The year was 1922 and Norma Talmadge and her producer husband Joe Schenck had come to L.A. from New York. It seems that Norma had looked and looked for a place to stay that suited her but couldn't find anything that was right. Whereupon Joe said, "Honey, I'll build you a building." And so he built the Talmadge—out of love. The manager goes on to say that Schenck—who never did things small—had plans to erect a duplicate of the Talmadge (shades of the Taj Mahal story) on the other side of Berendo Street with a footbridge connecting the two structures. However, the church that still stands on that corner supposedly refused to sell Schenck the land.

Meanwhile, the building permit mentions neither the name Talmadge nor Schenck but merely says that the Talmadge was built in 1923 for the Wilshire and Berendo (the names of the cross streets) Company. The architects are listed as Aleck Curlett and Claude Beelman, both important in their field at the time. In fact, it was Beelman who designed the monumental Irving Thalberg Building at MGM Studios in Culver City in the late 1930s. But did he and his partner do the Talmadge for Norma and Schenck? The name of the building would certainly imply that there was a connection between the star and the building . . . and the fact that no builders' names are given on the original permit is all the more reason to assume that a really big name was behind the project. Finally, most old-time picture people who are still around remember the Talmadge as having belonged to Norma and Joe—although some feel that the building was put up more for investment purposes than as a place for the star and her husband to live.

Whether or not the Talmadge sisters ever lived there, the Talmadge was and is a very impressive structure. Tall and imposing with its Beaux-Arts entrance angled to the corner, the

The Talmadge apartments

building has been beautifully maintained and features large luxurious apartments, a grand lobby, lovely gardens, and a patio
where glamorous parties were often held in the good old days.
Then, too, there's that portrait of Norma hanging above the
reception desk. Indeed, even if Norma Talmadge never did live
here—she's living here now.

19. MARY MILES MINTER MANSION
701 South New Hampshire Avenue

Scandal ended her career rather abruptly in the early 1920s
and today few people remember that Mary Miles Minter was one
of the silent screen's great beauties and most successful stars. So
successful, in fact, that this was the big brick mansion that the
nubile screen siren shared with her domineering stage mother,
Charlotte Shelby, at the height of her career. Today, the place is
reported to be a home for unwed mothers.

The scandal that ended the twenty-year-old Minter's brief
life at the top began on February 1, 1922, when Miss Minter's
director and supposed lover, William Desmond Taylor, was
discovered dead in his apartment (now demolished) on Alvarado
Street. There were two bullets in his chest—and it definitely
wasn't suicide. Since Taylor was also linked romantically with
another great star of the day—comedienne Mabel Normand—
the newspapers and the public went wild. And when it came out
that both Miss Minter and Miss Normand had stopped by the
dead director's apartment *before* the police on the morning after
his murder, the whole affair took on the aura of a real-life Agatha
Christie whodunit. Miss Normand's reason for entering the Taylor
flat was supposedly to retrieve some letters whose contents she

didn't want to be misconstrued. Miss Minter, on the other hand, is said to have been interested in removing some naughty nighties that happened to be monogrammed with the initials MMM—although she denied this up until her death in Los Angeles in 1984.

Taylor's most interesting "visitor," however, was a mystery man who was reported seen leaving the victim's apartment on the night of the murder. More than a little suspicious was the fact that this "man," wearing a raincoat, supposedly walked like a woman. Was it a jealous Miss Minter affecting a disguise? Or a jealous Miss Normand? Some speculated that it was neither but rather Miss Minter's mother who was enraged at having discovered Taylor's affair with her daughter. Others say that Mrs. Shelby's anger was really because she, too, was under Taylor's romantic spell.

The murderer was never found. But the damage done by all the headlines and hoopla that surrounded William Desmond Taylor's demise was irrevocable. The affair not only ruined Miss Minter's film career, it also had much to do with Mabel Normand's Hollywood downfall as well, since another of the case's revelations showed that Taylor helped supply Normand with the narcotics to which she was addicted. Nobody fared well in this one.

20. BULLOCKS WILSHIRE
3050 Wilshire Boulevard

It's around 1936, we're somewhere in Connecticut, and Marion Kirby (Constance Bennett) is being driven off for a wild weekend at a posh hotel by Cosmo Topper (Roland Young) in the original *Topper* film. The pair (she's a ghost, he isn't) arrive at the elegant Seabreeze Hotel, pull up under its magnificent Art Deco porte cochere, and check in. Soon, Marion's husband (Cary Grant, also a ghost) arrives in hot pursuit—and the Seabreeze is turned upside down by a series of hilarious ectoplasmic exploits.

As it turns out, the glamorous entrance to the Seabreeze was not some art director's fantasy created on the Hal Roach back lot. Instead, a real Los Angeles location was used . . . the rear entrance of Bullocks Wilshire Department Store. Built in 1929, this masterpiece of zigzag moderne architecture is an official historic cultural monument and one of the most beautiful buildings in Los Angeles. An architectural landmark in many ways, Bullock's was one of L.A.'s first large commercial buildings to be designed for shoppers arriving by car. In fact, the rear entrance (facing the parking lot) used in *Topper* is actually the store's main entrance.

Not seen in *Topper,* but worth a look for anyone visiting Bullocks is the colorful Herman Sacks' fresco on the ceiling of the porte cochere. A salute to the "Spirit of Transportation," the dazzling painting shows early airplanes, dirigibles, ships, and trains. Ironically, no cars are included. Around at the front of the store, another decorative element worth noting is the stylized

Bullocks Wilshire   *The Bryson apartments*

relief above the main doorway; it is said to have been the creation of MGM art director Cedric Gibbons. Besides his many movie credits, Gibbons also is known for designing the original "Oscar" statuette used by the Academy of Motion Picture Arts and Sciences.

Over the years, Bullocks Wilshire has been a favorite 1930s exterior for films and especially for TV movies. Besides its appearances as a hotel, Bullocks distinctive copper-trimmed façade has been seen on screen as everything from a period office building to an apartment house to what it really is: a department store!

21. BRYSON APARTMENT HOTEL
2701 Wilshire Boulevard

In its glory days, it boasted billiard rooms, music rooms, separate servants' quarters, and a ballroom on the ninth floor. Opened in 1913, the *L.A. Times* called it "the finest structure devoted exclusively to apartment-house purposes west of New York City." Today, none of the current staff of the Bryson can remember who some of the building's early celebrated tenants were, although no one doubts that there were many. What people do remember is that the building once had a celebrated landlord— Fred MacMurray, who bought the place in the forties and sold it in the seventies.

It was in the forties, too, that Raymond Chandler immortalized the Bryson in his novel, *The Lady in the Lake.* As Detective Philip Marlowe approaches the building, he finds: "a white stucco palace with fretted lanterns in the forecourt and tall date palms. The entrance was in an L, up marble steps, through a Moorish archway, and over a lobby that was too big and a carpet that was too blue. Blue Ali Baba oil jars were dotted around, big enough to keep tigers in."

Today, the carpet is faded, the Ali Baba jars are gone, and the Bryson provides basic low-budget housing at the edge of downtown L.A. Inside the lobby, a brass-and-glass cage elevator is like that of a vintage European hotel. The brass is tarnished black, however. Up on the ninth floor, the ballroom—paint peeling, plaster cracking, floor decaying—is inhabited only by pigeons and perhaps a few ghosts. Even in its neglected condition, the Bryson strikes a fine-looking silhouette along Wilshire Boulevard. Especially memorable are the two stone lions poised Sphinxlike atop the columns of the Bryson's grand main entrance. If only they could speak. . . .

There is currently some talk of major changes taking place at the Bryson, a rumor of totally restoring it—not as an apartment building but as offices.

22. VAGABOND THEATRE
2509 Wilshire Boulevard

This may be L.A.'s best revival house. Showing everything from the earliest of silents to the darkest of *films noirs,* the Vagabond frequently presents "legendary screen stars in person" as part of the program. Recent guests: Alice Faye, Esther Williams, Ella Raines, Jean Simmons, Tippi Hedren. The Vagabond also tries to secure the best available print of any film it screens and almost always features a double bill.

NOTE: *For schedule, call: 387-2171.*

23. PARK PLAZA HOTEL
607 South Parkview Street

Overlooking Douglas MacArthur Park (the place that inspired the 1960s Richard Harris and the 1970s Donna Summer hit song, "MacArthur Park"), the Park Plaza Hotel was built in the late twenties as an Elks Lodge. Architecture buffs are impressed by the building's monumental concrete façade which bursts forth with gigantic statues at the upper corners. Movie buffs may be interested in knowing that one of the architects, Claude Beelman, designed the Irving Thalberg Building at MGM Studios. Movie buffs will also be intrigued by the Park Plaza's extraordinary lobby. Dominated by a massive staircase, this grand Medieval-looking space has huge chandeliers, a frescoed ceiling, marble columns, and none of the splendor has been lost on Hollywood location managers and art directors. Among the many movies, TV movies, and TV series that have shot sequences in the Park Plaza's lobby and ballroom: *New York, New York, Blood Feud, Stripes, Young Doctors in Love, The Jack Dempsey Story, Dr. Detroit,* "Lou Grant," "Falcon Crest," "Kojak." In addition, it's been seen in many commercials as well as in music videos starring everyone from Pat Benatar to Steve Perry to Donna Summer.

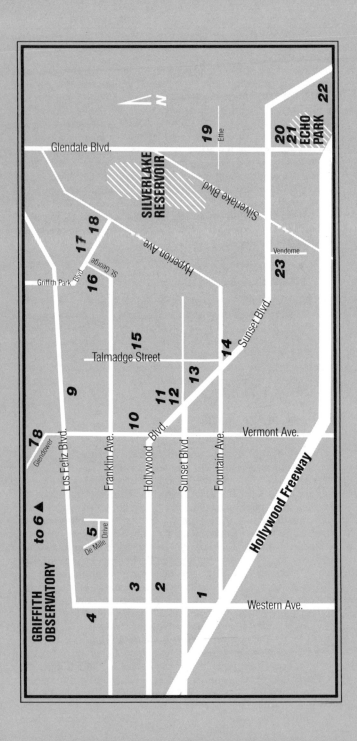

LOS FELIZ/
SILVERLAKE/
ECHO PARK

The Original "Hollywood"

5

*Lord of Los Feliz: Hollywood pioneer
Cecil B. DeMille at home
on DeMille Drive*

LOS FELIZ, Silverlake, and Echo Park are the names of three neighborhoods that lie between Hollywood and downtown Los Angeles. In the earliest days of the movie industry in Los Angeles, many of the first studios were based in these "East Hollywood" areas, especially around Silverlake, which was then known as Edendale. Today, most of these studios are gone but the names of some of their founders—Mack Sennett, D. W. Griffith, Walt Disney—are a part of film history. The names of others—Selig, Lubin, Spoor—may be remembered by only the hardest of hard-core silent movie afficionados.

For the serious film buff, fascinating vestiges of the Silverlake/ East Hollywood area's once formidable film activity can be discovered here: the original Vitagraph lot, for example, lives on as the home of ABC TV . . . the odd wedge of a building, once the private studio of Mack Sennett comedienne Mabel Normand, is now a scene shop. Other landmarks are less well preserved: a little sign on a supermarket parking lot is all that there is to mark the site of the first Walt Disney Studio—the birthplace of Mickey Mouse.

Whereas the studios tended to be clustered in and around Silverlake, Los Feliz—slightly to the north and considerably more exclusive—was where many early stars and moguls had their homes. Among the neighborhood's legendary residents, Cecil B. DeMille never moved from Los Feliz. Walt Disney, on the other hand, eventually made the switch to Beverly Hills when Los Feliz fell from fashion in the 1940s. Today, however, many of the newer stars—Lily Tomlin is one—have returned to Los Feliz and are helping to make it trendy, if not chic, once again.

Besides early studios and movie-star houses, Los Feliz, Silverlake, and Echo Park hold even more surprises for the movie lover. Many of these are famous film locations. Examples: the extraordinary Frank Lloyd Wright house that has been in many horror and science fiction flicks . . . the clutch of Victorian houses in Echo Park that has been used to represent everything from Depression-era Australia to today's Aspen, Colorado . . . the high school that is perhaps Hollywood's most photographed . . . and the stairs up which Laurel and Hardy tried to deliver a piano in their Academy-Award-winning short, *The Music Box.*

Finally, a visit to Los Feliz, Silverlake, and Echo Park— areas that are not on most travelers' itineraries—is a trip into ethnic L.A. In addition to discovering monuments to early filmmaking, movie lovers will come across South American grocery stores, Thai restaurants, Korean shopping centers, Ukranian bars, and Armenian lunch counters. A whole other Hollywood; call it the real world.

NOTE: *Car required for Los Feliz, Silverlake, Echo Park. The KCET Tour is highly recommended as is a walk or drive around Carroll Avenue.*

1. DELUXE LABORATORIES
1377 North Serrano Avenue

Before there was a Twentieth Century-Fox, there was a William Fox. His Fox Studios—opened in 1917—once occupied much of the block at the southeast corner of Sunset Boulevard and Western Avenue. Early Fox stars were super-vamp Theda Bara, cowboys Buck Jones and Tom Mix, plus Pearl White, Helen Ferguson, Colleen Moore, Jean Arthur, John Gilbert, Hope Hampton, Billie Dove, Janet Gaynor, Dolores Del Rio, and Carole Lombard.

William Fox started out in the picture business in 1904 when, at the age of twenty-five, he sold his cloth processing firm and opened a nickelodeon (price of admission, 5 cents) in a converted storefront in New York City. By 1913, Fox and his partners controlled a large chain of nickelodeons and the need for more films prompted them to start producing their own. In 1915, Fox moved to California and two years later opened his Sunset/Western studios. It should be noted that while Warner Brothers made history as the studio that introduced talking pictures, Fox immediately met the challenge with its Movietone (sound-on-film) system. Much more sophisticated, it was Fox's sound system that all the studios eventually adopted.

The early thirties were not kind to William Fox or to his studio. In addition to the catastrophic effects of the stock market Crash, the studio had serious legal troubles with the U.S. government. By 1935, when the company he founded merged with Joseph Schenck's two-year-old Twentieth Century Films, William Fox was no longer in the picture. Thus, Twentieth Century-Fox was born without Fox. Soon after the merger, the new studio's headquarters were moved to West Los Angeles, which remains their location today.

Today, all that is left of Fox's original Sunset/Western studios is the still-active Deluxe film lab ("Color by Deluxe"). A huge ZODY'S discount store and parking lot cover the rest of the site.

2. HOLLYWOOD PROFESSIONAL SCHOOL
5400 Hollywood Boulevard

Welcome to "Fame" West! Half of the Mouseketeers went to school here—and almost every one of "The Brady Bunch" was a Hollywood Professional School student at one time or another. Supposedly, Connie Stevens was "discovered" here—and former student Peggy Fleming used many HPS graduates in the cast of her "Peggy Fleming in Russia" television special. Other famous former students are Ryan O'Neal, Natalie Wood, Jill St. John, Donald O'Connor, Betty Grable, and Mickey Rooney.

Founded in 1930, the school was first called the Hollywood Conservatory of Music and Arts. It went into the business of serious education several years later when child-labor laws became tougher and insisted that even movie kids attend school a certain number of hours a day. Today, the school has classes from 8:45 to 12:45—which allows afternoons free for auditions and filming. The school also offers correspondence courses for performers whose jobs demand they be off campus and on location.

3. LE TRIANON
1752 North Serrano Avenue

Did Mary Pickford really build this fairy-tale chateau apartment building? That is the question. According to numerous legends and at least one real-estate brochure, Miss Pickford not only built Le Trianon in 1928 but had a vast penthouse apartment on the premises that featured "three levels of Old World Charm, hardwood floors, beams, archways, large rooms and more." But real-estate brochures have never been noted for their accuracy. The building permit makes no mention of Miss Pickford, lists the owner as the Chateau Holiday Corporation. A front? Who knows? Not Miss Pickford's husband of forty years, Buddy Rogers, who doesn't remember Mary ever having mentioned anything about the building. Of course, Rogers didn't marry Mary until 1937—and since she built, bought, and sold quite a bit of real estate in her time, it's quite possible that Le Trianon was no longer a part of her empire at the time of her marriage to him.

Meanwhile, one thing *is* sure about Le Trianon's beginnings: The building was designed by a very famous Los Angeles architect of the time, Leland A. Bryant. His most famous creation: the landmark Art Deco Sunset Towers apartment house on Sunset Boulevard. Today, Le Trianon has been beautifully restored and

Le Trianon today

looks just as good as it must have in 1928 when Mary Pickford may or may not have had that fabulous penthouse here.

4. THE AMERICAN FILM INSTITUTE
2021 North Western Avenue

Founded in 1967 "to advance and preserve the art of the moving image," the AFI has its administrative headquarters in Washington, D.C., and its campus in Hollywood. Here, aspiring directors, writers, editors, designers, and camera people learn the art and craft of contemporary filmmaking. Among AFI's recent graduates are screenwriter Tom (*Coal Miner's Daughter*) Rickman and director Michael ("Miss Lonelyhearts") Dinner.

NOTE: *Besides its classrooms and production facilities, the AFI campus is also home to the Louis B. Mayer Library. With an extensive collection of film books, periodicals, scripts, transcripts, clippings, and still photographs, this reference/research library is open to AFI students as well as to visiting scholars, researchers, advance graduate students, and all members of the motion picture and television industry. Library hours: Monday through Friday from 10:30 to 5:30. Phone: 856-7655.*

5. DeMILLE DRIVE
Between Los Feliz Boulevard and Franklin Avenue

Named for none other than old C. B. himself, DeMille Drive is a twisting hillside lane between Los Feliz Boulevard and Franklin Avenue. It was here that the pioneer director/producer lived in the same Spanish mansion—number 2000—from 1916 until his death in 1959. Over the years, some of DeMille's neighbors were Charlie Chaplin, who lived next door at 2010 in

Cecil B. DeMille outside his mansion on DeMille Drive

Griffith Park Observatory

the late teens, and W. C. Fields, who lived across the street at 2015 in the early forties.

Supposedly, long before DeMille came to Los Feliz, the area was a sacred Indian burial ground said to be inhabited by spirits. In 1942, DeMille's two-year-old grandson—by his daughter Katherine and her then husband, actor Anthony Quinn—drowned in a pond on the Fields property. Many attributed the child's death to an ancient Indian curse. Today, the former Fields house is shared by comedienne Lily Tomlin and writer-producer Jane Wagner. The DeMille house remains as it was when DeMille lived there and is occasionally opened up to the public for special tours.

NOTE: *Although there are no gates, numerous street signs announce that DeMille Drive is a private street and "not maintained by the city of Los Angeles." "Silent Policemen" (i.e., traffic bumps) further discourage sightseers from venturing into these parts.*

6. GRIFFITH PARK OBSERVATORY
Griffith Park

It's been seen time and again in all sorts of low-budget science-fiction films such as *When Worlds Collide* and *War of the Colossal Beast*—usually as the laboratory where scientists on earth are working feverishly to save the planet from alien invaders. But no film has ever used this Hollywood Hills landmark—built in 1935—as extensively as *Rebel Without a Cause*. It is here where the students of Dawson High—new kid on campus James Dean is one of them—come on a field trip early on in the film. During the planetarium sky show, Dean's clowning fails to endear him with one group of classmates who bully him in the parking

Sal Mineo and James Dean outside the Griffith Park Observatory in Rebel Without a Cause, *1955*

lot. The scenes at the end of the film are also played against the background of the Griffith Park Observatory and Planetarium. This time, a very frightened Sal Mineo is hiding from the police inside the Planetarium. Finally persuaded by Dean to come outside, Sal panics and is shot by one of the law officers. More than just a location, the observatory is used symbolically in the film, suggesting a cold and impersonal higher order of things that seems strangely uninvolved in the affairs of mortals.

Ennis-Brown house

Harrison Ford inside his Ennis-Brown house apartment in Blade Runner, *1982*

7. ENNIS-BROWN HOUSE
2607 Glendower Avenue

Of all the fantastic concrete-block houses that Frank Lloyd Wright built in Hollywood during the 1920s, the Ennis-Brown house is the most spectacular. Completed in 1924, the massive Mayan marvel enjoys a prized hillside location and can be seen from many points in the Hollywood flatlands. Possibly because it is so easy to see (and to photograph), the Ennis-Brown house has long fascinated Hollywood art directors and it has wound up in a number of movies. As far back as 1934, the place is said to have been the inspiration for the mysteriously moderne Hungarian castle that was the main location for Universal's horror classic, *The Black Cat,* the first picture to pair Boris Karloff and Bela Lugosi. Later, the Ennis-Brown house played the title role in Allied Artists' 1958 *The House on Haunted Hill.* Another of its memorable appearances was as the ultra-chic mansion of art director Claude Estee in the film version of Nathanael West's *The Day of the Locust.* It was also a location for *Terminal Man* in 1974. More recently, Harrison Ford, starring as a twenty-first-century bounty hunter in *Blade Runner* (1982), lived and loved inside this same 1924 Los Angeles landmark building.

NOTE: *The Ennis-Brown house is a private residence but house tours are given on the second Sunday of January, March, May, July, September, and November. For information and reservations, write: Trust for Preservation of Cultural Heritage, 2655 Glendower Avenue, Los Angeles, CA 90027—or call: 660-0051.*

8. FORREST J. ACKERMAN
2495 Glendower Avenue

Serious sci-fi film fans have no doubt already heard of Forrest J. Ackerman—long-time editor-in-chief of *Famous Monsters of Filmland* and the world's foremost collector of science-fiction and horror memorabilia. Ackerman lives in the Los Feliz hills in a Spanish villa that once belonged to actor Jon (*Ramar of the Jungle*) Hall. Taking over five basement rooms—his "dungeon"— is an incredible collection of some 125,000 stills from science-fiction and horror films, 18,000 lobby cards, more than 35,000 hard-cover books (close to 200 different volumes of Bram Stoker's *Dracula* and 200 of Mary Shelley's *Frankenstein*).

Ackerman also has a number of priceless artifacts, props, and costumes that have been used in or are associated with sci-fi and horror films. Among his treasures are the original creature costume from *The Creature of the Black Lagoon* (salvaged by a studio janitor), Lon Chaney's makeup kit, Claude Raines' *Phantom of the Opera* cape, Bela Lugosi's *Dracula* cape and huge ring (which Ackerman wears) with the Dracula family crest, the tiny costume worn by Johnny Eck (the half-man in *Freaks*), one of the only remaining models of the flying Martian death machines from *The War of the Worlds,* a perfect replica of one of the robots from Fritz Lang's *Metropolis,* and a part of *King Kong*'s giant paw.

Serious fans and collectors can make an appointment to visit Ackerman's fantastic realm (Saturday is usually the best day) by calling MOON-FAN. Ackerman also deals in movie stills, back issues of magazines, and lobby cards. Several years ago, Ackerman offered his entire collection to the City of Los Angeles. Since the collection proved too vast to be accommodated in any existing Public Library room, there are plans for a permanent museum to be created to house Ackerman's treasures. That has yet to happen—and for the moment, almost everything remains with "Mr. Science Fiction" himself.

9. MICHAEL'S RESTAURANT
4500 Los Feliz Boulevard

The last and least-known of the four Brown Derby restaurants opened in Los Feliz in 1941 and closed in 1959. Today a restaurant called Michael's occupies the same space—and remembers its predecessor by featuring the famous Brown Derby Cobb Salad on the menu.

NOTE: *Phone: 665-1181; open daily from noon to 9.*

10. LOS FELIZ THEATER
1822 North Vermont Avenue

An unprepossessing movie theater that is one of tinseltown's premier places to go to catch foreign flicks. In the 1950s

"Babylon" on Sunset, 1916

and 1960s, this kind of theater was popularly known as an "art" house.

NOTE: *Program information: 664-2169.*

11. "BABYLON" SITE
4473 Sunset Drive

Here, where the Vista Theater now stands—as well as on much of the land behind it—the great motion picture pioneer, D. W. Griffith, erected one of the greatest movie sets Hollywood has ever known: the towering city of Babylon. The year was 1916 and Griffith built his Babylon for a film originally called *The Mother and the Law*—but which has gone down in film history as *Intolerance*. The film was Griffith's follow-up to (and some say apology for) his immensely popular and controversial *The Birth of a Nation*. At the time of its release, *Intolerance* was touted as the most expensive movie ever produced. Lillian Gish reports that it cost almost $2 million but film historians feel that the budget, although exorbitant for its time, was decidedly less. Despite its cost, *Intolerance* was not a box-office success and wound up putting Griffith in severe financial straits. For several years after *Intolerance* was released, the massive Babylon set was not torn down and remained a Sunset Boulevard oddity and a tribute to Griffith's creative and financial excesses. In 1919, there was talk of preserving the set as a permanent landmark but nothing came of it and the legendary movie-set city of Babylon was eventually swallowed up by a city that was fast becoming equally legendary . . . Hollywood.

12. VISTA THEATER
4473 Sunset Drive

The pretty Spanish exterior of this little movie house belies the wild 1920s Egyptian decor inside. Originally part of the Lou Bard theater chain, the Vista (then known as the Bard) opened in 1923 with a mixed bill of vaudeville acts and silent movies. One explanation of the theater's schizophrenic architectural personality says that the owners intended to build a totally Spanish-style theater—but decided to go Egyptian in the middle of the theater's construction on hearing of the discovery of King Tut's Tomb in 1922. Today, the Vista is an important revival house in Los Angeles.

NOTE: *For program information, call: 660-6639.*

13. KCET STUDIOS
4401 Sunset Boulevard

The Cultural Heritage Board of the City of Los Angeles has designated the KCET studio site "Historic Cultural Monument No. 198." The oldest continually used studio in the country, the complex was established in 1912 by the Lubin Manufacturing Company, an early film producing organization that was based in Philadelphia. Subsequent occupants were such forgotten silent picture companies as Essanay (they produced twenty-one Westerns here), Willis and Ingles, and J. D. Hampton. By 1920, matinee idol Charles Ray took over the studio and eventually produced and starred in the ill-fated *The Courtship of Miles Standish* (1924), which bankrupted the actor as well as his production company. Many of the Spanish-style brick buildings that still occupy the KCET lot were built during the Charles Ray reign.

Monogram Studios' screening room in the 1930s

After various other tenants, Monogram Pictures came on the scene in the 1940s. Among the many "B" movies made by Monogram on this site were series such as "The East Side Kids," "The Cisco Kid," and "Charlie Chan." In the 1950s, through a merger, Monogram and its lot became another famous "B" studio—Allied Artists. The most memorable Allied Artists film shot and edited here was the original *Invasion of the Body Snatchers* (1957).

After serving as a rental lot for television productions in the 1960s, the studio was acquired in 1970 by KCET—the Los Angeles Public Broadcasting network. Since that time, KCET has been responsible for producing a number of nationally televised PBS series—including "Hollywood Television Theater," "Visions," and Dr. Carl Sagan's "Cosmos."

NOTE: *KCET operates a tour of its historic facilities on Tuesdays and Thursdays. Besides providing insights into how television shows are produced, the tour also offers a fascinating look at some of the vestiges of KCET's movie-studio days. One of the highlights of the tour is a visit to the 1933 screening room— a beautiful little theater with white columns, beamed ceiling, bricked walls and floors. For years boarded up and used as a storage space, the theater was "discovered" in the late 1970s and restored. For information on the KCET tour, call: 666-6500.*

14. TRIANGLE SCENE SHOP
1215 Bates Street

These days, stage sets for the Los Angeles Civic Light Opera are constructed inside this little wedge-shaped building with the high-high ceilings. Originally built for making movies back in 1916, this was once the personal studio of Mack Sennett's favorite

Triangle Scene Shop, formerly Mabel Normand's studio

on- and off-screen comedienne, Mabel Normand. Later, the same space was taken over by another silent screen great—cowboy star William S. Hart—who also used it for his own production company. More recently, yet another superstar has been linked to this historic site: Barbra Streisand; it was a location for her first film, *Funny Girl.*

Architectural note: The studio was originally built entirely of wood and had a canvas-topped roof that could be opened and closed to control the sunlight that lit the sets below. A permanent roof was probably added in the 1920s. The columned, stucco façade came in the 1940s.

15. ABC TELEVISION CENTER
4151 Prospect Avenue

Today, the name Vitagraph doesn't ring too many bells, but in the early part of the century it was a household word. One of the country's most important pioneer movie companies, Vitagraph traces its beginnings back to 1896 when two vaudeville comedians, Albert E. Smith and J. Stuart Blackton, decided to bring a projector and a couple of very short films into their act. When the movies proved more popular than their routines, Smith and Blackton realized that the future lay in the magical new medium of motion pictures—and Vitagraph was born. Based in the Flatbush section of Brooklyn, the two started filming everything from the Spanish American War to Teddy Roosevelt's inauguration. They also developed a powerful distribution system, signed the first actress ever to a movie contract (Florence Turner, "The

Vitagraph studios, 1924

Vitagraph Girl"), and like many early film companies, eventually established a California unit.

Vitagraph's first California films were shot in Santa Monica around 1912. In 1915, Al Smith purchased a large tract of land at Prospect Avenue and Talmadge Street which today is occupied by ABC Television. During the Vitagraph period, the lot was home to stars such as Anita Stewart, Corinne Griffith, Clara Kimball Young, Antonio Moreno, Bessie Love, Wallace Reid, Dolores Costello, Alla Nazimova, Adolphe Menjou, and Stan Laurel in his pre-Oliver Hardy period. In those days, Vitagraph's main entrance—now a brick wall with an ABC sign—was at the corner of Talmadge and Prospect. Here, players were paid (sometimes in gold coins) at the pay window at the front gate. Across the way, a small low shingled building was a commissary that featured home-cooked lunches. Today, what's left of the building stands abandoned and boarded up.

By 1925, Vitagraph, still headed by its founder Al Smith, was having financial difficulties. Enter an aggressive younger movie company called Warner Brothers. Warners not only bought the ailing Vitagraph but absorbed Vitagraph's stars and the copyrights to all its screenplays. The latter enabled Warner Brothers to remake many of Vitagraphs's old hits.

Since Warner Brothers had its main studios on Sunset Boulevard and later in Burbank, the former Vitagraph lot was always used by Warners as an annex studio. Nonetheless, all or parts of many important Warner Brothers pictures were shot here from the mid-twenties to the late-forties. Among them: *Trapped in the Snow Country,* starring the most popular box-office star of 1926—Rin-Tin-Tin; *The Jazz Singer* (1927); *The Glorious Betsy* (1928); James Cagney in *Public Enemy* (1931); *The Gold Diggers of 1933* with Ginger Rogers and Joan Blondell; and Errol Flynn in 1935's *Captain Blood.*

In 1948, the studio complex was bought and remodeled by the fledgling ABC Television Network. Since then, it has been used for locally produced ABC network shows and is sometimes rented by other networks and studios for their projects.

NOTE: *KABC is closed to the public but admits visitors to tapings of certain television shows such as "Family Feud." For information on tickets, call: 557-4398; or write: KABC, 4151 Prospect Avenue, Hollywood, CA 90027.*

16. JOHN MARSHALL HIGH SCHOOL
8939 Tracy Street

The archetypal American high school, this classic of "Collegiate Gothic" architecture has been Dawson High in *Rebel Without a Cause,* Rydell High in *Grease,* and numerous nameless highs in countless television commercials, movies of the week, and episodes of series. In reality, John Marshall was built in 1928, has 3400 students, and narrowly escaped demolition in the early

John Marshall High School

1970s because it did not meet earthquake code standards. Today, through the efforts of the community, the building has been stabilized and saved for future generations of students—and movie companies.

17. COURTYARD COMPLEX
2900–2912½ Griffith Park Boulevard

Legend has it that these enchanting storybook cottages were built by Walt Disney to house studio personnel. Located just around the corner from Disney's original Hyperion Avenue location, this story would seem plausible. City records, however, indicate that the courtyard complex was built by a Lois and Ben Sherwood around 1931. Another theory suggests that while Disney didn't build these little houses, he was influenced by their architecture, especially when he was preparing *Snow White and the Seven Dwarfs*. The Dwarfs' cottage in the film bears a striking resemblence to these Griffith Park Boulevard bungalows.

18. MAYFAIR SUPERMARKET
2719 Hyperion Avenue

Once it was a magic kingdom. Today, a supermarket and parking lot stand on the site of the original Walt Disney Studios. Housed in a charming white Spanish Colonial building, Disney's domain was described in the 1930s by reporter Janet Flanner as "the sanest spot in Hollywood ... remotely located in one of those endless suburban settings of Barcelona bungalows, pink roses and red filling stations that makes Southern California so

*Storybook cottages on
Griffith Park Boulevard*

picturesque. The studio looks like a small municipal kindergarten with green grass for the children to keep off of and, on the roof, a gigantic glorious figure of Mickey to show them the best way. ... With hysteria the seeming law for movie making, it's a wonder Mickey and Silly Symphonies succeed in this world at all, since the place where they're made is as sensible as a post office." (*Harper's Bazaar,* November 1, 1936)

Disney occupied his Hyperion Avenue quarters from 1926 until moving to the current Disney Studios location in Burbank in 1940. It was during the Hyperion period, however, that Mickey Mouse was born and that Disney's first feature-length film, *Snow White and the Seven Dwarfs,* was produced. Today, a small

Walt Disney's Hyperion Avenue studios, 1930

marker that looks like a no-parking sign is all there is to commemorate the magic that once went on here in Silverlake.

19. CENTER THEATER GROUP
1712 Glendale Boulevard

As the traffic swarms up and down busy Glendale Boulevard, few of the motorists making their way between the Glendale Freeway and downtown L.A. have any idea that the area of Silver Lake they're passing through was a lively center of motion picture production back in the early years of the twentieth century. In those days, the neighborhood had the romantic name of Edendale, and Glendale Boulevard was called Allesandro Avenue. The Selig Company was on Allesandro, as were the Pathé West Coast Studio and the Bison Studio. One of the largest and most successful of the Allesandro Avenue movie companies was the Keystone Comedy Company at number 1712. Founded in 1912 as a division of the New York Motion Picture Company, the Keystone studios were headed by the legendary Mack Sennett. It was here that he produced his Keystone Kops and numerous other comedies until 1927 when he moved his headquarters to Studio City in the San Fernando Valley.

In its heyday, the Keystone Comedy Company spread over both sides of Allesandro Avenue and featured stars such as Charlie Chaplin, Gloria Swanson, Roscoe "Fatty" Arbuckle, Buster Keaton, Ben Turpin, Louise Fazenda, Phyllis Haver, Marie Prevost, and Mabel Normand. The studio also featured one of the first enclosed concrete stages ever built. Today, that stage is all that is left of Sennett's historic domain. Set back from the street, the old studio looks like a big warehouse and can be seen easily since it sits on a small hill. No longer used for the making of movies, it was still involved in show business recently as a scene and costume shop for the Center Theater Group, a repertory theater company that works out of the Mark Taper Forum Theater at the Los Angeles Music Center in downtown L.A. More recently, the building was up for sale.

20. ANGELUS TEMPLE
1100 Glendale Boulevard

She wasn't a movie star—although many said she lived like one, her extravagances supposedly including mansions, money, and men. One thing is certain about evangelist Aimee Semple McPherson: She possessed "star quality" and marketed the commodity as effectively and successfully as any Hollywood personality in history. The clothes were always glamorous, the hair and makeup perfect, and the show—with music, mass baptisms, faith healings—was more spectacular than anything playing at Grauman's Chinese Theater. Thousands came to see and hear Sister Aimee at the great white semicircular temple that she built in 1923 across from Echo Park. With her name blazing in neon on the marquee outside and its huge auditorium within, the place seemed more a theater than a church. "No change," she roared, as the collection plates were passed, "greenbacks only!" Those who couldn't be there in person listened to her over the radio and sent in their contributions. Broadcasting from her own KFSG—the third radio station in Los Angeles and the first in this country's eventual long line of evangelical radio stations—she was one of America's first great radio stars.

Aimee Semple McPherson died (some say of a deliberate drug overdose) in 1944. Her legend and her church continue to this day. A television movie recently told her life story and starred Faye Dunaway; Nathanael West based the character "Big Sister" on Aimee in his *The Day of the Locust*—Geraldine Page played the part in the film version. The greatest monument to Aimee Semple McPherson's career, however, is the Angelus Temple. Extensively renovated in the early 1970s, it still occupies the same site across from Echo Park. If not one of the city's most beautiful houses of worship, it is certainly one of the most dramatic. Like its founder.

NOTE: *For anyone wishing to see the church's interior—which boasts the largest unsupported dome in North America—the doors are sometimes open. Otherwise, check to see when services are scheduled. A small religious bookshop is also on the premises and offers the official version of Sister Aimee's life.*

21. ECHO PARK

Not far from Mack Sennett's old Keystone Studios, this pretty park saw a lot of action back in the antic days of Sennett's Keystone Kops. If somebody landed in the drink at the end of a chase scene or via a mishap aboard a boat, chances are the body

Aimee Semple McPherson's Angelus Temple

Carroll Avenue: house used in Michael Jackson's "Thriller" video

of water they wound up in was Echo Park Lake. Edged by tall palm trees and filled with giant water lillies, Echo Park Lake was also the exotic L.A. locale where Jack Nicholson can be spotted aboard a rowboat in an early scene in the 1974 film *Chinatown.* The park, one of the oldest public parks in Los Angeles, was founded in 1891.

22. CARROLL AVENUE
1300 Block

Contrary to what many people think, Los Angeles wasn't always dominated by craftsmen's bungalows and dreamy Spanish-style architecture. Once upon a time, about a hundred years ago, the city was just as Victorian as the rest of the United States. While little of Victorian L.A. remains today, a notable exception is the hillside near Echo Park in the area known as Angelino Heights. Developed in 1886, Angelino Heights was downtown L.A.'s first "suburb" and was connected to the city via a cable car that ran along Temple Street. Today, some fifty beautiful Victorian residences and carriage houses—in various states of repair—still dominate this surprising enclave of another century.

Besides being listed in the National Register of Historic Places, the 1300 block of Carroll Avenue is also listed in most studio location scouters' notebooks as the place to go for an instant Victorian setting. Feature films, TV movies, and commercials are constantly being shot here. "The Thorn Birds," for example, used Carroll Avenue to recreate 1930s Australia in a sequence that was shot in Los Angeles. For the mini-series, "Aspen," fake snow was sprayed all over the street to duplicate the chic Colorado ski town. The TV version of "East of Eden" did up number 1320 Carroll Avenue as Kate and Faye's Bordello;

the same house also served as Marjo's rooming house in *Earthquake*. And for anyone wondering about the location of that "haunted house" that plays such an important role in the Michael Jackson "Thriller" video, it's at number 1345. More films and TV movies with Carroll Avenue sequences include "Every Day Was the Fourth of July," *Nickelodeon*, "Salem's Lot," "The Immigrants," "Splendor in the Grass" (the TV movie), and *Modern Problems*.

NOTE: *The Carroll Avenue Restoration Foundation sponsors house tours of the area every May and also at Christmas. They also have a walking-tour guide that's available to the public for a small charge. For information, write in care of 1316 Carroll Avenue, Los Angeles, CA 90026; or call 250-5976.*

23. "THE MUSIC BOX" STAIRS
932–935 Vendome Street

With the Depression in full swing, there wasn't much to laugh about in America in 1932—but producer/director Hal Roach and the famed comedy duo of Stan Laurel and Oliver Hardy gave movie audiences a hilarious lift with a little film called *The Music Box*. The film—in which "the Boys" try to deliver a piano to a house at the top of a long flight of stairs—won Roach an Academy Award as the best short (comedy) subject of 1931–1932. The stairs that Stan and Ollie grappled with are overgrown with ivy now, but are still standing between 932 and 935 Vendome Street, just south of Sunset Boulevard in Silverlake. A little known fact is that these same stairs were used in an earlier Laurel and Hardy film, *Hats Off,* a 1927 release that had them delivering vacuum cleaners. In the early eighties, the Los Angeles Cultural Heritage Board voted down a proposal to make the *Music Box* stairs an official cultural landmark.

Laurel and Hardy in The Music Box, *1932*

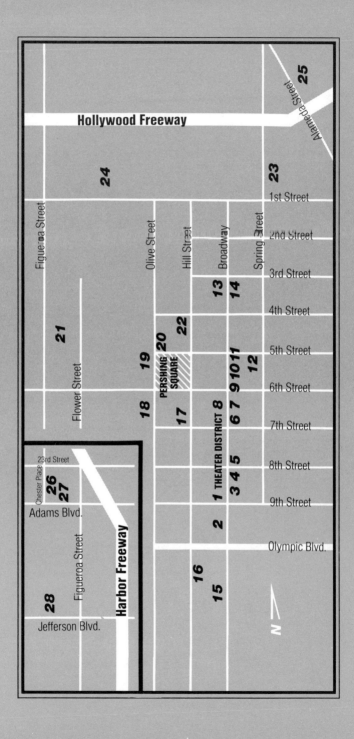

DOWNTOWN
LOS ANGELES

The Source

Comedian Harold Lloyd over downtown Los Angeles in Safety Last, *1923*

I T started with eleven families back in 1781. Recruited in Mexico as part of Spain's master plan to consolidate its empire and power in California, these early settlers—a band of Mexicans, blacks, and mulattos—named their new town "El Pueblo de Nuestra Senora la Reina de los Angeles" (Village of Our Lady Queen of the Angels). During its formative years, little of note happened in this small settlement with the long name. In 1826, owing to the revolution in Mexico, Los Angeles became Mexican rather than Spanish—but the change in administration had minimal effect on the town. More influential were the Anglos from the United States of America and its territories who started arriving around the same time. These included trappers, farmers, contractors, and at least one surgeon. Some learned the Spanish language; others didn't. In any event, English soon became the official language of Los Angeles, once California was ceded by Mexico to the United States following the Mexican War in 1848. By 1850, California was a full-fledged state and more and more Americans started moving in. It wasn't until two decades later, however, when transcontinental rail travel became a reality, that L.A.'s boom times really began. In 1870, the town's population numbered 5000 people; by 1880, it had grown to 11,000; and by 1890, it was close to 100,000.

All this is to say that Los Angeles was a well-established and fully functioning metropolis by the time the movies went West in the early part of the twentieth century. And when those first movie men arrived, they didn't head for Hollywood—most stayed right in downtown L.A. First on the scene was director Francis Boggs, who was with the Chicago-based Selig Polyscope Company of Colonel William Selig. After having shot some sequences on the Pacific coast at La Jolla in 1907, Boggs set up a temporary studio on a rooftop at 8th and South Olive Streets in downtown Los Angeles. About a year later, Boggs established what is considered to be L.A.'s first permanent studio; this time, he used a vacant Chinese laundry, again on Olive Street, and it was here where he shot *The Heart of a Racing Tout* (1909), the first dramatic feature film done entirely in California.

D. W. Griffith arrived in Los Angeles in 1910. Employed at the time by the American Mutoscope and Biograph Company of New York, Griffith worked mostly out of downtown L.A. until 1913 when he left Biograph. As more moviemakers came to Los Angeles, they founded studios in other areas: Silverlake, Santa Monica, Hollywood, Culver City. Nevertheless, for the first ten years of intensive moviemaking in L.A.—roughly from 1910 to 1920—it was downtown that was the nerve center as well as the social center for the new industry.

Downtown hotels were very important to the scheme of things in the early movie industry. Not only were these great meeting places for the movie colony, they were often "home," since there was much going back and forth between New York and L.A. in those early days. D. W. Griffith, for example, shot in

New York in the summer and fall, came West for the winter, and stayed in the Alexandria Hotel which still stands at 6th and Spring Streets.

Downtown movie theaters were important, too, for they were the sites of gala movie premieres years before these events happened in Hollywood. In fact, downtown is where the movie palace was born in Los Angeles—and where it flourished. Today, one of the great joys of visiting the downtown area is discovering a whole street that preserves some of the most fantastic movie theaters in the world.

The city of Los Angeles began downtown. In many ways, the movie business began here, too. Welcome to the source.

NOTE: *Downtown L.A. is best seen on foot. The first fourteen sites in this chapter can be covered in one or two hours. For those wishing a longer walking tour, items 15 through 22 should be added to the itinerary. A car will be necessary to visit the last six sites.*

1. THEATER DISTRICT
South Broadway, between 3rd and 9th Streets

By the 1930s, Los Angeles had more theaters than any other metropolitan area in the country—some 1500 of them to be exact. And nowhere was there a greater concentration of theaters—nickelodeons, movie palaces, vaudeville and legit houses—than along South Broadway in the middle of downtown Los Angeles.

Los Angeles Theater

The great surprise of the 1980s is that most of these theaters, built between the teens and the thirties, are not only still standing, but are still operating! These theaters endure, quite simply, because they still draw crowds—and the more lavish the theater, the bigger the take. In fact, L.A.'s Broadway—with its theaters, discount stores, fast-food operations, and vast central market—is said to do more business and to make more money per square foot than does posh Rodeo Drive in Beverly Hills! But Broadway is a far cry in ambience and spirit from Beverly Hills. This is another world—the center of Hispanic Los Angeles—and one is far more likely to hear Spanish than English, both in the streets and on the screen.

No matter what language is spoken here, L.A.'s Broadway theater district is a treasure of American theater history and architecture. In most cases, these theaters have been kept up rather than totally restored—so a little imagination may be necessary to picture what they must have been like in their heyday. At the same time, few of Broadway's theaters have suffered the horrors of any major "remodeling," a particularly devastating fate if it happened in the 1950s. All of this means that the architecture and the decor of these classic theaters are still pretty much intact and authentic even though the grandeur may be somewhat faded.

Several years ago, preservationists realized the unique privilege that Los Angeles enjoyed of still having so many magnificent theaters all in one area of the city. In an effort to further ensure their safety from the whims of future developers, these same preservationists succeeded in getting the Broadway theater and commercial district declared a National Historic District. It is the only district listed on the National Register of Historic Places in which theaters play such an important role.

NOTE: *To see Broadway, it's best to park the car and walk. In many instances, ushers will allow interested movie lovers to take a quick peek at the lobbies of some of the street's sumptuous theaters without buying a ticket. In other instances, it may be worth the price of admission to see a theater such as the United Artists, the Million Dollar, or the Los Angeles.*

One of the best ways of all to see the theater district is to take the two-hour Broadway tour organized by the Los Angeles Conservancy. These are usually given every Saturday at 10; tickets are $5. For reservations and/or information, write: The Los Angeles Conservancy, 849 S. Broadway, Los Angeles, CA 90014; or call: 623-CITY.

2. UNITED ARTISTS THEATER
933 South Broadway

Mary Pickford and Douglas Fairbanks had just returned from a grand European tour about the time that their production and distribution company—United Artists—was getting into the

United Artists Theater

motion picture theater business. Supposedly, Miss Pickford had
been particularly taken with the great cathedrals and castles she
had seen on the Continent and she insisted that her company's
flagship movie palace be just as splendid. Miss Pickford's fantasy
was made a reality by the Detroit architect C. Howard Crane,
who designed a spectacular theater that was somewhere between
a Gothic castle and a great Spanish cathedral. (The theater opened
on December 26, 1927, with Miss Pickford and Buddy Rogers—
her eventual husband—starring in *My Best Girl*.)

In the lobby of the United Artists—which is now decorated
with photos of Mexican movie stars—the ceiling is vaulted and
frescoed, the gold-edged mirrors enormous, and the banisters
fashioned of hand-carved teak. (When the theater opened in
1927, the carpets, specially woven in France, matched the frescoes
on the ceiling.) In the house itself, the walls appear to be made
of huge stone blocks and the ceiling—embedded with thousands
of tiny mirrors—creates a dazzling and magical lightshow. Two
huge murals on either side of the house depict heraldic Medieval
scenes. The mural on the right, however, is a wonderful spoof:
The faces all belong to various members of the board of directors
of the United Artists Corporation—including Pickford and
Fairbanks.

Today, the United Artists Theater is in remarkably good
condition and little has been done in the last half-century to alter
the essential splendor of the place. It is more than worth the price
of admission to experience that splendor.

3. ORPHEUM THEATER
842 South Broadway

Outside a sign reads, "Teatro Orpheum ... con titolos en Español; spoken in English." Inside, five chandeliers light the lobby—a combination of real and faux marble that was designed in 1925 by G. Albert Landsburgh to recreate the lobby of a European grand hotel. Today, vending machines and video games are also part of the scene. The house itself holds some 2000 spectators and is a spectacle of gold-leafing and stenciling. Two $45,000 (1925 dollars!) chandeliers are major decorative elements, along with Gothic arches and great round stained-glass panels under the balcony that are illuminated to provide atmospheric lighting. Of interest, too, are the theater's gleaming brass lobby doors, its lovely little brass box office, and the original "Orpheum" electric sign that tops the building. When it opened in 1925, the Orpheum was the last Orpheum vaudeville theater to be built in Los Angeles. Ironically, it turned out to be the place where vaudeville held out longer than practically anywhere else in the country. As late as 1950, vaudeville acts were still playing the Orpheum on South Broadway in L.A.

4. TOWER THEATER
802 South Broadway

S. Charles Lee—whose architectural credits include the Max Factor Building in Hollywood and the dazzling Los Angeles Theater down the street on South Broadway—designed the Tower Theater in 1927. It was the first theater in Los Angeles to be built

Tower Theater lobby

for talkies and to be "mechanically refrigerated." It was also extraordinarily handsome on the outside since its corner location allowed Lee to design essentially a complete building—rather than just a façade. With the Tower, Lee created a baroque fantasy of tile, sculpted niches, and pseudo-balconies—all dominated by an ornate corner clock tower (which was lowered substantially after the 1971 earthquake). Inside the theater, Lee tried to duplicate, on a small scale, the opulence of the lobby of the Paris Opera using stained glass, sculpted ceilings, and chandeliers. While this is an impressive space indeed, it only hinted at what Lee would do three years later inside the nearby Los Angeles Theater.

5. GLOBE THEATER
744 South Broadway

Opened in 1913 and originally run by Oliver Morosco (who was later to become a producer in New York and to have a theater named after him near the "other" Broadway), the Globe was one of the first legitimate houses to operate on Broadway in L.A. Now called "Teatro Globe" and featuring movies in español, the theater had an interesting life in the 1930s and 1940s as a newsreel theater. In those pretelevision days, it showed—as did many movie houses across the country—newsreels exclusively. At lunch, after work, between jobs, people would pop into this kind of theater to keep up with what was going on in the outside world.

6. CLIFTON'S CAFETERIA
648 South Broadway

A night or an afternoon at the movies on Broadway in the 1930s might also have included a visit to Clifton's Brookdale Cafeteria—not just to eat but to keep all of the fantasy going. When it opened in 1935, Clifton's tried to create the feeling of being in the great outdoors. Today, the place is still quite an experience. The main dining room has grottolike walls, a huge forest mural, four tiers of balconies with rough-hewn tables and balustrades, a waterfall that cascades into a burbling brook, plastic plants and flowers, a full-sized statue of a deer that watches over everything. Only the self-service cafeteria section at the rear of the restaurant seems considerably modernized. Also worth seeing is Clifton's *other* dining room upstairs: All done up Gay Nineties style with chandeliers and red-flocked wallpaper, it is a total departure from the neo-National Park decor below. More fun en route to the restrooms—look for tiny lights embedded in the stairs; and outside the building, a still-bright terrazzo sidewalk pictures the attractions—movie studios are among them—of Southern California.

NOTE: *The food ain't bad, either. Open daily, from 6 until 8.*

Clifton's Cafeteria terrazzo sidewalk

7. PALACE THEATER
630 South Broadway

This theater was designed by G. Albert Landsburgh for the powerful Orpheum vaudeville circuit. Called the Orpheum when it opened in 1911 as a vaudeville house, it is considered the oldest surviving Orpheum-built theater in the United States. Now called the Palace, the theater has shown movies since the 1920s and was used by director John Landis as a location for the Michael Jackson "Thriller" video. Especially attractive at the Orpheum/Palace is its French Renaissance façade and its deep exterior foyer with gold columns, mirrors, frescoed ceiling, and handsome "island" ticket booth.

8. LOS ANGELES THEATER
615 South Broadway

If Louis XIV had known about motion picture palaces back in the seventeenth century and had built one, it most likely would have been the Los Angeles Theater. Impressive on the outside with a terrazzo sidewalk and a massive columned façade, the Los Angeles is even more dazzling inside. The lobby alone provides a new definition of the word splendor—with glittering chandeliers, monumental mirrors, ornate staircase, fluted columns, crystal fountain.

Besides its dizzying decor, the theater offered amenities that gave a new definition to the word luxury. Smokers had their own private lounge with loge seats; infants could be dropped off in a "children's room" where an attendant would watch over them in a cheerful space that was decorated like the inside of a circus tent. There were also soundproof "crying rooms" where parents could see and hear the film and not worry about wailing tots. In the basement of this incredible theater, there was even a ballroom where a combo played and patrons could dance or have a bite to eat in the adjacent restaurant while waiting for seats. In this same ballroom, a special prism system projected the film being shown upstairs on a small screen. Finally, there were the bathrooms. In the ladies room, silver combs were handed out to women who could primp as long as they liked before vast marble vanities—and stalls were replaced by private rooms, each done in a different color marble.

Even the ushers had it easy at the Los Angeles: a special light-board system in the lobby showed them which seats were unoccupied. To achieve this, every seat of the 1000-seat theater was wired!

Designed by S. Charles Lee, the theater was the last great movie palace to be built on Broadway. It opened in 1931 with Charlie Chaplin's *City Lights*—one of the last great silent films ever made. One of L.A.'s most glamorous premieres, the gala event was marred only by the Depression-era breadline down the street. The Depression, ultimately, was not very kind to the Los Angeles Theater—for despite its splendor, it went bankrupt very quickly. One of the main reasons for this was the fact that the theater was not part of a chain and therefore was limited in the pictures it could show. Its owner is said to have wound up selling suits at Brooks Brothers.

Today the Los Angeles Theater shows citywide first-run movies in English. Still splendid, if somewhat threadbare, the theater is popular with film companies and can often be seen as a location in movies. In *New York, New York,* the ballroom of the Los Angeles doubled as the lobby of a grand hotel—and the entire opening sequence of Paul Mazursky's *Alex in Wonderland* starring Donald Sutherland was shot at the Los Angeles. The theater can also be spotted in "W. C. Fields and Me" and "Hold That Ghost." Best way of all to see it, however, is to go!

9. ARCADE THEATER
534 South Broadway

Look up above the marquee of the 1910 Arcade Theater and see its original name—Pantages—embossed in the cast-iron façade of the building that houses it. Alexander Pantages, who began his career producing dance-hall shows for gold miners in Alaska, went on to control one of the most important vaudeville circuits in the country. This was his first theater in L.A. The interior—still largely intact—tried to recreate an English Music Hall and was designed by the firm of Morgan and Walls who also did the Globe Theater on South Broadway, the El Capitan on Hollywood Boulevard, and the exterior of the Wiltern on Wilshire Boulevard.

10. CAMEO THEATER
528 South Broadway

If you ever wondered what a real nickelodeon looked like, this is it. The little Cameo first opened its doors in 1910 as a silent movie house that charged the whopping sum of a nickel to come inside and see the show. Ironically, most of those first "shows" came from back East since not too many filmmakers had as yet discovered the joys of Southern California. All that would change very quickly.

Today, the Cameo is into karate and dungeons-and-dragons-style feature flicks.

11. ROXIE THEATER
518 South Broadway

In a district of sumptuous theaters, the Roxie is notable for its lack of opulence. Inaugurated in 1931, it was the last theater to be built on Broadway and its stark "moderne" design reflected the austerity of the Depression era.

12. ALEXANDRIA HOTEL
501 South Spring Street

If we are to believe certain of the Alexandria's records, literally everybody who was anybody in early Hollywood stayed in this 1906 hotel at one time or another. Heading one list of former guests—or rather ending it, as the list is in alphabetical order—is the ubiquitous Rudolph Valentino (a refurbished suite

Los Angeles Theater lobby

bears his name). Then there's Fred Astaire, Theda Bara, the Barrymores, Sarah Bernhardt, Wallace Berry, Humphrey Bogart, Clara Bow, Francis X. Bushman—and that's just the beginning of the alphabet. Ironically, one luminary not on this list is D. W. Griffith—who definitely *did* make the "Alex" his base during his early L.A. sojourns.

There are many legends associated with the Alexandria in its early days. One holds that cowboy star Tom Mix once rode his horse into the lobby and over the hotel's much touted "million-dollar" Turkish carpet! Another says that Charlie Chaplin often did improvisations in this same lobby. And then there was the time in 1920 when Charlie Chaplin accused Louis B. Mayer of meddling in his divorce from Metro Studios contract player Mildred Harris. Chaplin eventually challenged Mayer to take off his glasses—at which L. B. did just that and solidly decked Chaplin, who wound up in a potted palm.

The movie crowd had deserted the Alexandria by the end of the 1920s. By then, the new Biltmore and Ambassador hotels had become the chic spots to stay and play—and Hollywood had a host of smart new hostelries of its own. The worst years for the Alexandria, however, were the 1930s when the Depression all but did the place in, forcing it to close for several years. When it reopened after that, it never regained its former place in the L.A. sun.

Today, the Alexandria seems to be going strong. While not one of the city's most lavish places to stay, the hotel was considerably upgraded by a $2 million refurbishing in the late 1970s. The best place to catch a feeling of what the Alexandria was like in its heyday is the restored Palm Court where a huge and very beautiful Tiffany stained-glass ceiling is the central decorative feature. In the lobby, an early remodeling lowered (i.e., covered up) the ornate original ceiling—but a climb up to the mezzanine level provides a closeup look at what's left of it.

13. MILLION DOLLAR THEATER
307 South Broadway

Five years before the Egyptian Theater premiered in Holly-wood and ten years before the Chinese, Sid Grauman created the Million Dollar Theater in downtown L.A. One of the first true motion picture "palaces" in the country, the Million Dollar opened in 1917 with cowboy actor William S. Hart starring in *The Silent Man.* (While Sid Grauman's name was "above the title" on all of the theaters he managed, Grauman never owned these theaters. He would get someone else to finance and build a house to his specifications and he would, in turn, lease it.)

The Million Dollar Theater is housed within the Million Dollar office building—which is said to have cost as much as its name boasted back in the late teens. Both the entrance to the theater on Broadway and the entrance to the building on 3rd

Million Dollar Theater, 1926

Street are exuberant expressions of an architectural style known as Churrigueresque—a New World offshoot of Spanish baroque that's even more baroque than baroque! It is within the auditorium of the 2200-seat Million Dollar, however, where all hell really breaks loose. Here, the feeling is one of being inside a great South American cathedral: there are numerous niches, statues, and organ-pipe covers that are reproductions of Spanish Colonial altar screens. There is also a functioning liquor bar on the second floor—one of the only real bars left in an L.A. movie house.

Ironically, this first of L.A.'s great picture palaces is the last movie theater in town to still have a live stage show as part of the bill. These feature Mexican and South American headliners (Maria Felix and Dolores Del Rio appeared at the Million Dollar in the seventies) as well as groups. For the price of admission, the audience gets to see both the movie and the show. Talk about your good old days!

14. BRADBURY BUILDING
304 South Broadway

It was the sleazy hotel that Jack Lemmon checked into as *Good Neighbor Sam,* the place where Edmund O'Brien met his murderer in the 1949 *film noir D.O.A.,* "Boston Blackie" 's office building, and the apartment house that was home to Sabastian, the "genetic designer" character in the sci-fi classic *Blade Runner.* Those are just a few of the films in which the Bradbury (office) Building has been featured prominently. Perhaps the most unusual building in all of Los Angeles, it is a dream of pink-marble

Inside the Bradbury Building

staircases, wrought-iron balustrades, open elevators that all rise around a light-drenched central atrium. Built in 1893, the Bradbury Building could have been the prototype for all the Grand Hyatt hotels on earth. And as far as movie art directors are concerned, it offers one of the city's most dramatic—and best lit!—interior locations.

The story surrounding the origin of this bizarre and wonderful L.A. landmark—which, surprisingly, looks totally unprepossessing from the outside—could have been the basis for a science-fiction film all its own. It seems that mining millionaire/real-estate developer Lewis Bradbury was in ill health and, realizing his days were numbered, wanted his last building to be something truly extraordinary. When the architect assigned to the project failed to come up with a design that pleased Bradbury, the aging millionaire turned to (no one knows just why) one of the architect's assistants. The assistant, thirty-two-year-old George Wyman (grandfather of sci-fi maven Forrest J. Ackerman), at first refused Bradbury's offer to design the building. Later, Wyman and his wife supposedly made contact with Wyman's dead brother via a Ouija-type board and received a message that said: "Take the Bradbury Building. It will make you famous." If instructions from the spirit world weren't enough, Wyman was further inspired by an 1887 science-fiction novel that described a sky-lit commercial building of the year 2000. The Bradbury Building—which some architects consider one of the most perfectly imagined interior spaces ever devised—was the only building of any importance that Wyman ever designed.

NOTE: *The Bradbury Building is open to the public, Monday through Saturday. There is a small admission charge.*

15. *HERALD EXAMINER* BUILDING
1111 South Broadway

Founded in 1903, the *Herald Examiner* was William Randolph Hearst's official Southern California voice up until his death in 1951. In addition to his newspaper empire, Hearst had a strong connection to the world of Hollywood through serving as executive producer for most of the pictures made by his movie-star mistress, Marion Davies. The couple was a major force in Hollywood social life during the 1920s and 1930s and together staged some of the town's most lavish parties. Hearst also influenced the Hollywood scene through star gossip columnist, Louella Parsons, who worked for the Hearst organization (and who often was "her master's voice" in her columns) throughout her career.

The *Herald Examiner* Building is an extraordinary structure that is classified as an example of the Mission Revival style by students of architecture. Inaugurated in 1912, it is the work of Julia Morgan—the first woman graduate of the prestigious Beaux-Arts school in Paris. In addition to its exuberant exterior, Morgan seems to have had a good time with the interior as well. The lobby especially—a lavish space of carved marble columns and arches—hints at the splendors Morgan would create in the 1920s when she was commissioned to design Hearst's famous "castle," San Simeon in Northern California.

16. MAYAN THEATER
1044 South Hill Street

The Mayan has one of the most fantastic façades of any movie house in Los Angeles—perhaps of any movie house in the

Lobby of the Herald Examiner *Building*

Mayan Theater façade

world. Somewhere between a pre-Columbian temple and a wedding cake iced by a madman, the Mayan's exterior is especially dramatic at night when it is floodlit. The Mayan opened in 1927, not as a movie theater but as a legit house. Anita Loos' *Gentlemen Prefer Blondes* was the premier attraction. Some twenty years and many incarnations later, the Mayan had become a burlesque house and, according to one source, briefly featured on its stage the woman who would become the most "preferred" blonde of the twentieth century. The woman went by the name of Marilyn Marlowe at the Mayan in 1948, writes Richard Lamparski in *Lamparski's Hidden Hollywood* (A Fireside Book, published by Simon and Schuster, 1981)—but she was really Marilyn Monroe. The strangest twist in all this is that Marilyn would later star as Lorelei Lee, the heroine of *Gentlemen Prefer Blondes,* in Twentieth Century-Fox's 1953 Hollywood musical version of the Anita Loos classic.

Movie lovers may remember the Mayan as the X-rated cinema where Jack Lemmon hung out in in the R-rated film, *Save the Tiger* (1972). Today, the Mayan is still X-rated—but many feel its architecture deserves an Academy Award.

P.S.: The intriguing building next door to the Mayan at 1050 South Hill Street is now the Metropolitan Community (a largely gay) Church. Originally, it was the Belasco Theater, a legit house that opened in the late 1920s.

17. THEATER JEWELRY CENTER
655 South Hill Street

Today, it's a kind of flea market filled with stalls selling jewelry at bargain prices. But a quick look around the inside of this souklike space reveals that it was once a theater—and a very grand one at that. The gilded ceiling of the lobby is still largely intact, as is the house itself where the massive proscenium is also gilded and the muraled ceiling is magnificent. Only the modern chandelier is a disappointment.

Back in 1920, this was Alexander Pantages' second vaudeville theater in downtown Los Angeles. Presenting films as well as live acts, the Pantages Theater was housed within the towering, Beaux-Arts-style Pantages Downtown Building. It was here that Alexander Pantages had his offices—and in 1929, the Pantages building figured in a sensational scandal when Pantages—who prided himself on his having exclusively female ushers—was arrested for allegedly raping one of them. The public was outraged—the woman who brought suit was just sixteen years old and Pantages was in his sixties. The jury must have been outraged as well because they found Pantages guilty. When a new trial brought about an acquittal two years later, the aging and physically broken Pantages had already served some of his fifty-year sentence. He died a few months later.

In the meantime, during the period of the Pantages trial, his theater was taken over by Warner Brothers who dropped the vaudeville acts in favor of just showing films. On its last legs in the early seventies, the theater closed down and later had a brief stint as a church. It was in the early 1980s that it began its new life as a shopping mall.

18. OVIATT BUILDING
617 South Olive Street

With mirrored pillars, illuminated glass ceiling, and silvery Art Deco doors, the spectacular entrance to the Oviatt Building is straight out of a Fred Astaire/Ginger Rogers musical. Although not a set, many movie stars did pass through this glamorous entrance to what was actually the establishment of Alexander & Oviatt—one of the most elegant haberdasheries in all of Los Angeles. Among the major male stars who kept their public images perfectly attired and accessorized here were Clark Gable, John Barrymore, Gary Cooper, and the actor who was considered Hollywood's best-dressed personality for decades—Adolphe Menjou.

James Oviatt—who built the exquisite thirteen-story landmark Oviatt building in 1928—did so with a flourish that matched the most flamboyant of Hollywood's early movie men. Oviatt spared no expense in the design and construction of his dream building. Impressed by a 1925 visit to Paris's famous "Exposition Inter-nationale des Arts Décoratifs et Industriels Modernes" (the design show that unleashed Art Deco on the world), Oviatt engaged the famed designer and crafter of glass, René Lalique, to create all of the glass panels and lighting fixtures that were used so lavishly in the Oviatt Building. It is said that some 30 tons of Lalique were installed in the original lobby—one of the largest commissions the French artisan ever received.

James Oviatt died in the early seventies and his building—already on the downswing by that time—quickly deteriorated even further after his death. In 1977, however, developer Wayne Ratkovitch and his partner Donald Bowers bought the Oviatt Building for a mere $400,000, managed to get it declared an Historic-Cultural Monument, and proceeded to sink some $5 million into its restoration. Today, the Oviatt's thirteen stories are fully rented and the original Alexander & Oviatt haberdashery on the first two floors of the building is the home of the ultra-elegant restaurant, Rex II Ristorante. So these days, movie stars dine—rather than shop—in this fabulous Los Angeles landmark.

P.S.: Proving that preservation can be profitable, Ratkovitch and Bowers reportedly sold the Oviatt Building to a Japanese real-estate corporation in early 1984 for the sum of $13.5 million!

19. BILTMORE HOTEL
515 South Olive Street

With almost 1000 guest rooms when it opened in October of 1923, the Biltmore was the largest hotel west of Chicago. Designed by architects Shultze and Weaver—who also were responsible for the Biltmore in New York City as well as the Waldorf Astoria—the L.A. Biltmore was instantly the city's grandest hotel and abounded with magnificent murals by artist Giovanni Smeraldi, a lavish lobby that duplicated a Spanish palace, and a galleria that was even more spectacular.

Many many stars have stayed at the Biltmore throughout its history but the hotel's greatest claim to fame as far as movie history is concerned has to do with a birth that some say occurred in its Crystal Ballroom on May 11, 1927. It was during an elaborate dinner to mark the founding of a new organization called the Academy of Motion Picture Arts and Sciences. Mary Pickford and Douglas Fairbanks were there; so were Louis B. Mayer, King Vidor, Jack Warner—and many more moguls and stars. MGM art director Cedric Gibbons was also there and during the dinner he is said to have done a rough sketch on a napkin of a little man who would go on to match (and even exceed) the fame of any movie star in history. The little man born that evening was eventually christened "Oscar."

As Oscar grew, he visited the Biltmore often—since the hotel was frequently the site of Academy Awards dinners. Oscar's Biltmore years: 1931, 1935, 1936, 1937, 1938, 1939, 1941, and 1942. Oscar also spent time at the Hollywood Roosevelt and Ambassador hotels during the early part of his career.

In 1969, the Biltmore hotel received a very special award all its own; it was named a Historic Landmark by the Cultural Heritage Board of the City of Los Angeles. Despite this great honor, the hotel itself was a bit down at heel. Dame fortune

Restored Biltmore Hotel lobby

showed her face, however, in the form of architects/developers Phyllis Lambert and Gene Summers, whose company acquired the landmark Biltmore in 1973 and eventually spent a reported $48 million in its restoration and refurbishment.

The classic beauty of the revived Biltmore's lobby, galleria, and ballroom has not been lost on Hollywood art directors. Since its restoration, the hotel has been used as a location for close to 250 feature films, television movies, series episodes, and commercials. Among the best known: *Chinatown, At Long Last Love,* "Rich Man, Poor Man," *The Last Tycoon,* the remake of *King Kong,* Streisand's *A Star Is Born, New York, New York, The Betsy, The Other Side of Midnight, The Buddy Holly Story, Airport 1979, Altered States, Splash,* "Scruples," "Movieola," *Foul Play,* "The Winds of War," "Falcon Crest," and "Dynasty."

20. AUDITORIUM BUILDING SITE
427 West 5th Street

Fronting Pershing Square at the northeast corner of 5th and Olive Streets, the Auditorium Building was the home of the Los

Actors dressed as Ku Klux Klansmen outside Clune's Auditorium to promote Birth of a Nation, *1916*

Angeles Philharmonic Orchestra for many years until its move to the L.A. County Music Center in 1965. For movie lovers, however, it is the auditorium's pre-Philharmonic history that is of interest. Opened in 1906 and often known as Clune's Theater Beautiful, this was the largest theater of its day in Los Angeles and the place where the public first saw a film that proved just how powerful and emotion-rousing a medium the movies could be. The year was 1915 and the film was D. W. Griffith's controversial (because of its racist overtones) *The Clansman*— which we know today as *The Birth of a Nation.*

Karl Brown—who was an assistant to Griffith's cameraman Billy Bitzer on the picture—wrote of the film's opening at Clune's in his *Adventures with D. W. Griffith* (Farrar, Straus & Giroux, 1973) as follows: "Griffith was given great credit for many things he had not done, while he was given no credit at all for the really enormous advances he had brought to the whole wide world of picture making. The greatest of these was the lifting of the lowly nickelodeon storefront theater, with its tinny honky-tonk piano and its windowless, foul-air smelliness, to the grandeur of a great auditorium with a great orchestra and a great picture that ran three hours and filled an entire evening with thrills and excitement in a setting of opulent luxury such as the great masses of working people had never dreamed possible for them. This sort of thing was for the idle rich who went to the opera to see and be seen. But after that first opening night at Clune's Auditorium in Los Angeles, anybody could be a millionaire for three hours and a Griffith snob for the rest of his life."

If we are to take Brown at his word, D. W. Griffith, *The Birth of a Nation,* and Clune's Auditorium all played a part in paving the way for the development of the great movie palaces that were soon to take over Los Angeles and the rest of the country in the later teens and twenties. (Brown does not mention the promotional gimmick that was used at the *Birth of a Nation* screening. It seems Griffith had actors dressed as hooded Klansmen assembled outside the theater on horseback. Enough said.)

Surviving into the 1980s, the auditorium building appeared quite different than it did in Griffith's day—because of major alterations in 1938 that totally moderne-ized the building's original Moorish façade. However, the interior of the building—designed by a nephew and student of famed Chicago architect Louis Sullivan—preserved many of the original Sullivanesque, Art Nouveau-like elements. The bad news is that the old auditorium building was razed in early 1985 to make way for a high rise.

21. WESTIN BONAVENTURE HOTEL
404 South Figueroa Street

The architecture of the twenty-first century arrived in downtown Los Angeles back in 1977 with the opening of this dazzling hotel designed by architect John Portman. A cluster of five thirty-five-story towers, each sheathed in mirror-glass, the 1474-room Westin Bonaventure has been frequently seen on both the large and the small screen—especially when the film or TV show takes place in the future. *Buck Rogers in the 25th Century* was one of the first science-fiction flicks to take advantage of the Bonaventure's fantastic façade and futuristic interior of sky-bridges, mirror fountains, and glass-bubble elevators. A likeness of the hotel also crops up briefly in *Blade Runner*—as part of the skyline of twenty-first-century L.A. The original *Blue Thunder* film used it, too.

No longer a newcomer to the downtown cityscape, the Bonaventure is often used in films and television as a backdrop

Bonaventure Hotel

that captures the spirit and look of contemporary L.A. Among the movies and TV shows in which the hotel has appeared as itself are *Breathless, Spinal Tap,* "Scruples," "Me and Mom," and "Male Model U.S.A."

22. SUBWAY TERMINAL BUILDING
417 South Hill Street

This is a reminder of how Los Angelinos once traveled—to work, to shop, and to the movies. The Subway Terminal Building stood above what served as the city's "Grand Central Station" from 1925 until 1955 when the last of the Red Cars of the Pacific Electric Railroad stopped running. Part of one of the most extensive public transportation systems in the country, L.A.'s Red Cars linked, in prefreeway days, downtown Los Angeles with the San Fernando Valley, Hollywood, West L.A., Santa Monica. Convinced for decades that the automobile was the only way to get around, it wasn't until the Energy Crisis of 1974 that Los Angeles started to think back to the good old days of the Red Cars. Today, the city is again planning to develop a rail/subway rapid-transit system to move its millions.

Although the Subway Terminal Building was restored in the early 1980s, little remains of its once spacious main concourse. Situated below ground, the concourse was divided up into offices once the trains stopped running. It's the lobby of the building—a grand marble-floored and marble-columned space—that merits a peek.

Los Angeles City Hall

23. CITY HALL
200 North Spring Street

This is the building that was the backdrop for all those doomsday press conferences in *The War of the Worlds* (1952). Later, in the same film, it wound up getting zapped by the death rays of invading Martian spaceships. This is also the high rise that for years served as *The Daily Planet* newspaper building in the long-running "Superman" television series and was also seen in the opening shot of "Dragnet" for ten seasons. For many years the tallest building in Los Angeles, indeed the only building allowed to rise above the 150-foot (usually ten stories) height limit imposed on all other structures between 1905 and 1957, City Hall was frequently called upon when the script called for a serious skyscraper. Among the 450-foot, twenty-eight-story building's other notable film and TV appearances are in *Mildred Pierce, D.O.A.,* and "The Rockford Files." How, you ask, did City Hall get to be so tall? No doubt, friends at City Hall helped.

24. DOROTHY CHANDLER PAVILION
135 North Grand Avenue

The largest of the three monumental marble buildings that make up the Los Angeles Music Center, the 3250-seat Dorothy Chandler Pavilion has been the site of the Academy Awards since 1969. It is also home to the Los Angeles Philharmonic. Architect of the Music Center is Welton Becket, the same man who did the landmark Capitol Records tower in Hollywood.

25. UNION STATION
800 North Alameda Street

Completed in 1939, this was the last of the great passenger train terminals ever built in the United States. And a great terminal it is indeed. On the outside, Union Station is a clean-lined Spanish structure that features pleasant patios and gardens as an integral part of its design. Inside, the main arrivals hall is a stunning space with four-story-tall ceilings that are frescoed and crossed with heavy beams. Here, one can easily imagine the glamorous "public" arrivals of movie stars with their secretaries, press agents, and loads of luggage as they alighted from the "Super Chief" back in the early forties. (Stars who wished anonymity exited the train a stop earlier at Pasadena.) One can imagine, too, the station's hubbub during the years of World War II as cavalcades of Hollywood's most famous personalities went off on War Bond drives—and as hordes of men and women in uniform went off to war.

Given its dimensions and its beauty, it is not surprising that Union Station has been used for countless films and television shows. The sheer scale of the place—perhaps the only interior in

© 1982 The Blade Runner Partnership

Union Station as the police station in Blade Runner

all of Los Angeles that can equal a soundstage in terms of size—is a cameraman's dream. This is the land of the endless "pullback" shot. Perhaps the film that used the terminal most extensively is a 1950 release that starred William Holden called *Union Station.* (The film was set in Chicago, however—not Los Angeles!) Other well-known theatrical and television films that have train-station sequences shot here are *The Hustler* (1961), *The Way We Were* (1972), *Gable and Lombard* (1975), *The Driver* (1977), *Oh God, Book II,* (1980), and *True Confessions* (1982).

One of the most interesting recent uses of the terminal was in *Blade Runner* (1982) in which it represented a police station in twenty-first-century Los Angeles. The film's director, Ridley Scott, is said to have chosen the location because he liked its "Art

E. L. Doheny mansion on Chester Place

THE SOURCE   153

Deco and neo-Fascist architecture and because of its immensity."
For the film, the producers built an actual office structure within
the terminal—and inadvertently blocked access to the ladies'
room in the process. It seems that filming needed to be interrupted
rather frequently owing to this oversight.

26. CHESTER PLACE
off West Adams Boulevard

In the heart of what was one of L.A.'s oldest of old-monied
areas, Chester Place is a cluster of marvelous mansions built
around the turn of the century. Of these, the most marvelous is
the Victorian Gothic chateau—number 8—that was owned by
the Doheny (oil) family for many years. The Doheny main house,
with its impressive marble stairs guarded by stone lions, is often
used for films and TV shows in which a mysterious mansion
figures in the plot. In the 1970s, the TV series "Colombo" was
constantly shooting at Chester Place and featuring the former
Doheny property.

Rarely used to represent Southern California, Chester Place
is far more likely to turn up on screen as a location in another
part of the country. Examples are its appearances in "Scruples"
(Boston), "Captains and Kings" (Philadelphia), "Testimony of
Two Men" (Hambleton, PA), *Godfather II* (New York City,
1917). In these instances, art directors often must "dress" the
palm trees to make them fit the landscape. This wasn't necessary,
however, in the made-for-television version of Tennessee Williams'
"A Streetcar Named Desire" which starred Ann-Margaret as
Blanche Dubois and featured Chester Place as New Orleans'
Garden District.

Today, Chester Place and many of its buildings—including
the Doheny mansion—form the downtown campus of Mount St.
Mary's College. When movie companies come to film here, they
are allowed to stay just one day so as not to disrupt the college's
academic activities to any great extent. Filming is also only
permitted on a certain number of days each month. All fees
collected from moviemaking here are used to help students
needing financial aid.

27. THEDA BARA MANSION
649 West Adams Boulevard

From the late nineteenth century and on into the early part
of the twentieth, West Adams was one of the most prestigious
boulevards in town. Just at the edge of Chester Place, this
handsome Tudor mansion at 649 West Adams was home to
several legendary silent movie celebrities. From 1915 to 1919,
super-siren Theda Bara lived here. Billed by the Fox publicity
people as the illegitimate daughter of a French artist and an
Arabian princess, Miss Bara was actually Theodosia Goodman

Former Theda Bara mansion

from Cincinnati! Besides Theda, this same house is said later to have been occupied by Roscoe "Fatty" Arbuckle—the comic whose career took a tumble in 1921 when he was implicated in the death of starlet Virginia Rappe. The young woman died after allegedly having been forced to perform some rather unusual sexual acts by Arbuckle in a San Francisco hotel room. Eventually "Fatty" was acquitted but his career never recovered. Joseph Schenck and Norma Talmadge are other names frequently mentioned as former famous residents of 649 West Adams. Today, the historic mansion is headquarters for the Vincentian Fathers.

The Shrine Auditorium

28. SHRINE AUDITORIUM
665 West Jefferson Boulevard

When it was built in 1927, it was the world's largest theater and held well over 6000 spectators. (Radio City Music Hall would match it in the next decade.) Designed by famed theater architect G. Albert Landsburgh, the Shrine resembles a gigantic double-domed Middle Eastern mosque on the outside, a massive Moorish palace on the inside.

As far as its movie history goes, ever since King Kong was brought back to civilization and put on display as "The Eighth Wonder of the World" at the Shrine (doubling as a Broadway theater in the 1933 RKO film), the mammoth auditorium has provided locations for a number of Hollywood classics. In the 1954 *A Star Is Born,* the Shrine is the site of the "Night of Stars" benefit at the opening of the film. It's here that Esther Blodgett (Judy Garland) first encounters Norman Maine (James Mason). Then, at the end of the same picture, Esther—now superstar Vicki Lester as well as Norman Maine's tragic widow—returns to the Shrine and utters her triumphant "This is . . . Mrs. Norman Maine" line as the camera slowly pulls back to reveal tiny Judy alone on the great stage.

In the 1970s, the Shrine was used in *The Turning Point* and *Foul Play.* More recently, Michael Jackson fans may recall that while filming a Pepsi Cola commercial at the Shrine in 1984 their idol was singed and taken to the hospital when a pyrotechnic effect went wild. The commercial aired nonetheless a few months later on the same Grammy Awards show (telecast from the Shrine) that saw Jackson win a record number of Grammies.

"King Kong" on stage at the Shrine in 1932

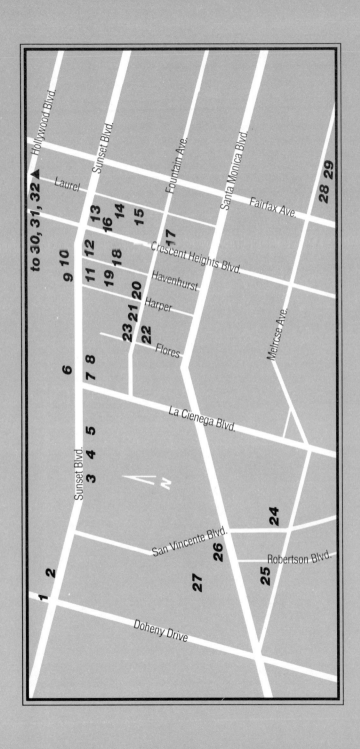

WEST HOLLYWOOD

Border Town

7

West Hollywood hot spot: Cafe Trocadero in the 1930s

ONE of the most enduring images of Hollywood at its most glamorous is that of the beautiful starlet, dripping in fur, exiting a limo with her handsome escort, and entering a glittering nightclub along the Sunset Strip. In the 1930s and 1940s especially, the Strip was the center of Hollywood's smartest nights on the town; and the names of its clubs and casinos—the Trocadero, Mocombo, Ciro's, the Clover Club, the Colony Club—were household words to the nation.

Why was so much of Hollywood's nighttime excitement centered around the Sunset Strip in West Hollywood? One of the reasons was the area's unusual status in the administrative scheme of Los Angeles. Originally called Sherman, West Hollywood was one of the few communities in L.A. County that voted against being annexed to the City of Los Angeles. At the same time, unlike Beverly Hills and Santa Monica—which stayed independent, incorporated cities—most of West Hollywood remained administered by the County of Los Angeles. With just the County and not the City watching over things, some say, all sorts of activities—gambling casinos and bordellos among them—thrived in parts of West Hollywood, whereas they would have had a much rougher go of it within the City of L.A. The Sunset Strip was also a preferred address for many of Hollywood's agents because County tax laws made collecting a 10 percent commission more lucrative here than practically anywhere else.

Today, the Sunset Strip remains one of West Hollywood's greatest attractions for the movie lover. The clubs with the famous names are gone now but many live on as restaurants, cabarets, and bars with new names, new owners. The Strip is also famous these days for its gigantic billboards used to promote both record albums and motion pictures. Edging the Strip, these monumental state-of-the-art advertisements are Hollywood's newest glamour symbols and provide an extra flash of drama to this historic part of L.A.

West Hollywood is more than just the Strip, however. The area also showcases some of L.A.'s most unusual architecture. A block south of Sunset, Fountain Avenue—with its incredible concentration of turreted French Norman apartment houses built in the 1920s—stuns the eye as some crazy kind of twentieth-century "chateau country." The fact that a number of movie people lived in many of these apartment buildings—as well as in the Spanish haciendas, the Moorish palaces, the Art Deco towers that are on and off Fountain—make the area even more intriguing.

Another West Hollywood attraction is Melrose Avenue, the alternative to Rodeo Drive for the well-heeled punk crowd as well as for the savviest of superstars. One of the latter group, Olivia Newton-John, recently was co-owner of a chic boutique along trendy Melrose Avenue. Today's West Hollywood is also the capital of gay L.A., with a large number of the city's male homosexual population centered here as well as many of the town's top gay nightclubs. It may be a far cry from that glamorous

Billboard on the Sunset Strip, 1983

image of the starlet getting out of the limousine in front of the Trocadcro . . . but the beat still goes on in West Hollywood. Only the drummer is different.

NOTE: *Many of West Hollywood's sights are best seen on foot. The serious sightseer might wish to spend a good two to three hours covering items 3 through 23, which take in the best of the Sunset Strip as well as the apartments on Fountain Avenue and its side streets. For those with less time, this itinerary can be shortened to include items 8 through 23. Melrose Avenue is another area of West Hollywood that makes for interesting walking, although its attractions are more for shoppers than for movie lovers. Finally, items 30 through 32 form a separate driving tour through Laurel Canyon and the Hollywood Hills. Technically not part of West Hollywood, Laurel Canyon is included in this chapter because of its proximity to the area.*

1. THE RAINBOW
9015 Sunset Boulevard

Once upon a time, this was an Italian restaurant known as the Villa Nova. The site of at least two notable romantic encounters, the Villa Nova saw Vincente Minnelli propose to Judy Garland here in 1945 and also provided the location for the 1953 blind date that paired Joe DiMaggio with Marilyn Monroe. In those days, the lighting was low and the music soft. These days, rock folk, designer-punk people, and serious singles hang out at what is now the Rainbow. The lights are still low, but the music is loud, and most of the "romance" takes place in the parking lot.

2. THE ROXY
9009 Sunset Boulevard

For the last decade, some of the biggest names on the rock, pop, country, and comedy scenes have appeared at the Roxy. Among them: The Bee Gees, Billy Joel, The Pointer Sisters, Frank Zappa, Bruce Springsteen, Bette Midler, Chuck Berry, Waylon Jennings, Linda Ronstadt. In the 1940s, however, according to a Hollywood old-timer, the same building housed the poshest grocery store in town. Called the West Side Market, this was where many of Hollywood's top stars did their marketing— and where the "regulars" were somehow able always to get the choicest cuts of beef, the richest cream and butter, and the best of whatever else was being rationed during the days of World War II. It was, in effect, a wide-open "Black Market" that billed customers by the month and that even delivered!

3. LE DOME
8720 Sunset Boulevard

A very elegant restaurant now occupies this handsome little neo-Colonial building that was erected in 1934 as the studio of interior decorator William Haines. Haines, a former MGM boy-next-door, was also a homosexual who did little to hide his lifestyle. When Louella Parsons started dropping hints about Haines' off-screen activities in her columns, this was too much for his boss, Louis B. Mayer. Supposedly Mayer told Haines to choose between his boyfriend and his MGM contract. Haines chose the former and wound up becoming one of the town's top decorators. One of his biggest star clients was MGM colleague Joan Crawford. Besides doing and redoing her Brentwood home many times, Haines also did her New York apartment. Other Hollywood people who lived in Haines-decorated mansions in-

Don Loper salon, 1946

cluded Constance Bennett, Leila Hyams, William Goetz, Jack Warner. Of his career change, Haines once had this to say: "I've never been divorced from showbusiness . . . many of my friends are my clients. I feel part of them. I'm still an actor who's hanging some curtains."

After Haines moved from his Sunset Strip studio in the 1940s, the premises were later taken over by Hollywood dress designer Don Loper. "I Love Lucy" fans may remember the episode where Lucy—sporting a bad California sunburn—appears in a Don Loper celebrity-wives fashion show wearing a tweed suit!

4. TROCADERO STEPS
8610 Sunset Boulevard

Three steps at the southeast corner of Sunset Boulevard and Sunset Plaza are all that remain of the Trocadero Cafe. The Troc—along with Mocambo and Ciro's—was one of the Sunset Strip's great nightclubs of the 1930s and 1940s. It was opened in 1934 by W. R. Wilkerson, publisher of *The Hollywood Reporter*— the film colony's trade paper/gossip sheet. When David O. Selznick needed a glamorous nightspot for a sequence in his 1937 *A Star Is Born,* he set it at the Troc. And when Selznick and Jock Whitney needed a place to celebrate the opening of *Gone with the Wind,* the Troc was again recruited. During its heyday, practically every star in Hollywood walked up its three steps at one time or another. There were even rumors of a secret gambling parlor downstairs—but most people who remember the Troc don't recall any gambling on the property. What they do recall is good food, good drinks, good entertainment (Nat King Cole had his own "room" here) . . . and they remember glamour. In 1946, after a change of ownership, the Troc closed down.

Trocadero Cafe, 1937

5. "77 SUNSET STRIP"
8524 Sunset Boulevard

In the late 50s and early 60s, this low-rise, half-timbered restaurant building was known as Dino's Lodge and was owned by Dean Martin. Its greatest claim to fame came not from its celebrated owner but from its weekly appearance on the popular television series, "77 Sunset Strip." It was here—under Dino's porte-cochere—that teen idol Ed "Kookie" Byrnes parked cars, combed his locks, and occasionally helped co-stars Roger Smith and Efrem Zimbalist, Jr., solve a case. Today, the porte-cochere of this television landmark looks just as it did when "Kookie" was working it.

6. THE COMEDY STORE
8433 Sunset Boulevard

Written on its outside walls are the names of the comics who have played here in the last fifteen or so years. Topping the list is Johnny Carson. One of the most vital comedy-workshop clubs in Los Angeles, the Comedy Store showcases established comedians who come to try out new material, as well as unknowns waiting to be discovered. Among the more successful in the latter category: Robin Williams, John Ritter, Richard Pryor, David Letterman, Gabe Kaplan.

While the Comedy Store is making entertainment history at 8433 Sunset Boulevard, another club that once flourished at this address will hold even greater interest for movie lovers. The name of the spot was Ciro's and it was founded in 1939 by *The Hollywood Reporter's* publisher, W. R. Wilkerson. Ciro's really hit its stride in the mid-1940s when a man named Herman Hover took it over and started to spend big money on publicity and promotion. Suddenly, Ciro's was the place to see and be seen and—above all—to be photographed! It is said that contract players were sent to Ciro's on dates arranged by their studio's publicity departments. Once their pictures were taken and it was established that they had indeed been there, these same "couples" would quickly slip out the back door and go their separate ways.

But Ciro's wasn't just for show. This truly was a place where the top stars of Hollywood could always be found both in the audience and on stage. Mae West performed here with her musclemen; Dean Martin and Jerry Lewis were often on the bill; and classy stripper Lili St. Cyr caused a minor scandal at Ciro's when her act was closed down by the police for lewdness.

The drama at Ciro's wasn't always limited to the stage. In the 1930s, Johnny "Tarzan" Weissmuller dumped a table of food onto the lap of his soon-to-be "ex" Lupe "Mexican Spitfire" Velez in one of the club's better known public brawls. Then there was the time in 1954 when Twentieth Century-Fox studio head

Ciro's in the 1950s

Darryl Zanuck stripped to the waist and tried to chin himself from a trapeze that had been part of the floor show.

Bar fights were not uncommon either—but there was a house rule that only permitted three fights per customer. After that, even the most regular of regulars would be permanently "eighty-sixed." Ciro's final drama took place in 1957 when the Internal Revenue Service claimed that Hoover owed the government an enormous sum of money for not collecting a 20 percent entertainment charge on private parties. Despite the fact that the courts later ruled that Hoover didn't owe the original sum—Ciro's and its owner had gone bankrupt. Sic transit gloria.

7. BUTTERFIELD'S
8426 Sunset Boulevard

Lush vegetation camouflages a pleasant patio restaurant that lies down a flight of steep redwood steps about 50 feet below the noise and traffic of the Strip. According to legend, the great American actor John Barrymore once resided in a bungalow on this hillside—and today the tiny guesthouse of Barrymore's former property now forms the dining room of Butterfield's restaurant. The room is a beauty and feels like a cottage in the country. Besides a fireplace, there is a giant blowup of a Louis B. Mayer birthday party in which all of MGM's stars are assembled seated around their master. There are also vintage photos of Barrymore and of Errol Flynn—who is said to have lived in the guesthouse for quite a number of months. Where else—but in Hollywood—can you have dinner in Errol Flynn's bedroom?

NOTE: *Phone: 656-3055.*

8. SUNSET TOWER APARTMENTS
8358 Sunset Boulevard

One of the most marvelous of moderne apartment houses in the world, the Sunset Tower has the same kind of streamlined glamour as the sleek Deco sets of 1930s black-and-white Hollywood films. Erected between 1929 and 1931, the fourteen-story Sunset Tower is one of the last important buildings of architect Leland A. Bryant. Of all the rich and famous tenants said to have lived here over the years, Howard Hughes was the richest and most famous. Supposedly, in addition to his own apartment, the eccentric millionaire kept a couple of extra pads in the building for his lady friends. Other name tenants were Billie Burke, John Wayne, Paulette Goddard, Carole Landis, Zasu Pitts, Joe Schenck, Preston Sturges, Lloyd Pantages (son of theater magnate Alexander Pantages), and gangster Bugsey Siegal (who, reportedly, was asked to leave).

Movie lovers can see the landmark Sunset Tower building in the 1944 RKO release *Murder My Sweet,* which was that studio's second film version of the Raymond Chandler novel, *Farewell, My Lovely.* (The first was *The Falcon Takes Over,* which was made in 1941 after Chandler had signed one of the worst contracts in history: RKO got practically unlimited rights to *Farewell, My Lovely* for a mere $2000.) In *Murder My Sweet,* Dick Powell as detective Philip Marlowe is taken to a lavish Sunset Tower suite, where, after being shown the beautiful view ("On clear days, Mr. Marlowe, you can see the ships in the harbor at San Pedro"), he is beaten up and held captive.

Deserted Sunset Tower Building, 1983

Today, the future of the Sunset Tower is problematical, even though it is listed on the National Register of Historic Places. In the early 1980s, new owners started moving people out, gutting most of the building in what was supposed to have been a co-op conversion. Then, all work stopped and former "Hogan's Heroes" star Werner Klemperer was often in the news for refusing to vacate his apartment in the building. Eventually everybody was forced to vacate—but as of 1985, no further work had been done and a "Friends of Sunset Tower" committee had been organized to petition the County of Los Angeles to help save the building. One wishes them luck because, despite its peeling paint and crumbling concrete, the Sunset Tower is still one of the Sunset Strip's most striking silhouettes—especially at sunset when it takes on a magical golden glow.

9. IMPERIAL GARDEN SUKYAKI
8225 Sunset Boulevard

In the 1940s, the multitalented Preston Sturges—writer and director of witty little Paramount comedies like *The Great McGinty* (1940), *Sullivan's Travels* (1941), *The Lady Eve* (1941), *The Palm Beach Story* (1942), and *The Miracle of Morgan's Creek* (1943)—opened a restaurant on the Sunset Strip. A highly sophisticated spot, Sturges' Players Club was a second home for many of the literary types—Robert Benchley, Dorothy Parker, George S. Kaufman, F. Scott Fitzgerald—who were holed up in the Garden of Allah across the street or in the Chateau Marmont next door. Very much an East Coast meets West Coast kind of place, the Players Club was popular with millionaires and their sons from Boston, New York, Philadelphia, and Chicago who hung out here in order to meet some of the prettiest starlets in Hollywood. The Players Club was also known for its drinks—the best and most potent in town. Sturges—who liked a good drink himself—wouldn't have had it any other way. Today, the former Players Club is yet another Japanese restaurant.

10. CHATEAU MARMONT
8221 Sunset Boulevard

A living legend—a vintage Hollywood hotel that's still luring celebrity guests. They come to this fabulous French chateau on Sunset Boulevard for its privacy, its quirky charms (no doorman, no dining room, no bar), and its history. Opened in 1929, the Chateau was described as "the newest and most luxurious apartment house in Los Angeles," despite the fact that Sunset Boulevard was a dirt road at the time. The Chateau Marmont had forty-three apartments back then—and each came decorated with expensive European and Oriental furnishings.

One of the Chateau's star long-term residents was Jean Harlow, who at age twenty-two was already on her third husband,

Chateau Marmont

Hal Rosson. Harlow shared suite 33 with Rosson for a year. Today, the suite is decorated all in white in honor of its former famous occupant. Another star who called the Chateau Marmont home was Boris Karloff. According to a long-time Chateau housekeeper, Karloff came for three weeks and wound up staying seven years.

When Billy Wilder came to Hollywood from Europe in 1934, the Chateau was his first Hollywood base. His room had a Murphy bed, cost $75 a month, and Wilder later used it as the model for the apartment that Fred MacMurray lived in in *Double Indemnity*. Marilyn Monroe is said to have stayed here, too. After she had abandoned Hollywood for New York and the Actors Studio, she supposedly holed up at the Marmont on her return to tinseltown to star in *Bus Stop*.

Heading the Chateau's frequent-guest category was Howard Hughes—who favored a penthouse suite that had a great view of the pool below. Hughes is reported to have often stood at his window, binoculars in hand, checking out the ladies down at the pool. Garbo also frequented the Chateau Marmont in her post-Hollywood period—checking in, as is still her custom, under the name of Harriet Brown. Garbo/Marmont stories abound and have her doing such things as making vegetable stews for breakfast, sleeping in the hotel lobby to escape the noise of a party near her room, and reporting that the Chateau Marmont was the only hotel in America where birds came and sang on her window sill.

New Hollywood loves the Chateau, too. Robert De Niro, Richard Gere, Bud Cort, Diane Keaton, Jill Clayburgh, Dustin

Hoffman, and Tom Wolfe are all Chateau Marmont fans and former guests. And, of course, there was John Belushi—whose drug death in a Chateau Marmont bungalow (number 2) made lurid headlines in March of 1982.

NOTE: *The Chateau Marmont has everything from single rooms to two-bedroom suites to cottages and bungalows. Many are equipped with kitchens. Today, the hotel has been renovated and still caters to both long- and short-term guests. It is the closest thing to living in the Old Hollywood manner that Los Angeles has to offer. Reservations and information: 656-1010.*

11. JAY WARD PRODUCTIONS
8218 Sunset Boulevard

A gigantic plaster statue of the one and only Bullwinkle the moose who along with Rocky the Flying Squirrel, Boris, Natasha, et al., conquered America on television in the 1960s—stands in front of the animation company that gave birth to them. Today, the studio produces animated television commercials.

12. GARDEN OF ALLAH SITE
8150 Sunset Boulevard

You name them—Bogie and Bacall, F. Scott Fitzgerald and Sheilah Graham, John Barrymore, Errol Flynn, Clara Bow, Tallulah Bankhead, Marlene Dietrich—they all either stayed or played here—or both. Alas, a parking lot and a Great Western Bank now stand where the fabled Garden of Allah once sprawled across the southwest corner of Sunset and Crescent Heights Boulevards. A cluster of twenty-five low Spanish bungalows built around a main house that belonged to silent screen actress Alla Nazimova, the Garden of Allah was opened as a hotel by Nazimova in the late twenties.

Besides being popular with the top stars of the day, the place was also a haven for the literati that flocked to Hollywood in the

The Garden of Allah

1930s. Robert Benchley, Dorothy Parker, George S. Kaufman, F. Scott Fitzgerald all helped earn the Garden of Allah its reputation as the "Algonquin Round Table West." Round Table member Alexander Woollcott referred to the place as "the kind of village you might look for down the rabbit-hole." The Garden of Allah was also known for the hard drinking that went on—in its bar and bungalows as well as around its pool. Robert Benchley, upon falling into the pool (built in the shape of the Black Sea—a tribute to Nazimova's Russian background), is credited with the famous line: "Get me out of these clothes and into a dry martini."

By the time the 1940s rolled around, the Garden of Allah had started losing some of its appeal—as many of the personalities who had made it famous had moved on in their careers and no longer hung out here. By the 1950s, the place was rapidly deteriorating and the hookers had moved in. In 1959, it all came to an end when the nostalgic old Hollywood compound was razed for the bank that now stands on the former Nazimova property. Instead of sparking massive protests (as would be the case today), the demolition of the Garden of Allah was heralded with a festive farewell party. A thousand guests turned up—many of whom were celebrities dressed up like the celebrities of the 1930s who had given the Garden of Allah its name. Today, all that remains of the magical Garden of Allah is a model that is housed in a glass bubble in the back of the Great Western Bank. A model—and a lot of memories.

13. SCHWAB'S SITE
8024 Sunset Boulevard

Forced to close in late 1983 because of financial difficulties, Hollywood's most famous drugstore recently was scheduled to resurface as a nightclub called L.A. Heartbreakers. Only "Schwab's" neon sign from a 1950s remodeling remains as a reminder of this important Sunset Strip hangout for "underemployed" actors,

Schwab's, 1956

*F. Scott Fitzgerald's former
West Hollywood apartment*

writers, and directors. In the film *Sunset Boulevard,* Schwab's is
referred to as "headquarters" by out-of-work screenwriter Joe
Gillis (William Holden). In addition to the several scenes from
Sunset Boulevard that take place at Schwab's, according to
director Billy Wilder, there was also a Schwab's scene with
Hollywood columnist/Schwab's fixture Sidney Skolsky—but the
scene was cut from the final version of the film.

Many of the regulars at Schwab's—especially the breakfast
bunch—resided at the neighboring Garden of Allah or Chateau
Marmont. And since the latter had no room service, Schwab's
often provided this vital amenity for Chateau guests who preferred
neither to eat out nor cook in. Although most of the world now
knows that Lana Turner was not discovered at Schwab's, we
repeat it here one more time—just for the record.

14. F. SCOTT FITZGERALD APARTMENT
1403 North Laurel Avenue

F. Scott Fitzgerald spent the last years of his life in Hollywood,
the last months of his life in number 6 at the rear of this West
Hollywood apartment house that was inspired architecturally by
the chateaux of Normandy in France. It was here that Fitzgerald—
his health having failed him after many years of hard drinking—
worked on a film script, some short stories for *Esquire,* and his
Hollywood novel, *The Last Tycoon.*

Fitzgerald's last lady friend, Sheilah Graham, lived a block
away at 1443 North Hayworth. In her book, *Beloved Infidel*
(Holt, Rinehart and Winston, 1959), Graham speaks idyllically
of their days as neighbors/lovers in West Hollywood: "I found
him an apartment . . . on the street next to mine. To economize,

The Villa d'Este apartments

we shared the same maid, each paying half of her salary. We dined at each other's apartment on alternate nights: one night she cooked his dinner and I was his guest, the next, she cooked mine and he was my guest. Again, like a married couple, we went shopping at night in the supermarkets on Sunset Boulevard, or spent an hour in Schwab's drugstore, five minutes away, browsing among the magazines and ending our visit sipping chocolate malted milks at the ice-cream counter. On the way home we chanted poetry to each other, swinging hands as we walked in the darkness, Scott declaiming passionately from Keats. . . . Sometimes a passerby stared at us and I would burst out laughing, but Scott would maintain a stern demeanor."

That was in the summer of 1940—a period Graham describes as their happiest time together. For one thing, Fitzgerald hadn't touched alcohol for a year. Still, it all came to an end very quickly. Fitzgerald succumbed to a heart attack a few days before Christmas of that same year. He was forty-four years old. He never finished *The Last Tycoon,* although it was published posthumously and even made into a movie in the 1970s.

15. VILLA D'ESTE
1355 North Laurel Avenue

One of the most beautiful courtyard apartment complexes in all of Los Angeles, the Villa d'Este was where Dean Jones and Carol Lynley lived in the 1963 Columbia film, *Under the Yum Yum Tree.* Erected in 1928, this haunting Mediterranean building is the work of the brothers F. Pierpont and Walter S. Davis and has seduced many Hollywood celebrities over the years with its tiled fountains, its jungly courtyards, its peace and quiet. No

*The Granville,
formerly the Voltaire*

wonder the exotic silent screen beauty Pola Negri felt at home here. And rumor has it that the great producer/director of historical epic films—C. B. DeMille—also kept an apartment at the Villa d'Este for his "private" purposes. Today, the building is beautifully maintained and remains one of West Hollywood's poshest addresses.

16. THE GRANVILLE
1424 North Crescent Heights Boulevard

Until recently known as the Voltaire, this marvelously maintained "chateau" was once owned by the Skouras family (the late Spyros Skouras was the Twentieth Century-Fox studio executive held largely responsible for the debacle known as *Cleopatra* in the early 1960s). Besides Skouras, other Hollywood names connected with the Voltaire are Ann Sothern, Jack Lord, Arthur Treacher, and Janet Gaynor—all of whom were former tenants.

In late 1954, Marilyn Monroe had separated from Joe DiMaggio and was about to abandon Hollywood and her Twentieth Century-Fox contract for a new life on the East Coast. At the time, her lawyers suggested she lie low and out of reach of Fox's lawyers until the moment she was ready to get on the plane. She followed their advice as suddenly newspaper headlines started asking: "Where Is Marilyn?" Marilyn, it turned out, was staying with a friend of hers at the Voltaire—the building that belonged to the family of one of the heads of the studio she was quitting!

Today, the Voltaire has been turned into a luxury hotel and has been rechristened the Granville.

17. SITE OF "OLEANDER ARMS" APARTMENTS
Southeast corner of North Crescent Heights Boulevard and Fountain Avenue

Remember the "Oleander Arms"—the apartment that Esther Blodgett (Judy Garland) lived in when she was a minor band singer in *A Star Is Born?* It was while staying at the Oleander Arms that Esther/Judy decided not to follow the boys in the band for that gig up in San Francisco in favor of Hollywood. And because of her decision, both a star and a motion picture plot were born!

Well, until June of 1984, the building that had been used as the Oleander Arms stood at the corner of Fountain and Crescent Heights. It was fairly well maintained—and movie lovers could recognize it by the distinctive fencelike balustrades that ran the length of the balconies. Then, suddenly, a wrecking crew arrived. They didn't level the building so much as dismantle it, chop it up. Next thing anyone knew, big sections of the building were loaded onto trucks. (One made the papers when it got stuck in traffic.) When questioned as to where the trucks were headed, a driver answered, "114th and Figueroa."

Interested in the building's whereabouts, a writer doing a book on Hollywood drove some ten miles south to the spot the truck driver had mentioned—and there, indeed, stood a couple of hunks of the old Oleander Arms looking like abandoned railroad boxcars. No one was on the site—so the writer asked a service station manager across the street what was going to happen to the hacked-up buildings. "People buy 'em," was the answer. And so, if we are to believe the man at the gas station, somewhere, in God only knows what parts of the city, lie scattered the vestiges of a great Hollywood movie. Somewhere, there's a someone . . . living in Judy's *Star Is Born* apartment.

The "Oleander Arms" being hauled away, 1984

18. COLONIAL HOUSE
1416 North Havenhurst Drive

In recent years, Bette Davis made Colonial House her West Coast base. On the National Register of Historic Places, this staid bit of Britain in otherwise architecturally exotic West Hollywood was once home to Carole Lombard and her first husband, William Powell. The famous couple resided here from 1931 to 1933. Lombard—who went on to marry Clark Gable—was in her early twenties during her Colonial House years. The building's most famous fictional resident was Budd Schulberg's Sammy Glick, the success-obsessed title character of Schulberg's 1941 Hollywood novel, *What Makes Sammy Run?* In the book, Schulberg describes Sammy's Colonial House apartment as "one of the smallest in the building and even that must have been way beyond his means . . . but he wrote off only part of the expense to shelter, the rest to prestige."

19. VILLA ANDALUSIA
1471–1475 North Havenhurst Drive

Arthur and Nina Zwebell designed this enchanting Spanish/Moorish masterpiece in 1926. Not visible from the street are the apartment building's various patios—one with an elevated swimming pool, another with an elegant tiled fountain and magnificent exterior fireplace. The apartments themselves have beamed ceilings, tiled floors, and staircases. Clara Bow lived here—as did Katy Jurado, Jean Hagen, Caesar Romero, Teresa Wright, Jack Weston, Marlon Brando Sr. (Marlon's father), Anna Kashfi (Marlon's former wife), John Ireland, and Claire Bloom. This is 1920s Hollywood architecture at its best.

20. VILLA PRIMAVERA
1300–1308 North Harper Avenue

Yet another creation of the combined architectural efforts of Arthur and Nina Zwebell, the Villa Primavera has the look of a Mexican hacienda and enjoys one of the most expansive front lawns of any apartment building in West Hollywood. One of the reasons for this lavish use of land may have been that Villa Primavera dates back to 1923, which makes it one of the area's first buildings. The interiors of the apartments in the complex are just as appealing as the exterior; all face a central courtyard and have fireplaces, beamed ceilings, wonderful little niches and secret spaces. Current residents insist that James Dean had a pad here—and go on to tell of the bizarre sexual behavior (bondage) that supposedly went on in the closet of his apartment. Katharine Hepburn is said to have been another former tenant. The 1950 film *In a Lonely Place,* starring Humphrey Bogart, used Villa Primavera as a location.

P.S.: For a look at yet another 1920s Zwebell masterpiece,

the Patio del Moro Apartments is just around the corner at 8229 Fountain Avenue. The fantasy behind this design is all-out North African—and the building not only has a spectacular front gate that would be very much at home in Marrakech but a miniature mosque tower in back as well. Actress Joyce Van Patten once lived at El Moro.

21. ROMANY VILLA
1301–1309 North Harper Avenue

Design for living: In 1930, Marlene Dietrich, newly arrived in Hollywood, takes an apartment in the same building (Romany Villa) as that of her discoverer, director, and mentor—Josef von Sternberg (the exact nature of their personal relationship was— and still is—the subject of much speculation). Von Sternberg, estranged from his wife Riza at the time, is torn between the two women. Practically as soon as Marlene arrives on the scene, Von Sternberg wires Riza in New York to come to California. Riza comes, moves into Joe's apartment—and the sparks start flying! Marlene, hating Hollywood and suffering from a very bad case of homesickness (remember, she has left a husband and daughter back in Germany), threatens to return home. Von Sternberg, with a big professional investment in seeing Marlene succeed in Hollywood, spends hours in her apartment every evening trying to calm down the temperamental star. Riza is not amused—and eventually asks her husband why he doesn't marry Marlene. To this, Von Sternberg is quoted as replying: "I'd as soon share a telephone booth with a frightened cobra." No matter. Riza returns to New York, files for divorce . . . and later sues Marlene for alienation of her husband's affections as well as for libel because of something Marlene reputedly has said about her in a magazine interview. The press has a field day—but eventually Riza drops her suits against Marlene and polite letters are exchanged between

Romany Villa

Villa Celia

the two Teutons. So it went . . . and, according to an old Hollywood friend of Riza von Sternberg, some of it started right here at the Romany Villa.

Some thirty years later, another glamorous European-born Hollywood star, Zsa Zsa Gabor, lived for a year in this same building—during one of her brief periods between husbands—after a fire had gutted her Beverly Hills manse. Charlie Chaplin is rumored to have been one of Romany Villa's original owners.

22. VILLA CELIA
8320–8328 Fountain Avenue

One of Fountain Avenue's loveliest chateaux, Villa Celia is said to be a copy—on a smaller scale—of Chateau Azay Le Rideau in France's Loire Valley. It's therefore fitting that famous French actress Michèle Morgan once lived in this 1928 West Hollywood castle. More recently, Al Pacino also had an apartment at Villa Celia during the filming of the 1983 remake of *Scarface.*

23. LORETTA YOUNG VILLA
8313 Fountain Avenue

For many years, Loretta Young owned the modern villa that stands semisecluded behind these high Fountain Avenue walls. In the 1960s, Joan Crawford often stayed in a small apartment on the premises. Present owners and residents of the property are former Warner Brothers glamour girl Alexis Smith and her husband, Craig ("Peter Gunn") Stevens.

24. PACIFIC DESIGN CENTER
8687 Melrose Avenue

Known as the Blue Whale to both its critics and its fans, the Pacific Design Center building houses some of L.A.'s top decorators as well as a number of the firms that purvey fabrics, furniture, wallpapers, bathroom fixtures, etc. to the decorating trade. An architectural wonder of blue mirror glass, this 1976 building upstaged another striking mid-seventies phenomenon—model Margaux Hemingway—in the Dino de Laurentis-produced film, *Lipstick*. In the film, the Design Center—with its criss-crossing escalators and glassy galleria roof—furnished the visually exciting location for a climactic chase sequence in the last reel. Besides the building, one other appearance was notable in *Lipstick*—that of Margaux Hemingway's younger sister, Mariel, who played Margaux's younger sister in the film.

25. STUDIO ONE
652 North Lapeer Street

A former sheet-metal factory in West Hollywood was the unlikely setting for a movie-star nightclub—but the year was 1967 and anything could happen back in those crazy days of the late sixties. Known as The Factory, this cavernous private play-place had various bars, a pool room, dance floor, big dining room, small dining room, even an art gallery. The Factory also had names like Sammy Davis, Jr., Paul Newman, and Peter Lawford on its Board of Directors—and all of their chums were members. Originally announced at $1200 a year, the club's annual membership fee quickly dropped to $500—and it was rumored that many good-looking ladies got in for free.

Despite the hype and the supposed exclusivity, The Factory was a bomb. When it proved difficult to fill this vast space with famous faces, the management dropped all pretention and let literally anybody inside. By the beginning of the 1970s, it was all over. A few years later, however, The Factory was reborn as Studio One. A sign of the times, Studio One was a gigantic predominantly gay disco that rivaled New York City's Studio 54 and attracted a fair share of straight celebrities to its dance floor and laser shows. Today, Studio One, as well as a number of other bars and restaurants housed within this former West Hollywood factory building, appear still to be going strong.

26. TONY DUQUETTE STUDIO
824 North Robertson Boulevard

Everyone says that this barny 10,000-square-foot building was once a movie studio owned by Norma Talmadge and that some of the lovely clapboard bungalows surrounding it were dressing rooms. While there seems little in the way of hardcore evidence to back up this legend, the fact that one of the little streets in this charming West Hollywood neighborhood is called Norma Place would indicate some Norma Talmadge connection.

Whatever the building's beginnings (the original building permit seems to have been lost), its recent history is of equal interest to movie lovers. For inside this vast place is one of Hollywood's most theatrical interiors—a magical world of exotic artifacts and one-of-a-kind set pieces assembled by L.A. artist, costume/set designer Tony Duquette. Duquette—who won a Tony Award for his Camelot costumes in 1962—took over what may or may not have been Norma Talmadge's former studio and made it his own base of operations back in 1956. To celebrate his move to these new headquarters, Duquette and his artist wife (Beegle Duquette was responsible for the paintings that Elizabeth Taylor supposedly painted in *The Sandpiper*) threw one of the town's most glamorous parties. The guest list—a mix of international society and the last of Old Hollywood—included everyone from Her Serene Highness Princess Gina of Liechtenstein to Rosalind Russell, Marion Davies, Louella Parsons, and—in one of her rare public appearances—Mary Pickford. For the affair, the women all wore diamonds, furs, and elegant gowns. The evening's *divertissements* included an original ballet as well as Agnes Moorehead impersonating the divine Sarah Bernhardt in *Phèdre*. And in the tradition of Hollywood's great parties of the 1920s and 1930s, there was an incident that made front-page news the next morning.

The incident involved the Davies/Pickford group. It seemed that the two legendary ladies and their husbands—Horace Brown and Buddy Rogers, respectively—wound up on the driveway of Pickfair in the wee hours of the morning. There, for some reason, Brown—who just happened to be carrying a pistol—was demonstrating how to fire it correctly. When the little gun went off, the bullet ricocheted and grazed Miss Pickford, who was taken to a hospital and treated for a very minor head injury. "America's Sweetheart" told the press the next day that Mr. Brown was contrite and had assured her he would never carry a gun again. Oh, those Hollywood parties!

NOTE: *The Tony Duquette Studio is occasionally open for group tours. For information, call: 274-6736.*

27. DOROTHY PARKER HOUSE
8983 Norma Place

From 1957 to 1963, writer/great American wit Dorothy Parker lived in this small white West Hollywood house with her writer husband, Alan Campbell. The two—who lived off and on in Hollywood for several decades—collaborated on screenplays. Their most famous collaboration was the script for the 1937 *A Star Is Born* which resulted in an Oscar nomination for the pair.

Campbell died on Norma Place in 1963. Parker died a recluse in New York City in 1967. Of Hollywood, Parker once said: "The only 'ism' Hollywood believes in is plagiarism."

28. FANTASIES COME TRUE
7408 Melrose Avenue

For Walt Disney buffs, a shop that specializes in Disney-ana. It's all here—vintage photos, puppets, pins, games, jewelry, statues, radios, record players, projectors, lamps, Mouseketeer hats, glasses, dishes, silverware . . . everything imaginable that could be decorated with Mickey Mouse, Donald Duck, Goofy, and the gang.

29. KOALA BLUE
7366 Melrose Avenue

In the fall of 1983, West Hollywood's Melrose Avenue was booming as Los Angeles' top shopping spot for trendy fashions, food, and fixtures. And in the fall of that same year, Australia had just won international yachting's greatest trophy—the America's Cup—and taken it out of America for the first time in history. Meanwhile, Hollywood-based superstar/professional Australian Olivia Newton-John decided to cash in on both the Melrose Avenue boom and the Australia craze (America had just discovered Australian movies and movie stars, too) by opening a chic boutique on Melrose called Koala Blue. The shop's stock in trade: things Australian—from Down Under designer fashions to Aboriginal art, stuffed koala bears, Aussie milkshakes and candy bars.

30. LAUREL CANYON/HOUDINI RUINS
2398 Laurel Canyon

South of Sunset Boulevard, Laurel Avenue is a sedate West Hollywood street of pretty apartment buildings and private homes. Just north of Sunset, Laurel Avenue goes through a distinct transformation. It changes its name for one thing—to Laurel Canyon Boulevard, and becomes a road rather than a street as it starts winding up into the Santa Monica mountains. The architecture changes, too. The hillside-clutching houses and bungalows of Laurel Canyon and its numerous narrow twisting side roads have a decidedly rustic look to them. The whole feeling is one of being in the great outdoors—rather than in the middle of the second largest city in the United States. Laurel Canyon is not glamorous: it's real. It is not a place of great wealth or ostentation. In the sixties, hippies lived here. As for the movie colony, those film folk who have lived here have tended to be screen writers rather than screen stars.

One of the most unusual sites in Laurel Canyon is what's

Errol Flynn's Mulholland House

left of the once great Italianate estate of magician Harry Houdini.
It can be seen off to the right at the intersection of Laurel Canyon
Boulevard and Lookout Mountain Avenue. Besides being a
magician and escape artist, Houdini had a very brief career as a
movie star in the late teens and early twenties. His silent screen
epics were fast-action adventure yarns that featured sensational
stunts and dramatic escapes. Today all that is visible of his
Hollywood home is a set of elaborate stone steps and balustrades,
now crumbling and overgrown. The main house is gone anyway;
only these steps and the servants quarters remain. Many say that
Houdini's ghost haunts his Laurel Canyon estate—and, from the
looks of its present condition, there may well be something to
the story.

   NOTE: *The best/only way to see Laurel Canyon is in a car;
the same holds true for the Mulholland Drive sites that follow.*

31. MULHOLLAND HOUSE
3100 Torreyson Place

   To reach the former estate of Errol Flynn, it's necessary to
drive all the way up to the top of Laurel Canyon Boulevard and
turn right onto Mulholland Drive. The view of the San Fernando
Valley from atop Mulholland is spectacular—and is worth pulling
over to the side of the road to see. The cluster of large hangerlike
buildings that dominates the landscape is the CBS-MTM Studio
in Studio City; they were originally Mack Sennett's studios in
the late 1920s and were later Republic Studios of "B" Western
movie fame.

   The Errol Flynn estate can be seen just beyond Torreyson
Place. Again, the car should be stopped for a good view. It's off
to the right—a large ranchlike compound with stables and gatehouse below, main living quarters above. Flynn built Mulholland
House in 1942 and it was the scene of all sorts of wild and

Ann Harding/Rudy Vallee house, tennis court, and ballroom

wicked goings on—especially in the bedrooms which Flynn equipped with one-way mirrored ceilings so that both participants and spectators could have full views of whatever went on in bed. Since Flynn's death, Mulholland House has had several other famous occupants—including, at separate times, Richard Dreyfuss and Ricky Nelson.

P.S.: Off to the right of Mulholland House, the flying-saucer-shaped structure that shoots up from a great fat pedestal embedded in the hillside is the private residence "Chemosphere." Designed in 1960 by John Lautner, this bizarre bit of Space-Age architecture has been used as a location for both TV series and TV movies.

32. RUDY VALLEE ESTATE
Pyramid Place

To catch a glimpse of this great Hollywood Hills estate, continue east along Mulholland Drive until it is intersected by Woodrow Wilson Drive. The huge pink structure that looks like the clubhouse of a country club actually supports Rudy Vallee's tennis court and private ballroom. The pink Mediterranean villa above is where Vallee lives. Before Rudy Vallee lived here, actress Ann Harding once called the same house home.

NOTE: *To return to Hollywood, continue on Mulholland until it comes down into Cahuenga; then turn right.*

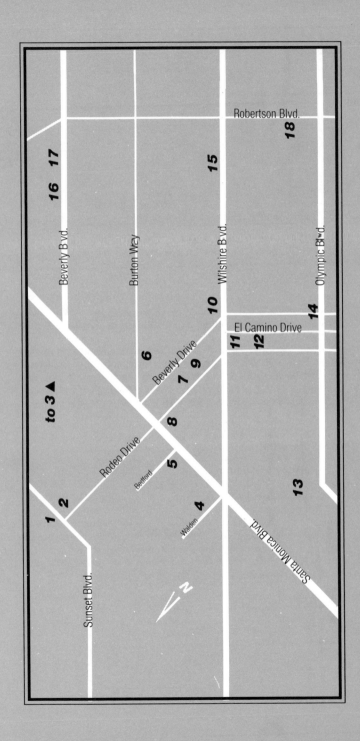

BEVERLY HILLS

**Hollywood's
Golden Ghetto**

8

Will Rogers, former honorary mayor of Beverly Hills

I T'S been called the most fabulous six square miles on earth. It's the land of Rodeo Drive, movie-star houses, extraordinary wealth, and fame—and if the streets aren't paved with gold, they are constantly filled with the most expensive automobiles in the world. In Beverly Hills, Rolls-Royces, Mercedes, and Maseratis truly are the rule—rather than the exception.

Beverly Hills got off to a slow start. Originally a Spanish land grant called Rodeo de las Aguas (the gathering of the waters), the area that today comprises Beverly Hills saw several owners and a number of development schemes during the nineteenth century—from wheat fields to oil fields to a plan to establish a town for German immigrants. All of these schemes met with failure, however, and by the end of the century, Rodeo de las Aguas was known for its lima bean fields—if it was known at all.

At the beginning of the twentieth century, a group of wealthy businessmen were again convinced that there was oil under Rodeo de las Aguas. Headed by Burton E. Green, the new Amalgamated Oil Company acquired the bean fields and started drilling. Alas, no oil was found—supposedly because the equipment used to tap it couldn't drill deep enough. On the other hand, an equally important—and valuable—discovery was made ... water. And so the Amalgamated Oil Company segued into the real-estate business under the banner of the Rodeo Land and Water Company.

The new development company officially founded Beverly Hills in 1907. (It is said that Beverly Hills was named after Beverly Farms in Massachusetts—either because Burton Green had visited the place and liked it, or because he had read of President William Howard Taft's visit there.) Despite its classy "Eastern" name, for awhile it looked as if Beverly Hills was also headed for failure. By 1910, there were only a handful of houses in what was to have been Burton Green's dream city of lush parks, tree-edged boulevards, and handsome homes.

Seeing how poorly things were moving, Green and company next decided to erect a grand hotel to promote their beautiful Beverly Hills—and in 1912, the Beverly Hills Hotel was opened. The hotel helped somewhat—but by 1920, the population of Beverly Hills was a mere 700. It took a Douglas Fairbanks and a Mary Pickford to really put Beverly Hills on the map—which is exactly what the movie-star newlyweds did when they set up housekeeping in "Pickfair" in 1920. From then on, Pickfair came to symbolize all of the fantasy, magic, and luxury of the film world for millions of movie fans. Pickfair also started a trend within the movie colony—as suddenly stars and moguls bought land in Beverly Hills and built their own fantasy realms.

It is no surprise, therefore, that the top sights in Beverly Hills remain its movie-star mansions. The movie community did more than build homes here, however. Many took an active part in the city's affairs and influenced its history. The main reason that Beverly Hills remains an independent city and was never annexed by Los Angeles was the campaign led by some of the major names in the motion picture industry in the early 1920s. Several years later, the town would even have a film celebrity as its honorary mayor. More than just a bedroom community for Hollywood, in many ways and for many people, Beverly Hills is "Hollywood."

NOTE: *This chapter is divided into two sections. The first covers the basic attractions of Beverly Hills of interest to movie lovers; the second section deals with the city's legendary movie-star houses. Items 7 through 11 in the first section—all on or near Beverly Hills' famous Rodeo Drive—can be seen on foot. To see the other sites mentioned in this chapter, a driving tour is suggested. (While items 16 and 17 technically are not in Beverly Hills, they are included here for convenient sightseeing.)*

1. BEVERLY HILLS HOTEL
9461 Sunset Boulevard

This great pink palace, a classic example of the architectural style called Mission Revival, is one of the oldest hotels in Los Angeles. When it opened in 1912, there was literally nothing but bean fields and empty lots surrounding it. That was the problem, indeed why the hotel was built in the first place—because the newly launched real-estate development of Beverly Hills wasn't doing so well. Few people were even looking at, much less buying, the lots that Burton Green's Rodeo Land and Water Company were selling. But with a hotel, where people could come and see the wonders of Beverly Hills first-hand, all that would change. At least that was the idea—and to make sure that the Beverly Hills Hotel would be a hit, Green and company managed to hire Mrs. Margaret Anderson away from the popular Hollywood Hotel to come and manage the new Beverly Hills.

When many members of the movie colony, led by Mary Pickford and Douglas Fairbanks, started moving to Beverly Hills

The Beverly Hills Hotel

Lauren Bacall and Gregory Peck by the pool at the Beverly Hills in Designing Woman, *1957*

in the 1920s, the Beverly Hills Hotel immediately felt their impact. Besides becoming a social center for film folk, the hotel often took care of their progeny—with special showings of movies just for kids and their nannies as well as with a private children's dining room.

In the 1930s, in fact, that same little dining room became one of the hotel's most famous public rooms—the Polo Lounge. Hollywood was passionate about polo back in those days—and the Beverly Hills Hotel was where the Sunday chukkers crowd often wound up after the matches. Darryl Zanuck, Will Rogers, and Walter Wanger were among the town's top polo enthusiasts—and were part of the group who gave the Polo Lounge its name. Always a popular place, during the 1960s and 1970s, the Polo Lounge succeeded the Brown Derby in Hollywood as the top spot in town to be paged while having lunch or cocktails. Booths came equipped with telephones in the center—and tables all had jacks. Like the Brown Derby, eventually most of the pages were more for show than anything else—but that didn't diminish the cachet of the Polo Lounge. The phones are still there and the pagings go on. (The hotel's star page boy, Buddy Douglas—"Johnny" of "Call For Philip Morris" fame—retired in the early 1980s.)

Through the years, the Beverly Hills has had its share of movie-star guests—and movie-star scandals. Marilyn Monroe and Yves Montand made gossip columns during the filming of *Let's Make Love* when both took their film's title literally in a Beverly Hills Hotel bungalow. John F. Kennedy is also said occasionally to have checked into a bungalow at the Beverly Hills—without Jackie.

Besides star guests, the Beverly Hills Hotel at one time had a couple of very well-known owners. That was back in the early 1940s when a private consortium purchased the hotel from the Bank of America. Among the names involved in this transaction were Irene Dunne, Loretta Young, and Harry Warner.

The hotel has appeared in many films—its pool and cabanas often standing for Hollywood living at its lushest. Much of the opening of *Designing Woman* (1957) with Lauren Bacall and Gregory Peck takes place poolside at the Beverly Hills. The 1937 *A Star Is Born* also features this famous pool patio. The Polo Lounge has also figured as a Hollywood location in many a Hollywood flick—*American Gigolo, Shampoo, Valley of the Dolls,* and *The Way We Were* to name a few. Then there's Neil Simon's *California Suite,* in which the entire action of the film takes place at the Beverly Hills Hotel. Based on his play of the same name, the film version actually shot only one sequence on location at the Beverly Hills—a scene in which Jane Fonda is on the terrace of her room. Since the hotel no longer permits filming in its public areas, the rest of the hotel—from its classic porte-cochere to its pool, lobby, and Polo Lounge—was carefully studied by art directors and set designers and then duplicated at the Burbank Studios and the Columbia Ranch. That's Hollywood!

2. WILL ROGERS MEMORIAL PARK
Sunset Boulevard at Canŏn Drive

Just across Sunset from the Beverly Hills Hotel, a pretty little park takes over the triangle of land bounded by Cañon Drive, Beverly Drive, and Sunset Boulevard. A peaceful enclave of green lawns, glorious gardens, and tall palm trees, this was once called Sunset Park and is the oldest municipal park in Beverly Hills. In 1952, it was renamed in honor of not only one of Beverly Hills' most famous citizens—but also its first honorary mayor: humorist Will Rogers. Of his job as mayor, he once said that his main official duty was directing folks to Pickfair.

3. GREYSTONE PARK AND MANSION
905 Loma Vista Drive

Movie buffs will remember it from *The Loved One*—the 1965 Tony Richardson-directed film version of Evelyn Waugh's novel of the same name that satirized the funeral customs of Southern California. In the film, both Greystone's mansion and its grounds were used to represent "Whispering Glades," the Forest Lawn-like cemetery around which much of the plot revolved. Besides *The Loved One,* Greystone has been used in many other films, TV movies, series, and commercials.

Greystone was originally the name of the huge 400-acre Beverly Hills ranch of the Edward L. Doheny (oil and later real estate) family. Doheny built the magnificent fifty-five-room stone mansion in the late twenties for his only son, E. L. Doheny, Jr. Three weeks after the younger Doheny moved into Greystone with his wife and five children, both he and his male secretary were found dead in Doheny's bedroom. The official version of the story says that the secretary shot Doheny and then himself when Doheny refused to give him a raise. Another version of the events suggests that Doheny and his secretary were lovers . . . and that it was Doheny who fired both shots—possibly because he feared that their affair was about to be discovered by his family.

No matter what really happened in 1928 in Doheny's bedroom, Greystone remains one of Beverly Hills' most impressive estates—and unlike its counterparts, this is one great property that is open to the public. That's because the City of Beverly Hills bought Greystone and eighteen of its original 400 acres in the mid-1960s. (Most of the rest of the acreage has been used for the ultra-exclusive development called Trousdale Estates—where Richard Nixon and Elvis Presley were former residents.) In 1971, Greystone's grounds were made a public park—while the main house served as the headquarters for the American Film Institute's film school. After the AFI moved to East Hollywood in 1983, the City of Beverly Hills embarked upon a long program that hopes to restore Greystone mansion to its original condition. If all goes according to plan, the mansion will eventually be open to the public on a limited basis.

NOTE: *Greystone Park is open from 10 to 5 daily during the winter months; 10 to 6 during the summer. Information: 550-4627.*

4. WITCH'S HOUSE
516 Walden Drive

Beverly Hills' most bizarre house—a fairy-tale cottage where everything from peaked roofs to leaded windows is wonderfully askew. One almost expects to see Margaret Hamilton wandering about the front lawn in full *Wizard of Oz* witch's drag. Just who was responsible for all of this whimsy right in the middle of Beverly Hills? The answer: a movie studio several miles to the

Witch's house, Beverly Hills

Church of the Good Shepherd

south over in Culver City. The crazy cottage was originally built as the offices for Irwin C. Willat Productions—and was moved to Beverly Hills in the early 1930s when the studio went out of business. Although it has been a private residence ever since, the house may be familiar to movie lovers from its appearance in MGM's *The Loved One* (1965) in which it was used as the Hollywood abode of the character played by Sir John Gielgud.

5. CHURCH OF THE GOOD SHEPHERD
505 North Bedford Drive

If you're Catholic and live in Beverly Hills, this is your church. Famous parishioners have included/include Desi Arnaz, Charles Boyer, Rosemary Clooney, Gary Cooper, Jeanne Crain, Jimmy Durante, Peter Finch, Jose Ferrer, Jack Haley, Alfred Hitchcock, Jose Iturbi, Carmen Miranda, Bob Newhart, Maureen O'Sullivan, Rosalind Russell, Jane Wyman, and Rudolph Valentino.

In May of 1950, an eighteen-year-old Elizabeth Taylor was married at the Church of the Good Shepherd to Mr. Conrad Nicholson ("Nicky") Hilton, Jr. It was a fairy-tale wedding that would not be matched until Grace Kelly married Prince Rainier in Monaco some six years later. For Elizabeth's wedding, MGM insisted on having designer Helen Rose do the "costumes." Also, the opening of Elizabeth's new film, *The Father of the Bride,* was deliberately scheduled for the month after her real wedding so as to get the maximum benefit of the publicity.

According to Kitty Kelley in *Elizabeth Taylor: The Last Star* (Simon & Schuster, 1981), Elizabeth delighted the guests at the ceremony with one of the most dramatic and longest postvows kisses in the church's history. And when the ceremony was over, while scores of photographers were recording it all for the world to see, Elizabeth was heard to say to her mother: "Oh, mother, Nicky and I are one now—forever and ever." It was Miss Taylor's first "forever" and this one lasted about three months.

Besides marriages, Good Shepherd has seen some pretty spectacular Hollywood funerals in its time. The biggest was undoubtedly for Rudolph Valentino in 1926. Gary Cooper, Jimmy Durante, Peter Finch, Alfred Hitchcock, and Rosalind Russell had Good Shepherd send-offs as well. One of the best known Good Shepherd funerals, however, was staged—it was that of Norman Maine (James Mason) in the 1954 *A Star Is Born*. In one of the film's most wrenching and frightening sequences, Vicki Lester (Judy Garland) collapses when she is set upon by reporters and fans as she is leaving the church; she barely makes it into the waiting limousine.

The Church of the Good Shepherd—dedicated in 1925—is the oldest church in Beverly Hills.

6. LYTTON INDUSTRIES
7370 Little Santa Monica Boulevard

MCA—the Music Corporation of America—was founded as a band-booking agency in 1925 by Dr. Jules Stein, an ophthamologist who decided early in his career that show business was more fun (and more profitable) than medicine. By the late 1930s, MCA had grown to become one of Hollywood's most important talent agencies—and when it came time for MCA to build new headquarters, Dr. Stein wanted something that wouldn't look like an office building. Translating Stein's dream into reality was the work of distinguished black L.A. architect, Paul R. Williams— who came up with this graceful neo-Georgian structure that is now the home of Lytton Industries.

There are many myths surrounding the former MCA building. One says that the sweeping double staircase in the main lobby was used in *Gone with the Wind.* Definitely not true! Another is that the Tuscan colonnade in the plaza at the rear of the original MCA building was salvaged from Ocean House—the great Santa Monica estate (144 rooms!) of William Randolph Hearst and Marion Davies, most of which was demolished in 1956. This, it turns out, may well be true—since, according to several former and current MCA officials, Dr. Stein bought many treasures at Ocean House's predemolition auction.

As for MCA, the company grew and grew and in the 1950s became heavily involved in television production. No longer a talent agency, MCA today is a huge entertainment conglomerate. Now based in Universal City, MCA counts, among its corporate holdings, Universal Studios.

7. RODEO DRIVE

The residential part—north of Santa Monica Boulevard—once had a bridle path in the middle; it has long since been landscaped with grass and palmettos. Besides horses, at least one very famous jogger used the bridle path, according to director Billy Wilder who remembers often seeing Greta Garbo running along Rodeo in the mid-thirties.

Garbo did more than jog on Rodeo. She—along with her good friend, health-food activist Gaylord Hauser—wound up buying a nice hunk of the commercial part of it south of Santa Monica Boulevard. Since the area has become one of the most expensive shopping streets (and pieces of real estate) on earth, Garbo is assured of doing what she likes best—being left alone—for ever and ever and ever.

8. ARTISTS AND WRITERS BUILDING
9507 Little Santa Monica Boulevard

Will Rogers was one of the forces behind this little building that went up in 1921 to provide creative artists with work space in Beverly Hills. Today, the Artists and Writers Building is a fashionable, if somewhat inconvenient (the place has no hot water or air conditioning) address for Hollywood writers, producers, and directors. Among the recent tenants: director Billy Wilder, actor/producer Jack Nicholson, game-show maven Chuck Barris, science-fiction writer Ray Bradbury, and comedian/director Bill Bixby.

9. THE DAISY
326 North Rodeo Drive

It's had a number of lives—including a stint in the mid-sixties as one of Beverly Hills' trendiest private after-hours spots, when, as The Daisy, it was a second home to Sinatra, Sammy Davis, Jr., Peter Lawford et al. Its most glamorous era, however, began in the late 1930s when this was the first location of Romanoff's. The creation of one of the world's greatest imposters, Romanoff's supposedly belonged to His Imperial Highness, the Prince Michael Alexandrovitch Dmitry Obolensky Romanoff. Although Mike Romanoff claimed to be a member of the Russian Royal Family, immigration officials listed him as Harry F. Gerguson, a Lithuanian immigrant who came to the United States with his parents around 1900. No matter what his origins, in Hollywood, Romanoff managed to pull off being a Russian Prince with little difficulty. His restaurant—which remained an important place to see and to be seen until his retirement in 1962—was originally founded with the financial backing of such Hollywood heavyweights as socialite producer John Hay Whitney, Garden of Allah-based writer Robert Benchley, Twentieth Century-Fox's Darryl Zanuck, and Joseph Schenck.

NOTE: *Romanoff's was at 326 North Rodeo Drive from 1939 through the 1940s; after that, the restaurant was on the south side of Wilshire at 140 South Rodeo Drive—which today is Liu's Chinese restaurant.*

10. ISRAEL DISCOUNT BANK
206 North Beverly Drive

Where else but in Beverly Hills would an Israeli bank be housed in a mosque? The bank building—with its huge dome and soaring minarets—was actually the Beverly Theater when it opened back in 1925. This Islamic-moderne architectural folly was the first real movie palace to be built in the City of Beverly Hills—and meant that all of the film people who had moved there in the 1920s could now go to the movies without driving five miles to Hollywood or ten to downtown Los Angeles.

11. BEVERLY WILSHIRE HOTEL
9500 Wilshire Boulevard

When Miss Piggy and Kermit the Frog come to L.A., they stay in cabana number 1 by the pool at the Beverly Wilshire. When Elvis Presley was starting to indulge his star power during his early Hollywood days, he kept a suite here—and kept security guards on their toes what with all of the comings and goings of ladies of the evening. And when Liz Taylor had conquered Richard Burton in *Cleopatra* and returned to Hollywood with him, she continued to shock the world when she and Burton shared the Presidential Suite of the Beverly Wilshire—even though

The Beverly Theater, 1925

she was officially Mrs. Eddie Fisher at the time. Warren Beatty didn't just stay here—he lived in a Beverly Wilshire penthouse suite for over a decade and considered the hotel "the only place to live in L.A." Steve McQueen lived here, too—right before he took off for Mexico and the Laetrile treatments that did not cure the cancer that had taken over his body. The staff remembers McQueen as very kind, gentle: He gave away all his plants to the maids before his departure.

Besides stars, the Beverly Wilshire has hosted royalty, presidents, the highest of high society. The hotel dates back to 1928—when its serious nine-story Beaux-Arts façade confirmed the fact that Beverly Hills had truly arrived as a city. Whereas the Beverly Hills Hotel was built (in 1912) to lure visitors to what was then just a real-estate developer's fantasy, the Beverly Wilshire was erected because that fantasy had become a reality that exceeded everyone's wildest expectations.

Today, there are really two Beverly Wilshires. The original 1928 building—and a towering addition that was built behind it in 1971. The addition—named the Beverly Wing—was part of the master plan of the star of the Beverly Wilshire, Hernando Courtright. A friend of the rich and the famous and often on the list of America's Best Dressed Men, Courtright is a Hollywood celebrity in his own right. One of L.A.'s most famous hoteliers, he headed the Beverly Hills Hotel from 1941 to the late 1950s. Courtright entered the Beverly Wilshire picture in the early 1960s, bought the place—with a little help from friends such as Kirk Douglas, Gregory Peck, and Jimmy Stewart—and quickly set to refurbishing everything with all the gusto and flamboyance of an old-time movie mogul. It was in the new wing of the hotel where Courtright—with the help of his late wife, Marcelle—really pulled out all of the stops. Here, he used Carrera marble as if it were lineoleum, created a ballroom to rival Versailles, and did whole

The Beverly Wilshire Hotel

floors of "theme" rooms—from Italian Renaissance to "Avant Garde Moderne." Courtright named many of the suites in the new wing after some of his best celebrity friends—and saw that these were decorated to match their namesakes' personalities. The "Dolores Del Rio Suite," for example, is an exuberant mix of Spanish Colonial furniture with Aztec-patterned bedspreads and curtains. The "Jimmy Stewart Suite" is somewhat more subdued. Other star suites at the Beverly Wilshire are named for Irene Dunne, Yves Saint Laurent, Bob Hope, and Hernando Courtright. The celebrity theme is continued down in the pool area, too, where the pool is an exact copy of one that was once owned by Sophia Loren. It may be Beverly Hills—but it's pure Hollywood!

12. WILLIAM MORRIS AGENCY
151 and 150 El Camino Drive

Did you hear the one about the actor who had murdered his wife? With the law closing in on him, he went to his most trusted friend and asked what he should do to disappear. His friend's answer: "Sign with William Morris." The largest (get the joke now?), oldest (it was started in 1898 by a vaudeville booking agent named William Morris), and most famous talent agency in the world, William Morris has had as much influence on the history of Hollywood as any studio. In the early days, the William Morris agency controlled the careers of mega-stars like Mae West, Al Jolson, Spencer Tracy, Katharine Hepburn, James Cagney, Judy Garland, Fanny Brice—and collected 10 percent of their and many others' considerable earnings.

It was a William Morris agent, Johnny Hyde, who would get a legend known as Marilyn Monroe off the ground. Generally credited for moulding her career, Hyde landed Marilyn the roles in *The Asphalt Jungle* and *All About Eve* as well as negotiated the Fox contract that put her on the map. It was both a professional and a personal relationship—and "Johnny Hyde's girl" was with him in Palm Springs when he suffered the heart attack that cost him his life at the end of 1950. Marilyn also had a room in Hyde's Beverly Hills home—which she was forced by Hyde's family to vacate immediately after his death.

In those days, William Morris was located on Cañon Drive. The company moved to its present location in 1954—and recently built the matching structure across the street. With offices in six other cities (New York, Nashville, London, Rome, Sydney, and Munich), William Morris employs some eighty agents in its black-glass Beverly Hills headquarters. Here, it is estimated, they look after the careers of some 1200 artists.

13. BEVERLY HILLS HIGH SCHOOL
255 South Lasky Drive

It's one of the top high schools in the U.S.A. It has its own Drama Department, its own cable TV channel, a gym where the floor opens up to reveal a swimming pool. If that isn't enough, it even has its own oil wells which have been helping to keep school taxes low ever since 1927 when Beverly Hills High School was established. Originally administered by the Los Angeles School Board, Beverly Hills High—with its neo-Norman classroom buildings sprawling over 26 acres at the southwestern border of Beverly Hills—was taken over by the city of Beverly Hills in 1935.

Of the thousands of children of the movieland elite that Beverly Hills High has educated, some have gone on to fame and fortune on their own—from Desi Arnaz, Jr., to Shaun and Patrick Cassidy, Rob Reiner, Carrie Fisher, Marlo Thomas, Tish Sterling, and Jack Linkletter. Other former Beverly Hills students that have done pretty well for themselves are Richard Chamberlain, June Haver, Rhonda Fleming, Joel Grey, Richard Dreyfuss, Bonnie Franklin, Burt (Batman's Robin) Ward, Paramount Pictures' exec Barry Diller, ballerina Maria Tallchief, tennis star Louise Brough, and writer Nora Ephron.

14. MONUMENT TO THE STARS
Beverly Drive and Olympic Boulevard

Water played an important role in the early lives of most of the communities in the Los Angeles Basin. In many instances, it simply came down to the fact that the city of Los Angeles controlled the main water supplies—which meant that many communities had the option of being annexed by L.A. or dying of thirst. Hollywood, for example, voted to become part of Los Angeles in 1910 for just this reason.

Monument to the Stars

Academy of Motion Picture Arts and Sciences

When the company that furnished Beverly Hills with its water claimed that it could no longer provide adequate amounts of the stuff in the early 1920s, the question of annexation became a hotly debated issue. The rallying cry for the proannexation forces was "Annexation or Stagnation." The antiannexation group was led by eight of filmdom's most illustrious citizens: Mary Pickford, Douglas Fairbanks, Will Rogers, Conrad Nagle, Tom Mix, Harold Lloyd, Rudolph Valentino, and director Fred (*Ben Hur*) Niblo. The issue came to vote in April of 1923—and the star-led faction won 507 to 337. To this day, Beverly Hills is a totally independent community within the County of Los Angeles.

In 1959, a monument was erected in honor of the eight luminaires who had helped save Beverly Hills from Los Angeles. Topped by a huge metal sculpture depicting a spiraling piece of movie film, the Monument to the Stars shows each of the actors in the group wearing a costume from one of his/her famous films. The monument is yet another reminder that Beverly Hills is a very special place.

15. ACADEMY OF MOTION PICTURE ARTS AND SCIENCES
8949 Wilshire Boulevard

It was founded in 1927 by Mary Pickford, Douglas Fairbanks, Louis B. Mayer, and a crowd of other film notables—all of whom felt that the image of the motion picture industry and of motion pictures needed upgrading. (Many sources say that Mr. Mayer's real motive in establishing the Academy was to use it as a means of keeping unions out of the motion picture business.) Since that time, the Academy has done much more than hand out Oscars. Based in its striking seven-story mirror-glass headquarters on Wilshire since 1975, the nonprofit organization is involved in such diverse activities as film preservation, lecture and seminar programs, and the development and encouragement of new talent through scholarships and grants. The Academy also boasts one of the world's finest research libraries specializing in the history and development of the motion picture. Besides some 14,500 volumes—many of them rare books published when the industry was in its infancy—the Academy's Margaret Herrick Library also has extensive collections of clippings, periodicals, photographs—plus production files on more than 60,000 films. Among its special collections are the personal papers, scripts, stills, and scrapbooks of Mary Pickford, John Huston, George Cukor, Hedda Hopper, Louella Parsons, Edith Head, Mack Sennett, and William Selig.

NOTE: *The Academy library is open to Academy members, the press, students, film researchers, and the general public. Hours: Monday, Tuesday, Thursday, Friday, from 9 to 4:30. Movie lovers should also check out the Academy's main lobby—frequently the scene of exhibits on the motion picture industry. Phone: 278-4313.*

16. CHASEN'S
9039 Beverly Boulevard

This is Ronald Reagan's favorite restaurant. The chili is a legend and may be the most expensive on earth. The decor is of the Great American Restaurant variety: pine-panelled walls, big banquettes covered in red leather. A big favorite with the who's who of Old Hollywood, Chasen's counts the Jimmy Stewarts, the Gregory Pecks, Buddy and Beverly Rogers, the Frank Sinatras, and Elizabeth Taylor among its regulars. In fact, according to

Chasen's

Mrs. Maude Chasen, Liz was so keen on the chili that she had buckets of the stuff shipped to her while on location overseas with *Cleopatra.*

One of Hollywood's classic restaurants, Chasen's was founded by Dave Chasen in 1936—with $3500 borrowed from his friend, *New Yorker* editor Harold Ross. Chasen's got off to a great start and everything was going smoothly until World War II intervened and Dave was served with a draft notice. With no one qualified to run Chasen's in his absence, his wife Maude persuaded him to show her the ropes—which he did, and suddenly Maude Chasen found herself in the restaurant business in a big way. Today, she still is—and has run Chasen's single-handedly since Dave's death in 1973. On any given night, you'll find Maude out there seeing that all the celebrities who still flock to Chasen's are kept happy and well fed.

HOURS: *Open daily, for dinner only; reservations: 271-2168.*

17. INTERNATIONAL CREATIVE MANAGEMENT
8899 Beverly Boulevard

Created in 1974 through the merger of two sizable talent agencies (Ashley Famous and Creative Management Associates—the latter founded by David Begelman who would go on to be the principal figure in Columbia's *Indecent Exposure* scandal in the late 1970s), ICM is William Morris' leading competitor.

In 1981, ICM's leading star, La Streisand, clashed with its top agent, Sue Mengers (whose rise from secretary to million-dollar flesh peddler is the stuff Judith Krantz novels are made of). What seems to have happened is that Streisand agreed to do a supporting role in Mengers' director husband's first U.S. film, *All Night Long.* For her services—which she considered a personal favor to help Mengers and mate—Streisand would receive $4 million plus 15 percent of the profits. Everything was fine until it came time to pay Barbra. Before handing over Babs' check, Sue took out her customary 10 percent commission, i.e., $400,000. When Streisand saw what Mengers had done, she got angry because she had lent her name and talents to the project only as a favor. Mengers wound up giving back the $400,000 to Streisand. Streisand wound up firing Mengers. And that's show biz.

18. JANE FONDA'S WORKOUT
369 South Robertson Boulevard

It started here. Before the book, before the record, before the videotape, before the millions of dollars, there was this little gym in the heart of the design/interior decorator area of Beverly Hills where Ms. Fonda started out in the exercise business. Today, she still drops by to teach an occasional class.

NOTE: *Phone: 652-9464.*

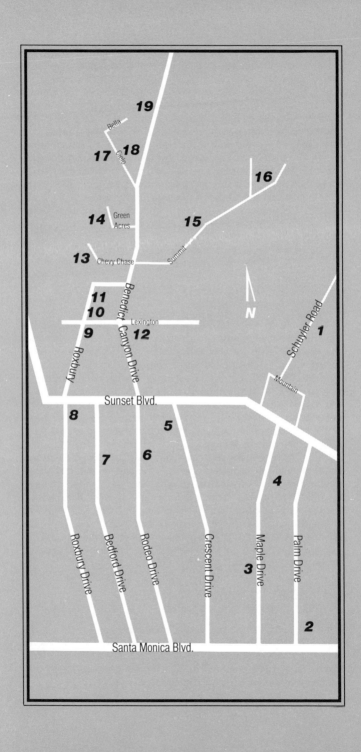

STAR HOUSES

THE movie-star residences of Beverly Hills have long been among the top tourist attractions of Los Angeles. For those coming to Hollywood in hopes of seeing glamour, money, fame, and fantasy—Beverly Hills is one part of town that lives up to everybody's expectations of what a movie capital should be.

To list all the houses in Beverly Hills that have had star owners or renters would be impossible. For one thing, movie people are not known for their stability as far as where they live is concerned—and often stay in a house for just a few years, sometimes just a few months—depending on the vagaries of career, finances, and domestic situation.

Another problem with Beverly Hills houses as far as sightseeing is concerned is that many of these legendary places are not visible from the street. Needless to say, their occupants—already in the public eye—would choose homes that offer as much privacy as possible.

The houses mentioned here have been selected first of all because most can be seen from the street—and second because most have played some part in the history and legends of Hollywood. Finally, many of the homes that follow are notable for their architecture. These are the best of Beverly Hills—the classics.

NOTE: *When touring these or any other of the private residences and properties mentioned in this book, movie lovers should take the utmost care to respect the privacy of their occupants. For convenience, it is suggested that you add items 1 through 4 from the previous Beverly Hills section to the itinerary that follows.*

Movie-star maps for sale at Sunset and Doheny, 1935

1. ELIZABETH TAYLOR
1330 Schuyler Road

The big beautiful Spanish mansion that Elizabeth Taylor shared with her third husband, Mike Todd. This is where Taylor was living in 1958 when Todd's private plane, "Lucky Liz," went down over New Mexico, killing Todd and the three others aboard. Liz had planned to be aboard, too, but had stayed home nursing a cold. As the world knows, Eddie Fisher helped Liz through the difficult days that followed.

2. MARILYN MONROE
508 North Palm Drive

Portrait of a marriage: It was April of 1954 when Marilyn Monroe and her husband of three months—Joe DiMaggio— moved into this "Elizabethan cottage" just north of busy Santa Monica Boulevard in the "flats" of Beverly Hills. They had tried living with Joe's family up in San Francisco—but that hadn't really worked out. Besides, Marilyn now had to be in Hollywood to do *There's No Business Like Show Business*. While the setting appears blissful enough, the marriage was not. The quarrels had already begun, as had Marilyn's taste for champagne—at all hours of the day. Things came to a head in September, when Marilyn flew to New York City to do location shooting for *The Seven Year Itch*. Joe followed. There was the famous sequence shot on Lexington Avenue: Marilyn—in white dress with panties to match—shows all. For DiMaggio, all was too much—and he quickly returned to L.A. The marriage was over. When he moved out of the Elizabethan Cottage shortly thereafter, photographers and reporters were then en masse to document his exit. By November, Marilyn had moved out, too—and 508 North Palm Drive was ready for another set of tenants, another story.

Marilyn Monroe/Joe DiMaggio former home

3. LOUELLA PARSONS
619 North Maple Drive

She was feared, hated, fawned over. She was one of the most powerful women in Hollywood—and this unpretentious stuccoed Spanish villa was her home base from the 1930s until the mid-1960s when failing health necessitated moving her to the first of a series of nursing homes where she would spend her last days as a lonely, senile old lady.

4. GEORGE BURNS/GRACIE ALLEN
720 North Maple Drive

If it looks familiar, perhaps it's because a duplicate was used in the famous husband-and-wife comedy team's TV series in the 1950s.

5. VINCENTE MINNELLI
812 North Crescent Drive

Standing across Sunset Boulevard from the Beverly Hills Hotel, this stately Mediterranean mansion was Vincente Minnelli's home for most of his post-Judy Garland years. According to the terms of the Minnelli-Garland divorce in the early fifties, little Liza was to spend six months of each year with her father and six with her mother. Among the many things Princess Liza enjoyed when in residence at her poppa's palazzo was a backyard playhouse specially decorated for her by artist Tony Duquette. She also had a closet full of costumes from famous films—*Gone with the Wind, The King and I, An American in Paris*—all in little-girl sizes. According to Candice Bergen in her autobiography, *Knock Wood* (Linden Press/Simon & Schuster, 1984): "I remember always asking to go to Liza's to play dress-up because in her

George Burns/Gracie Allen home

Marlene Dietrich former mansion

closet hung little girls' dreams." It wasn't all a dream, however. Liza once said of her early years bouncing around Beverly Hills between parents and stepparents: "It was a childhood to be reckoned with."

6. LUPE VELEZ
732 North Rodeo Drive

"Casa Felicitas" ("happy house" in Spanish) was definitely the wrong name for this Bev Hills hacienda where actress Lupe Velez resided in the 1940s. For it was here that the Mexican-born screen star—former lover of Gary Cooper, John Gilbert, and Randolph Scott; former wife of Johnny "Tarzan" Weissmuller—carried out one of Hollywood's most bizarre suicides. After dinner with a few close friends, Lupe retired to her glamorous Beverly Hills bedroom—in which she had placed masses of flowers and lighted candles—and she proceeded to take an overdose of sleeping pills. While Louella Parsons reported on the dignity of Lupe's demise, Kenneth Anger tells the story differently in his book, *Hollywood Babylon* (Straight Arrow Books, 1975). According to Anger, Lupe's maid discovered her dead mistress—not in her satin bed, but in the bathroom. Evidently the pills had made her violently ill and sent her off to the bathroom vomiting. Here, she stumbled, landed head first in the toilet bowl, and met death by drowning—not Seconals. Whatever really happened, Lupe was dead at the age of thirty-six. At the time, she was supposedly carrying the child of a man who had refused to marry her.

7. LANA TURNER
730 North Bedford Drive

It was one of the biggest stories of 1958—and it happened here. On April 5, Lana Turner's daughter, Cheryl Crane, stabbed Lana Turner's lover, Johnny Stompanato, to death while Lana

Lucille Ball/Desi Arnaz home

and Johnny were embroiled in an argument in which Stompanato threatened Turner's life. The media had a field day with the revelations regarding Lana's love life that the trial brought out into the open.

8. MARLENE DIETRICH
822 North Roxbury Drive

La Dietrich's Deco digs during the 1930s. Rita Hayworth and her third husband, the Aly Kahn, are said to have spent time here, too—a decade or so later.

9. JIMMY STEWART
918 North Roxbury Drive

Stewart not only owns the house—but also the corner plot next door where gentleman Jim grows his own vegetables. This may be the only working farm left in Beverly Hills.

10. LUCILLE BALL
1000 North Roxbury Drive

This has been Lucy's home for decades. Recently, Beverly Hills' celebrity citizens fought to get tour busses banned from their city. They succeeded. One person, however, definitely would not have approved of the move: Lucy Ricardo—especially when one remembers the lengths to which she and Ethel often went just to catch a glimpse of a star back in "I Love Lucy" days.

11. JACK BENNY
1002 North Roxbury Drive

Another familiar house—because, like Burns and Allen's, it was sometimes seen on Benny's television shows in the 1950s.

12. MARION DAVIES
1700 Lexington Road

In the mid-1920s, William Randolph Hearst bought this beautiful mansion for his mistress, Marion Davies. Just to keep everything on the up and up—on paper anyway—the house was bought in the name of Marion's mother, Rose, who also lived there. Because Marion loved to entertain lavishly, a ballroom was immediately added to the house; according to Hollywood legend, this was accomplished in a week's time with carpenters and craftsmen working around the clock. According to silent screen actress Eleanor Boardman, it was here that she married director King Vidor in 1926. It was to have been a double wedding—the other couple being John Gilbert and Greta Garbo. Garbo, however, chose not to attend. Gilbert thus proceeded to get very drunk—until, finally, Louis B. Mayer pulled him aside and counseled him just to sleep with Garbo, and not to bother about marrying her. This further incensed Gilbert, who lunged at Mayer and knocked him out. It was a bad move—because after the episode, Mayer supposedly did everything in his power to muck up Gilbert's career—including, according to many sources, tampering with Gilbert's voice in his first talkie. Gilbert died in 1936. He was forty-one, a hopeless alcoholic and a has-been.

13. GRETA GARBO
1027 Chevy Chase Drive

Garbo had many L.A. addresses during her Hollywood days. She lived in this hedge-hidden Beverly Hills bungalow for about a year from 1929 to 1930—sharing it with a chow chow, four cats, a parrot, and a Swedish couple who were her staff. Supposedly, Garbo liked the pool—but not the neighbors who kept looking into her garden.

14. HAROLD LLOYD
1740 Green Acres Place

One of Beverly Hills' greatest estates, Harold Lloyd's "Green Acres" was built in 1928 and was home to the famous comedian from that year until his death in 1971. Today, the forty-four-room (not counting twenty-six bathrooms!) property is on the National Register of Historic Places.

15. CHARLIE CHAPLIN
1085 Summit Drive

One of Chaplin's numerous L.A. addresses, this was the only house he built from the ground up. And not well, according to some accounts that say Chaplin tried to save money by employing studio carpenters as construction workers. Supposedly he had so

Harold Lloyd's Green Acres

many problems with the place owing to its shoddy construction that it was dubbed "Break-away House" by his friends. Recently, the former Chaplin house belonged to actor George Hamilton.

The Chaplin house can only be glimpsed through the driveway; it is mentioned here because it's en route to Pickfair.

16. PICKFAIR
1143 Summit Drive

The most famous Beverly Hills mansion of them all. This is where Douglas Fairbanks and Mary Pickford reigned as king and queen of Hollywood from 1920 up to their divorce in 1936. In Pickfair's grandest days—the 1920s—an invitation to this fairy-tale realm was no less important than an invitation to the White House. At Pickfair, Doug and Mary received the world—kings, queens, dukes, duchesses, and international socialites, as well as the cream of Hollywood. And because Pickford and Fairbanks were two of the first big stars to desert Hollywood and downtown Los Angeles to live in Beverly Hills, they were directly responsible for popularizing the place and for luring other movie industry residents.

After her divorce from Fairbanks, Pickford continued to live at Pickfair with her last husband, Charles "Buddy" Rogers. Increasingly reclusive in her later decades, Miss Pickford died at Pickfair in 1979. While there was some talk of turning Pickfair into a museum at the time, Rogers ultimately sold the estate to sports entrepreneur Jerry Buss; reportedly, Pickfair went for $5 million.

Although Pickfair is surrounded by walls, it can be seen through the main gate. Movie lovers should note the charming cherubs that top the pillars at both the main and rear entrances.

Doug and Mary go canoeing in Pickfair's pool

17. SHARON TATE
10050 Cielo Drive

As one goes further up into the hills of Beverly Hills, the land seems lonelier, wilder. It was here—at practically the end of Benedict Canyon—that one of the most horrible events in Hollywood's history took place in the late 1960s. From the road, only the driveway of the former rented estate of actress Sharon Tate and her husband, director Roman Polanski, is visible—but this is somehow haunting enough when one remembers that the Manson Family made their way up this driveway one evening in the summer of 1969 and savagely murdered Sharon Tate, her unborn baby, Abigale Folger (of the "Mountain Grown" coffee family), super-stud hairdresser Jay Sebring, Voytek Frykowski, and Steven Parent.

18. VALENTINO STABLES
10051 Cielo Drive

Across from the former Tate/Polanski driveway, this private residence was created from the former stables of Rudolph Valentino's fabulous Falcon Lair estate. Falcon Lair is further up in the hills.

19. FALCON LAIR
1436 Bella Drive

If the former Sharon Tate/Roman Polanski property seems a bit off the beaten track, Falcon Lair is positively isolated. But total isolation was exactly what Rudolph Valentino required when

Valentino's Falcon Lair

he moved to this Benedict Canyon mansion in 1925. At the height of his popularity, Valentino wanted to get as far away from his adoring—and often annoying—fans as possible. Falcon Lair—named for his film *The Hooded Falcon*—was to have been Valentino's dream house, "as near to ideality as you can find in a place," he wrote to a fan magazine at the time. As for the decor, Valentino furnished his dream house with classic movie-star extravagance—and mixed Middle Eastern furniture, precious Renaissance art objects, Oriental carpets, Medieval tapestries, weapons, and armor.

Alas, like so many Hollywood dreams, Falcon Lair never lived up to its owner's idyllic expectations. For one thing, by the time he moved in during 1925, his marriage to his second wife Natacha Rambova had broken up. For another, the pains in his stomach were becoming more frequent and more debilitating—a forewarning of the ulcer that would kill him the following year on August 23, 1926.

After Valentino's death, Falcon Lair was sold to an owner who never lived there. Come the Depression, the once great estate was sold again—this time for the ridiculous sum of $18,000! More recently, the property belonged to famous heiress Doris Duke.

NOTE: *While little can be seen of the main house from the road, a visit to this hilltop retreat is interesting nonetheless—especially when one considers what the trip must have been like in the 1920s when Valentino piloted one of his glamorous touring cars up what must have been a very dusty canyon road at the time. Visitors to Falcon Lair should note the words "Falcon Lair," barely visible above the pillars of the main gate. Visitors should also make sure not to disturb the caretakers.*

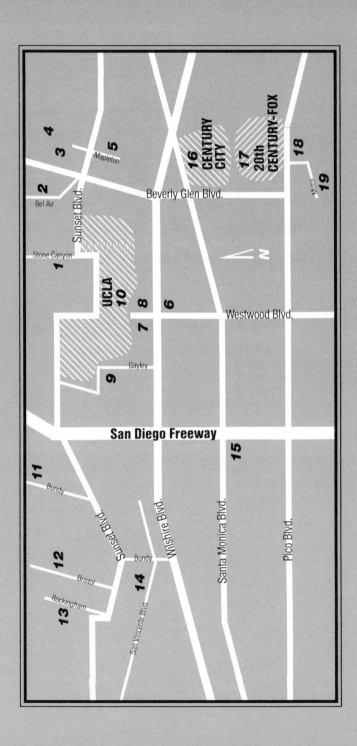

THE FASHIONABLE WESTSIDE

Between Beverly Hills
and Santa Monica

9

*Joan Crawford,
Brentwood's meanest mama*

WHEN Angelinos today speak of "the Westside," they can mean any of a group of wealthy communities that lie between Beverly Hills and Santa Monica. Bel-Air, the Holmby Hills, Westwood, Brentwood, Century City, and the Cheviott Hills are all posh Westside places—and harbor a number of sites relevant to the movie history of Los Angeles. Of these, the most important Westside attraction may well be the Twentieth Century-Fox Studios where the 1890s New York Street set built in the late sixties for *Hello Dolly!* still stands on the studio parking lot for all the world to see. Other Westside musts range from Westwood Village (which today has more first-run movie houses and studio premieres than any other part of Los Angeles) to Joan Crawford's *Mommie Dearest* mansion in Brentwood to James Dean's frat house at UCLA to the little cemetery where Marilyn Monroe is laid to rest.

NOTE: *This chapter covers a lot of ground—and every site mentioned here will involve a car. The one exception: Westwood Village—which is one of L.A.'s most pleasant areas for strolling.*

1. BEL-AIR HOTEL
701 Stone Canyon Road

L.A.'s ultimate hideaway—a fantasy realm of romantic Spanish bungalows, exotic foliage, quiet courtyards, gurgling fountains, and a serene lake that has swans gliding across it. Since the 1940s, some of the greatest names of Hollywood have sought seclusion in this dream world. Names like Garbo, Dietrich, Gable, Peck, Grant, Grace Kelly. This, too, is where Howard Hughes carried on so much business in the hotel's wood-panelled bar that it became known as his unofficial "office."

The Bel-Air Hotel

The "Beverly Hillbillies" Bel-Air mansion

Today, the Bel-Air still lures the rich and the celebrated—especially after a recent and costly makeover carried out by the hotel's new owner, Mrs. Caroline Hunt (of the Texas Hunt oil billions) Schoelkoff. The Bel-Air was not always a hotel. Its main building, long since remodeled, was originally the sales office of the real-estate company of another oil millionaire, Alfonso Bell. It was Bell who developed the ultra-exclusive gated community of Bel-Air on what was his former ranch.

In those days—the 1920s—Bel-Air did not sell lots to movie people, nor to minority groups such as Jews, blacks, or orientals. Things "opened up" after the Depression, however, when a few movie people, some of them Jewish, managed to make it to the inside of Bel-Air's great wrought-iron gates. By the 1940s, anybody who could afford to live in Bel-Air did. It was also in the 1940s when the Bel-Air real estate office and grounds were converted to the movie-set hotel that today makes every guest feel like a star.

2. "BEVERLY HILLBILLIES" HOUSE
750 Bel Air Road

This spectacular forty-room French mansion was the prime-time residence of television's "Beverly Hillbillies" from 1962 to 1970. A long run by Hollywood standards—both for a TV series and for one family to live at the same address in tinseltown.

3. CLAUDETTE COLBERT
615 North Faring Road

No one can fault Claudette Colbert's taste. Her long-time L.A. home was this attractive Holmby Hills Colonial mansion designed by the noted architect, Lloyd Wright. Besides being beautiful, the home must have been very convenient for Miss Colbert's husband, Dr. Joel Pressman, who was a leading surgeon at the nearby UCLA Medical Center. Pressman died in 1968—and today Miss Colbert lives most of the year in a handsome restored plantation house on the Caribbean island of Barbados.

4. WESTLAKE SCHOOL FOR GIRLS
700 North Faring Road

One of the poshest private girls schools in town. Candy Bergen, Jill Schary, Shirley Temple, Vicki Milland all went. Former May Queen Candice Bergen remembers it as the kind of place where "dirty saddle shoes were a misdemeanor and a pair of loafers could get you sent home." Insiders say that, for many years, Westlake had a "quiet quota" system that set the school's WASP-Jewish ratio in order to keep the former group decidedly in the majority. Jill Robinson-Shaw, writer daughter of Dore Schary, remembers trying to get into Westlake at various times and always being rejected. But when her father made Hollywood headlines in 1951 by succeeding Louis B. Mayer as top man at MGM, a place at the school seems miraculously to have turned up for her.

5. BOGEY AND BACALL
232 South Mapleton Drive

Gable and Lombard, Lucy and Desi, Mary and Doug, Liz and Dick—sometimes it takes two people to make a Hollywood legend. And of all of Hollywood's couples, none was more famous than Bogey and Bacall. In fact, a recent popular song paid tribute to the legendary duo with the lyrics: "We had it all—just like Bogey and Bacall."

They met on *To Have and Have Not* in 1944. She was nineteen; it was her first picture. He was twenty-five years older, had been a big name for some time. It was the kind of on-screen chemistry that directors and studio heads dream of. They went on to make three more films together: *The Big Sleep* (1946), *Dark Passage* (1947), and *Key Largo* (1948). Off-screen, the chemistry was just as potent. They married in 1945—and from 1946 until 1957 lived in this handsome Holmby Hills home and raised two children.

Here, too, Bogey and Bacall played vital roles in a sociological phenomenon of mid-fifties Hollywood known as the Holmby Hills "Rat Pack." Frank Sinatra was president of the group, Judy Garland (she and her husband Sid Luft lived just up the street from the Bogarts) was vice president, Bacall was den mother, literary agent Irving "Swifty" Lazar was treasurer, and Bogey was the rat in charge of public relations. Other members included Peter Lawford, Sammy Davis, Jr., David Niven, Mike Romanoff, Noel Coward, Dean Martin. Together, they drank, hit all the glamour spots on the Sunset Strip, drank, and didn't give a damn about Hedda, Louella, or any other columnist in town. What did it mean to be a "rat"? To PR man Bogart, in an interview with writer Ezra Goodman, it meant "staying up late and drinking lots of booze. We're against squares and being bored and for lots of fun . . . we don't care who likes us as long as we like each other. We like each other very much."

Beautiful house, beautiful children, great careers, great friends, great marriage. Bogey and Bacall did indeed "have it all"—until Bogart's painful death from cancer took it all away in 1957. Alone, Bacall went on to become a Broadway actress and people remember Bogart as a tough guy in the movies. But together, they are the stuff that myths and great movies are made of.

6.   WESTWOOD MEMORIAL PARK
1218 Glendon Avenue

Her body lay unclaimed at the L.A. County Morgue until Joe DiMaggio got into the act and took over the funeral arrangements. It was a small ceremony—DiMaggio had invited only a handful of people—and it took place in the chapel of a little Westwood cemetery that's hidden behind a high rise, a bank, and a parking lot off busy Wilshire Boulevard. Despite its secluded location, Marilyn Monroe's loyal fans somehow manage to find her above-ground crypt that lies just beyond the "Sanctuary of Tranquility." Alas, even in death, it seems that Marilyn (1926–1962) missed out on the peace she so desperately sought. Joe DiMaggio no longer sends the roses that kept coming several times a week for some twenty years—but a constant stream of fans assures that Marilyn never lacks floral tributes. Besides flowers, some fans leave lipstick prints on the outside of her cold marble vault.

Not far from Marilyn's tomb, her former studio boss at Twentieth Century-Fox, Darryl Francis Zanuck (1902–1979), is buried next to his wife Virginia in the grassy center section of the

*Mann's Fox Village
Theater, Westwood*

cemetery. The famous Twentieth Century-Fox logo—blazing kleig lights on either side—has been incorporated into the inscription on Zanuck's marble marker. Natalie Wood Wagner—"Beloved daughter, sister, wife, mother, and friend"—is buried nearby. Her grave is covered with the tiny pots of flowers, votive candles, and Russian icons that characterize a Russian Orthodox burial. Like Marilyn Monroe's death, Natalie Wood's drowning off Catalina Island in December of 1981 made headlines and left many questions unanswered. Also like Marilyn, Natalie's fans are very faithful and pay their respects regularly.

NOTE: *The entrance to the Westwood Village Cemetery is a half-block south of Wilshire Boulevard, just east of Glendon Avenue. The cemetery is open from 8:30 to 5 daily.*

7. FOX VILLAGE THEATER
961 Broxton Avenue

It now belongs to the Mann theater chain, but it still goes by its old name—"Fox"—both on the marquee and atop the tall Spanish Colonial tower that crowns this handsome Westwood movie palace. The theater's Spanish design is no accident, since Westwood Village was built in the 1920s as a master-planned commercial center. Part of the plan required that all of Westwood Village's buildings—from banks to shops to gas stations—conform to a Spanish Colonial architectural theme. The Fox theater— which opened in 1931—fits right in. Besides its striking columned tower, this beautifully maintained first-run movie house is notable for its four-sided neon-lit marquee, its spacious forecourt, and its tiled ticket booth. Inside, the Spanish fantasy continues—with vaulted ceilings, flamboyant murals, brightly tiled water fountains. One of the most glamorous of Westwood's movie houses, the Village Theater is frequently the scene of studio premieres.

8. MANN'S BRUIN THEATER
923 Broxton Avenue

The work of star theater designer S. Charles Lee, the Bruin opened in late 1937. By this time, other architectural styles— such as this sleek example of late-1930s moderne—had begun to deviate from Westwood Village's Spanish Colonial master plan. The Bruin's semicircular neon marquee is original—but inside the theater, the marvelous murals that glowed in the dark have been painted over.

9. SIGMA NU
601 Gayley Avenue

College try: When eighteen-year-old James Dean left Fair-mont, Indiana, for Los Angeles in June of 1949, he planned to enroll in UCLA's theater arts program that fall. Besides his

Sigma Nu fraternity, UCLA

passion for acting, another reason Dean chose to attend college in Los Angeles was because his father lived there. Indeed, Dean had once lived there, too—since his father and mother had moved from the Midwest to I.A. when Jimmy was five years old. But when his mother died of cancer three years later, he was shipped off to Iowa, where he was raised by an aunt and uncle and by his paternal grandparents.

When Dean arrived back in Los Angeles in 1949, it was the first time he had been there since his mother's death. The plan was for Jimmy to live with his father and stepmother while he attended UCLA. But Dean's dad had other plans. Since he was living in Santa Monica, it made much more sense for his son to attend Santa Monica City College. Also, the theater was out of the question. So, James Dean spent his freshman year of college at SMCC—as a physical education major.

The following fall, however, Jimmy managed to realize his dream and he registered at UCLA—in theater arts. He also moved out of his father's home and into the Sigma Nu fraternity house on Gayley Avenue. Dean's fraternity days proved to be short-lived. According to his biographer, David Dalton, in *James Dean: The Mutant King* (St. Martin's Press, 1974), Dean's fraternity brothers razzed him about his theatrical activities one time too often and he retaliated by punching one of them out. The end of the story: The movies' most famous "Rebel" was expelled from his fraternity.

Dean's academic career was practically as brief as his fraternity experience. He dropped out of UCLA and, after doing a couple of bit parts in movies, he left Los Angeles for New York in the fall of 1951. There, he was determined to become an actor—for real. The move paid off: When he returned to Hollywood a mere three years later, it would be to star in *East of Eden*. But once again, it would be another abortive Southern California stay—

because after just a year and a half and two more pictures (*Rebel Without a Cause* and *Giant*), it would all come to an end.

Or would it? Speaking at Jimmy's funeral back in Fairmont, Indiana, the Reverend Xen Harvey put it this way: "The career of James Dean has not ended. It has just begun. And remember, God himself is directing the production." Today, the career, the production, the legend of James Dean go on—and on.

10. UNIVERSITY OF CALIFORNIA AT LOS ANGELES

The Los Angeles campus of the University of California was established in Westwood in 1929. One of the state's most prestigious institutions of higher education, UCLA has a student body of close to 30,000. The University also has an especially strong motion picture/television curriculum which draws upon the talents and facilities that its proximity to "Hollywood" offers. UCLA has in turn contributed an impressive number of major talents to the Hollywood scene: actress Carol Burnett, director Francis Ford Coppola, screenwriters Colin (*Harold and Maude*) Higgins and Robert (*Chinatown*) Towne are all former UCLA students.

UCLA's film archives is strongly involved in the preservation of early motion pictures. Right now, major efforts are being made to transfer a number of silent films from their original—fast decomposing—nitrate film onto safety film. Another recent UCLA project involved the painstaking restoration of the first commercial feature film shot in three-strip Technicolor, *Becky Sharp.*

NOTE: *The UCLA film archives shares many of its films with the public—and has screenings of classic and contemporary, well- and little-known movies at its Melnitz Hall Theater, practically every day. Sometimes, an artist who worked on the film being presented is on hand to speak and answer questions. Many of these programs are free; others have a small admission charge. For information, call: 825-2345.*

11. MOUNT ST. MARY'S COLLEGE
12001 Chalon Road

When Hollywood needs to go abroad, it often heads no further than to the beautiful Chalon Campus of Mount St. Mary's College. Encompassing 56 acres high up in the hills behind Brentwood, this glorious enclave of lavish lawns, gardens, and tile-roofed buildings (the first was built in 1929–1930), has long provided magnificent Mediterranean settings for films, TV shows, and commercials. For example, the 1960s TV series, "Mission Impossible," with many episodes that took place overseas, frequently shot at Mount St. Mary's, turned the campus into France and Spain, as well as various fictional Eastern European countries.

Besides the beauty of the architecture and foliage of Mt. St. Mary's, another reason that film companies like to shoot here is because its high-up location assures some of L.A.'s best available,

*Mount St. Mary's
College chapel*

smog-free light. The light factor is especially important when filming commericals, since companies want to show off their product to its best advantage. Car companies, especially, often use the courtyard of Mt. St. Marys—with its arches and colonnades—as a background for TV spots as well as for print ads. Near the courtyard, another often photographed locale: Mt. St. Mary's chapel. It was the site of Jane Wyman's trip to the altar in a 1984 episode of "Falcon Crest," also witnessed Ali MacGraw's and Jan-Michael Vincent's on-screen nuptials in the 1983 miniseries "The Winds of War." For anyone who missed the weddings, they may have seen the campus play a decidedly different role in Mel Brooks' 1977 film, *High Anxiety.* In the Brooks spoof of various Alfred Hitchcock flicks, Mt. St. Mary's doubled for the Psycho-Neurological Institute for the Very Very Nervous.

NOTE: *The Mount St. Mary's campus is not a tourist attraction and it offers no parking for visitors who are not expected. The college has a policy that allows filmmakers only one day of shooting on the premises so as to disrupt campus life as little as possible. All monies collected from shooting fees go toward helping students needing financial aid.*

12. JOAN CRAWFORD HOUSE
426 North Bristol Avenue

This sprawling but unprepossessing Brentwood mansion was the scene of Miss Crawford's often turbulent domestic life for some three decades. It started quietly enough in 1929 when she moved into the house with her first husband, Douglas Fairbanks,

Jr. He was twenty, she was supposedly twenty as well, although her real age was closer to twenty-five. Many suspected Joan's motives in marrying Doug, Jr., felt she was trying to marry up—and into the glamorous world of Doug's dad and stepmother at Pickfair. If that was the case, Joan's plan backfired because it was a long time before she even got an invitation, much less was socially accepted by the lord and lady of Pickfair.

Nonetheless, Joan tried hard at playing the role of the Perfect Wife. No matter that it was she who had paid for their Brentwood base (Fairbanks was in debt at the time of their marriage), she appeared to adore her young husband, was photographed gazing up worshipfully at his bust on the fireplace. It was all very cozy and cutesy: She called him Dodie, he called her Jodie, they called their house "El JoDo" à la Pick-Fair. A few years later, the name-calling was no longer so romantic. Dodie moved out, Jodie redecorated, and Jodie and Dodie officially called it quits in 1934.

Joan remained queen of Castle Crawford through two more husbands (Franchot Tone and Philip Terry), many more remodelings, and four adopted children. One of those children, Christina, would go on to describe in chilling detail La Crawford in a new role . . . that of "Mommie Dearest" raising her Brentwood brood. Interesting: The house used in the film version of *Mommie Dearest* bore little resemblance to the real thing.

Crawford sold her Brentwood place in 1959 after she had been widowed by her fourth husband, Pepsi Cola executive Alfred Steele, with whom she had lived in New York. Far from leaving her a rich widow, Steele died with quite a few bills outstanding—which was one of the reasons why Joan bailed out of Brentwood. Donald O'Connor and his family were subsequent residents of 426 North Bristol.

Joan Crawford's long-time Brentwood base

Former home of Shirley Temple and family

13. SHIRLEY TEMPLE HOUSE
231 North Rockingham Road

Shirley Temple was born in Santa Monica in 1928. Her father worked for a bank and they lived in a modest little house. A mere seven years later, little Shirley had already made close to twenty films, been awarded a special Academy Award, and been signed to a $4000 a week contract that, with bonuses, made her the highest paid child in the world. At the same time, her great success enabled her family to move into this beautiful, vaguely French "farmhouse" in exclusive Brentwood. Here, Shirley had her own "doll house"—which was actually a full-sized guest house where the little tot kept her huge doll collection and where she had her own soda fountain. Later, when her child-star days were over, a seventeen-year-old Shirley Temple moved into her "doll house" with her new husband, actor John Agar, before he went off to World War II. They were divorced several years and one daughter (whom David O. Selznick instantly tried to put under contract!) later.

In 1950, Miss Temple went on to marry Charles Black of the Northern California/Pacific Gas and Electric Company Blacks. Despite the fact that Black was dropped from the Social Register for marrying an actress, the union worked. Today, Shirley Temple Black's grown-up accomplishments include several stabs at hosting a television series, a stint as an interior decorator, and the posts of U.S. Representative to the United Nations, U.S. Ambassador to Ghana, and U.S. Chief of Protocol. She resents being called a "former" child star—but, on seeing one of her clips at a film festival, once announced to the audience, "That little girl had a good time, too."

14. MARILYN MONROE HOUSE
12305 5th Helena Drive

Where it all came to an end on August 5, 1962. Marilyn had been living in this one-story villa at the end of a cul-de-sac off Helena Drive in Brentwood for about six months. Urged by her psychiatrist to "put down roots," she had found the house and bought it—all by herself. She had liked the house, gone to Mexico to look for its furnishings and fabrics. She especially liked the garden where she often played with her poodle Maf. But the house, the garden, the dog just weren't enough to compensate for the many areas of her life that were not going well, not working out. For one thing, she had been fired from *Something's Gotta Give,* the film she had been working on with Dean Martin. For another, she was supposedly involved with a very public figure who was also a very married man. Finally, she was ill—both physically and emotionally. The drugs helped somewhat—got her through the bad days, and worse nights. But the drugs weren't the answer either—and in the end, one of them, Nembutal, was what "officially" did her in. But, in truth, the end had been a long time in coming.

15. NUART THEATER
11272 Santa Monica Boulevard

A revival house that emphasizes—but is not limited to—foreign and experimental films. Every show is a double feature—except the midnight screenings on Fridays and Saturdays of cult films such as drag queen Divine's *Pink Flamingos.*
NOTE: *Program information: 478-6379; 479-5269.*

16. CENTURY CITY

Part of it was Chicago, another part was Algiers, still another harbored a South Seas lagoon. It was one of Hollywood's greatest

Century City

back lots—but in 1961, Twentieth Century-Fox was practically bankrupt from the production delays and massive costs of its then uncompleted *Cleopatra.* Realizing at the time that its real estate was worth more than its movies, Fox sold off a huge chunk of its back lot to the Aluminum Company of America for the development of a massive complex of offices, shops, condos, theaters, and restaurants that is now known as Century City.

Ironically, Century City quickly reverted to its former back-lot status when film and television production companies discovered that its state-of-the art architecture was wonderfully photogenic and easily could be made to look like practically any Thoroughly Modern Metropolis in America. Century City's walkways, landscaped plazas, and high rises have been seen in literally hundreds of series and television movies. Recent feature films that used Century City are *Against All Odds* and *The Man Who Loved Women.* In both of these movies, the locale was Los Angeles. But in the 1977 film about the world of professional dance, *The Turning Point,* Century City's ABC Entertainment Center doubled as New York City's Lincoln Center. And in *Conquest of the Planet of the Apes* (1972) Century City played a city of the future where human workers were pitted against slave apes.

17. TWENTIETH CENTURY-FOX STUDIOS
10202 West Pico Boulevard

Of all the major studios that are off-limits to visitors, Twentieth Century-Fox is the most intriguing to look at from the outside. Standing in front of the studio's main entrance off Pico Boulevard, for all the world to see, is Fox's vast New York City set that was created for *Hello Dolly!* in the late 1960s. Granted. the set—built

Twentieth Century-Fox Hello Dolly! *street, 1983*

to ¾ scale since the camera makes everything look larger than life—has seen better days; but like D. W. Griffith's great Babylon set for *Intolerance*—which stood on Sunset Boulevard for several years back in the teens—Fox's New York City is a landmark that celebrates the essential magical nature of filmmaking. In addition to being a landmark, the *Hello Dolly!* street is still used as a set, and occasionally turns up on a television show—especially when the script calls for a dilapidated inner-city neighborhood.

The history of the Twentieth Century-Fox lot goes back to William Fox, who bought the land along Pico Boulevard in 1925. At the time, his Fox Film Corporation—based at Sunset Boulevard and Western Avenue in Hollywood—needed additional shooting space for the Tom Mix Westerns that were the studio's mainstays. (Today, Tom Mix's barn is still on the lot and is used as an office.) A decade later, when financial difficulties had pushed Fox out of the company and prompted the Fox Film Corporation to merge with Joseph Schenck and Darryl Zanuck's two-year-old Twentieth Century Pictures, the new Twentieth Century-Fox organization decided to make Fox's Pico Boulevard property its headquarters. Eventually, Darryl Zanuck became the new studio's chief and remained a major mogul at Twentieth Century-Fox on and off up until the early 1970s.

Twentieth Century-Fox's biggest moneymaker in its early years was Shirley Temple, whose pictures provided the studio with a strong financial base. Today, Miss Temple's back-lot cottage is the studio hospital and the studio commissary still has a private dining room named after the top tot star. Other top Twentieth Century-Fox stars in the late 1930s were Tyrone Power, Alice Faye, Carmen Miranda, Don Ameche, Will Rogers, Janet Gaynor, and Sonja Henie. Later, Betty Grable, Anne Baxter,

Shirley Temple's bungalow on the Twentieth Century-Fox lot in the 1930s

Jennifer Jones, Victor Mature, Gregory Peck, and Marilyn Monroe would join the Fox fold.

Among the greatest Twentieth Century-Fox pictures made on the Pico property were *Cavalcade* (Fox's executive office building has balconies that resemble a ship's which were used in this shipboard film), *The Story of Alexander Graham Bell, In Old Chicago, The Grapes of Wrath, How Green Was My Valley, The Song of Bernadette, State Fair, Forever Amber, Gentlemen's Agreement, All About Eve, The Robe* (in which Fox introduced CinemaScope), *How to Marry a Millionaire, The King and I,* and *Hello Dolly!*

The present Fox lot, however, is only a shadow of its former self. In 1961, the studio was again in financial trouble—especially with the massive costs that *Cleopatra* was running up—and much of the original back lot was sold to the Alcoa Corporation for the Century City complex. The good news for movie lovers is that what's left of Fox Pico facilities has survived as long as it has—since frequent rumors have Fox selling off all its valuable Westside real estate and moving to the San Fernando Valley. Since there may be a great deal of truth to these rumors, movie lovers should catch a glimpse of the famous New York street set while they can—before it becomes another "lost" city like D. W. Griffith's Babylon.

P.S.: Anyone driving by the Twentieth Century-Fox Studios on Pico Boulevard to see the *Hello Dolly!* set should also turn north onto Fox Hills Drive in order to check out the studio's western wall. At Tennessee Avenue, the original main gate of the studio is now an auxiliary entrance; and at Orton Avenue, there's a good view of the back of Darryl F. Zanuck's former office building. It is said that the room within the cupola is where Mr. Zanuck's "casting couch" was located.

18. HILLCREST COUNTRY CLUB
10,000 West Pico Boulevard

Many people are under the impression that this famous country club—just south of Twentieth Century-Fox Studios—was founded by Jewish movie folk like Al Jolson, Jack Benny, George Burns, and George Jessel because they couldn't get into the WASP-only Los Angeles, Wilshire, and Bel-Air country clubs. False. The actual fact of the matter is that Hillcrest was founded in 1921—not by movie people, but rather by Jewish businessmen, lawyers, and doctors who couldn't get into the aforementioned WASP-only clubs. Later the movie moguls and movie stars also joined—including not only all the above names but eventually a couple of pretty well-known gentiles as well. The most famous of the latter: Frank Sinatra. Besides famous members, Hillcrest is famous for its food—which is said to be better than any restaurant in Los Angeles.

19. "BIG BUSINESS" HOUSE
10281 Dunleer Drive

In one of Laurel and Hardy's last silent films—*Big Business* (1929)—the boys are selling Christmas trees. When the owner of this house on Dunleer Drive destroys their sample tree, Stan and Ollie retaliate by destroying the man's house. According to an interview given by Hal Roach that appears in Kevin Brownlow's *Hollywood, The Pioneers* (Alfred A. Knopf, 1979), the *Big Business* crew started shooting the film at the wrong house! Its owners were away at the time—but returned just as their place was being devastated by Laurel and Hardy. On witnessing the sight, they, too, were devastated.

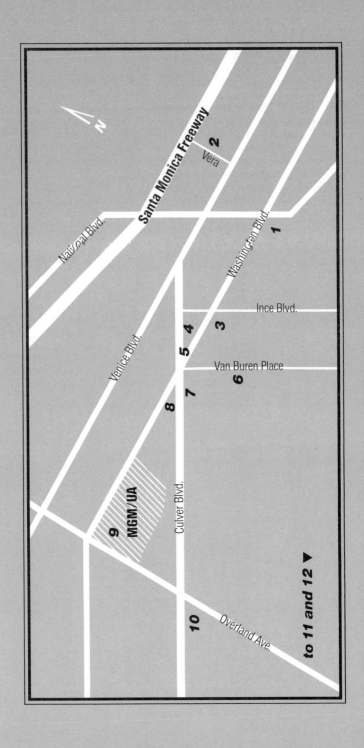

CULVER CITY

"The Heart of Screenland"

Made in Culver City: Gone with the Wind

ASPLASHING fountain and gleaming stainless-steel sculpture in the shape of a loop of motion picture film proclaim Culver City "The Heart of Screenland" over at the corner of Overland Avenue and Culver Boulevard. A plaque at the base of this monumental piece of public art goes on to say: "Dedicated by the Citizens of Culver City—the Motion Picture Capital of the World."

Culver City? What are they talking about? What's going on here? Actually, quite a bit went on here—especially in the 1930s and 1940s when, at one time, this little middle-class Los Angeles community, about six miles southwest of Hollywood, produced over half of the movies made in America. This dramatic statistic was largely owing to the presence of Metro-Goldwyn-Mayer which was Culver City's single greatest industry. But Culver City's film fame wasn't just because of MGM. Hal Roach, David O. Selznick, as well as a number of smaller Culver City studios enabled city officials to adopt the slogan: "Culver City—Where Hollywood Movies Are Made." For some civic boosters, slogans weren't enough—they wanted nothing less than to change Culver City's name. The name they chose? "Hollywood!"

Unlike many areas of Los Angeles, the movies didn't "come" to Culver City, they were brought there. The man responsible for this was the town's developer, Harry H. Culver—who as early as 1915 saw the potential of the movie industry and went about enticing studios to set up shop in his new real-estate development. First on the scene was the Kalem Motion Picture Company—which later was known as Essanay. They didn't stay long, however—but the highly successful producer/director Thomas Ince did. In fact, it was Ince who built the studio that eventually became MGM. It was also Ince who built another historic studio that wound up being home to such greats as Cecil B. DeMille,

"Heart of Screenland" fountain, Culver City

David O. Selznick, RKO, and even Lucille Ball and Desi Arnaz's Desilu Productions. Today, both of Ince's former studios are not only still standing, they are still turning out films. The Hal Roach Studios, however, have been torn down—but for the Laurel and Hardy fan, many of the locations used in both their silent and sound Hal Roach comedies can be found in downtown Culver City. For film buffs, this rarely visited pocket of Los Angeles must be visited—indeed, if you haven't seen Culver City, you haven't really seen Hollywood. Hoo-ray for . . . Culver City!

NOTE: *The sites of downtown Culver City—from numbers 3 to 10—can be seen easily on a walking tour of about forty-five minutes to an hour. The last two items in this chapter—the Holy Cross and the Hillside Memorial cemeteries—are technically not in Culver City, but are included here because of their proximity.*

1. HAL ROACH STUDIO SITE
West Washington Boulevard at National Boulevard

At the southwest corner of Washington and National boulevards, there's a postage-stamp-sized park with a picnic table, two benches, and a simple marker that bears the following inscription: "Site of the Hal Roach Studios . . . Laugh Factory to the World . . . 1919–1963." And that it was—for it was here that Roach produced (and often directed) early Harold Lloyd films, the Our Gang comedies, the Laurel and Hardy series, and the "Topper" films. Besides all of Roach's funny fare, he sometimes did serious films such as *Captain Fury* (1939), *Of Mice and Men* (1939), and a great number of propaganda movies during World War II. Called "Fort Roach" during the war years, the studio boasted Lieutenant (later Captain) Ronald Reagan as its leading leading man.

Proving how far we've all come since World War II, today, behind the little park, the area where Roach's studios stood has been taken over by Culver City Mazda.

House used in Laurel and Hardy's Perfect Day

Selznick International Studios, 1935

2. "PERFECT DAY" HOUSE
3120 Vera Avenue

It was anything but a *A Perfect Day* in this Laurel and Hardy classic that saw the boys trying to set off on a picnic only to have one disaster after another keep them from ever getting anywhere. The house in front of which most of the action of the film takes place—a cozy Cotswoldlike cottage with bulging roof—has changed little since *A Perfect Day* was released in 1929.

P.S.: Die-hard Laurel and Hardy fans may also recognize the house next door (3116 Vera) and the house across the street (3115 Vera)—both of which also appear in *A Perfect Day*.

3. LAIRD INTERNATIONAL STUDIOS
9336 West Washington Boulevard

Remember that shot of the white mansion with the elegant columns that preceded every David O. Selznick film in the late 1930s and early 1940s? It wasn't Tara—although many assumed that it was, since Selznick's most famous production was *Gone with the Wind*. The mansion was actually the main office building of Selznick International Studios. Selznick set up his own company in Culver City in 1936 after having been a vice president and producer at MGM. One of Selznick's principal backers in this venture was John Hay "Jock" Whitney (Gloria Vanderbilt's cousin) who served as Chairman of the Board of Selznick International.

Selznick produced an impressive group of motion picture classics from his Culver City base. *Little Lord Fauntleroy* (1936), *The Garden of Allah* (1936), *A Star Is Born* (1937), *Nothing Sacred* (1937), *The Prisoner of Zenda* (1937), *Intermezzo* (1939), and *Rebecca* (1940) were all filmed here—as was much of *Gone with the Wind* (1939). In fact, the hills directly behind the studio are those seen in the sequence where Scarlett and Melanie flee Atlanta.

It was not Selznick, however, who built the great white mansion that became the trademark for his films. The building and the studio were actually founded back in 1919 by the pioneer director-producer Thomas Ince—who had his greatest early success with a string of Westerns that starred William S. Hart. Among the famous Ince films done on his Culver City lot were *The Typhoon* (1920) with Sessue Hayakawa and *Human Wreckage* (1924), which was inspired by silent superstar Wallace Reid's fatal bout with drug addiction and which starred the late actor's wife, Dorothy Davenport.

After Ince's untimely death in 1924, the studio he built had a series of occupants before Selznick arrived. One of those interim tenants was Cecil B. DeMille, who had broken away from Paramount in 1925 to form his own company, which he set up on the former Ince lot. It was here that DeMille leased his classic story of the life of Christ, *King of Kings,* in 1926–1927.

After DeMille returned to Paramount in the late 1920s, Pathé—which via mergers became RKO-Pathé—took over. At this time Joseph P. Kennedy and Gloria Swanson were partners in the picture business (associated with RKO) and Gloria's 1930 Art Deco bungalow is now the office of independent producer Blake Edwards. Some of RKO's greatest pictures were shot at this little Culver City studio: *What Price Hollywood?* (1932), *King Kong* (1933), *Becky Sharp* (1935), *Top Hat* (1935). And when Selznick burned Atlanta for *Gone with the Wind,* part of what he set aflame was the old jungle set from RKO's *King Kong!*

It should be noted that even during the Selznick era, RKO continued to shoot films such as *Citizen Kane* (1941) at Culver City, since Selznick only leased the studios from RKO. Thus, when Selznick International disbanded in 1943, the lot was still part of RKO and remained so until 1957 when Lucille Ball and Desi Arnaz acquired it for their mushrooming Desilu empire. When that same empire was dissolved in the late 1960s, the

Blake Edwards' office in former Gloria Swanson/Joseph Kennedy bungalow at Laird International Studios

The Culver City Hotel

Culver City studio became a rental lot—which is what it is today under the name of Laird International Studios. (Steven Spielberg shot much of *E.T.* at Laird.)

Perhaps no other studio in Los Angeles preserves as much history as this one. Stored inside the slat-sided silent stage that Ince built in 1919 are props and set pieces that range from the mockup of the plane John Wayne flew in *Jet Pilot* to the oval panels from Scarlett O'Hara's *Gone with the Wind* bedroom to the bases of Tara's columns. Another stage houses all the props from *Citizen Kane*. At this writing, there is the possibility that Laird may establish a museum—either on studio property or somewhere else in the area. In the meantime, movie lovers visiting Laird must make do with checking out the famous mansion that appeared at the beginning of all those Selznick pictures—and imagining all the wonderful movies that have been shot on the premises.

4. HOTEL ADAMS
3896 Main Street

Besides appearing in at least two Laurel and Hardy films—*We Fall Down* (1928) and *Liberty* (1929)—this is one of the places where the Munchkins were housed in 1938 during the filming of *The Wizard of Oz* at MGM six blocks away. Today, a sign in the seedy lobby admonishes tenants: "no cooking or extension cords in rooms."

5. CULVER CITY HOTEL
9400 Culver Boulevard

According to Judy, "They got smashed every night and the police had to pick them up in butterfly nets." She may have exaggerated a bit—but when 124 Munchkins hit Culver City in 1938, the small L.A. community had its hands full. Most stayed at the Culver City Hotel where, according to one story, a policeman was needed on every floor to break up their wild sex orgies. According to other stories, their raucous behavior was not limited to their hotel. Evidently one of them caused quite a disturbance at MGM when he bit a guard in the leg. Others were said to carry knives—and several of the women supposedly propositioned *The Wizard of Oz* stagehands on various occasions. In her book, *The Making of the Wizard of Oz* (Alfred A. Knopf, Inc. 1977), Aljean Harmetz concludes that while some of the stories about filmdom's most famous little people (they ranged in height between 2'3" and 4'8") may have been true, many ranked among Hollywood's tallest tales.

6. HOTEL WASHINGTON
3927 Van Buren Place

"What a dump!" The line forever belongs to her *Whatever Happened to Baby Jane?* costar, Bette Davis—but it aptly describes Joan Crawford's first L.A. digs. Just a couple of blocks from MGM where she was making $75 a week, the hotel saw Joan (*née* Lucille Fay Le Sueur) check in in early 1925. Today, the Washington advertises "nice rooms for nice people," requires that rents be paid by the day or by the week—in advance—just to make sure that no nice tenant runs up a big bill.

7. CITY HALL
9770 Culver Boulevard

Culver City officially became a city in 1917 and this beautiful Beaux-Arts building has served as City Hall ever since 1928. It has also served as a Laurel and Hardy location a couple of times as well. In *County Hospital* (1932), City Hall doubled as the hospital of the film's title ... and in *Going Bye-Bye!* (1934), it was called on to be a courthouse.

8. CULVER THEATER
9820 West Washington Boulevard

With its gigantic billboard-like façade, this is one of the ways that they designed movie houses in the era just after World War II. Now split up into three theaters, the Culver is also an example of how movie theater owners dealt with the challenges presented by television, cable, and home video. The Culver Theater was often used by nearby MGM for sneak previews.

9. MGM/UA
10202 West Washington Boulevard

"More stars than there are in the heavens." That's what MGM claimed during its glory years in the 1930s and 1940s.

Making Leo the Lion roar in the late 1920s

And, in fact, the claim wasn't so far-fetched—since this was the studio that employed Judy Garland, Mickey Rooney, Clark Gable, Jean Harlow, John Gilbert, Greta Garbo, Marion Davies, Joan Crawford, Norma Shearer, Greer Garson, Myrna Loy, Spencer Tracy, Katharine Hepburn, Elizabeth Taylor—to mention but a few. Name a legend—and chances are, he or she was under contract at MGM. Indeed, if Hollywood had had no studio other than Metro-Goldwyn-Mayer, the town still would have been the movie capital of the world.

MGM had more than just super-stars. It also had some of the finest technical people in the business—set designers, costumers, special-effects men. It counted among its great directors George Sidney, George Cukor, King Vidor, Sidney Franklin, Victor Fleming, Clarence Brown, W. S. Van Dyke II, Stanley Donen, and Vincente Minnelli. In some ways, even more important than its directors were MGM producers. Early on, for example, one of the most vital forces at the studio was Irving Thalberg—who was its first head of production. Working in this capacity from 1924 up to his death in 1936, Thalberg was responsible for the string of successful films—including *Ben Hur, Flesh and the Devil, Anna Christie, The Big Parade, Grand Hotel, David Copperfield*—that quickly made the studio's name and fame.

Another ultra-important name at MGM was Arthur Freed—whose "Freed Unit" produced most of those lavish musicals that have come to be synonymous with the letters MGM. Freed's top productions: *The Wizard of Oz* (in association with Mervyn LeRoy), *Babes in Arms, Strike Up the Band, Babes on Broadway, Girl Crazy, Meet Me in St. Louis, The Pirate, The Harvey Girls, Easter Parade, Singin' in the Rain, Show Boat, An American in Paris,* and *The Band Wagon.*

Finally, the biggest name of all at MGM—not counting the studio's mascot/symbol, "Leo the Lion"—was the infamous Louis B. Mayer. For almost thirty years he ruled his studio and Hollywood with an iron hand—and was respected, feared, often hated, rarely loved. In 1951, he fell from power. Nonetheless, a frequently told story about his funeral in 1957 says that the reason it was so crowded was because everybody wanted to make sure he was really gone.

A former junk dealer, Mayer got into the picture business in 1907 when he bought a movie house in Massachusetts. He quickly acquired more theaters and before he knew it he owned a chain. By 1918, Mayer was in Los Angeles making his own movies under the banner of Louis B. Mayer Pictures. MGM came about in 1924 through a three-way merger that brought together Mayer's company, Samuel Goldwyn's studio, and Metro Pictures. It was decided at that time that Goldwyn's lot in Culver City would be Metro-Goldwyn-Mayer's headquarters—and the company has never budged since. In fact, it is the only one of the major studios that is still operating from its initial location.

Originally built for Thomas Ince's division of Triangle Pictures in 1915, the MGM property grew along with the new studio's success. For anyone visiting it, the most impressive MGM structure that can be seen from the street is the Irving Thalberg building. Erected in the late 1930s in honor of Thalberg—who died in 1936 at the age of thirty-seven—this massive white WPA-moderne office building looks as though it would be more at home in Washington, D.C., than in Southern California. Indeed, architecturally, it is much more a tribute to Louis B. Mayer's sense of self-importance than to Thalberg's creative genius. Over on Washington Boulevard at the other side of the studio, the more graceful, colonnaded building that was Triangle's headquarters in 1916 provides a vivid contrast to the Thalberg/Mayer monolith. To the right of this building are the tall narrow arches that loom above MGM's original main gate.

Many changes have taken place at MGM since the grand days of the 1930s and 1940s. For one thing, Metro-Goldwyn-Mayer now goes by the name MGM/UA—owing to a hookup with United Artists in the early 1980s. Then, too, the present MGM/UA lot is much smaller than it used to be. That happened in 1969 when the studio—under new ownership—took a cue from Twentieth Century-Fox and sold off its back lots to real-estate developers. Gone went the "Andy Hardy" street, the huge artificial lake used for *Mutiny on the Bounty* (1935) and *Showboat,* and the sets of *Meet Me in St. Louis* and *Raintree County.* Today, one of the developments on the old MGM back lot is called the "Raintree Apartment and Condominium Complex." All in all, MGM went from 183 acres to 30 acres in this real-estate deal.

In 1970, even more of MGM was lost when the bulk of the studio's props and set pieces were auctioned off. The years 1969

MGM's original main gate

and 1970 were sad times for movie lovers. Still, as long as there are movies, there will always be an MGM—a magical land where Mickey and Judy sang and danced, where Greta Garbo was the most ravishing creature on earth, and where almost all endings were happy ones. The studio may be down to 30 acres—but the great MGM movies are as big and lavish as they always were: *They* are forever—and they happened here.

10. FILM STRIP U.S.A.
Culver Boulevard at Overland Avenue

The most exuberant tribute to Culver City's vital role in the film history of Los Angeles, this fountain/sculpture was erected in 1981 in front of the Veterans Memorial Building, across the street from the housing development that used to be an MGM back lot. Natalie Krol is the sculptor.

11. HOLY CROSS CEMETERY
5835 West Slauson Avenue

This enormous grassy hillside looking out on MGM off to the north is the final resting place of some of Hollywood's most famous stars of the Roman Catholic faith. Of these, one of the brightest was Rosalind *Auntie Mame* Russell—whose grave is marked by a large white cross in section "M." In the mausoleum higher up on the hill are Joan Davis, Spike Jones, and Mario Lanza.

The greatest concentration of names of Holy Cross, however, can be found around the cemetery's artificial, but very pretty, "Grotto"—which is to the left of the main entrance. Here lie Zasu Pitts, Jack Haley, Bela Lugosi, Jimmy Durante, Charles Boyer. Here, too, a haunting reminder of the Manson Family's madness: the grave of Sharon Tate Polanski (1943–1969) and that of her unborn child, Paul Richard Polanski.

Rosalind Russell memorial, Holy Cross Cemetery

The biggest star around the Grotto may well be Harry Lillis "Bing" Crosby (1904–1977) who is buried alongside his first wife, Wilma W. Crosby (1911–1952) who was better known as the singer Dixie Lee. A few markers down from the Crosbys is the cemetery's most bizarre grave site. The marker reads: "Carmel Gene Gallegos . . . Going Bing's Way . . . A Road to Jesus." Only one year—1924—is inscribed on the marker. According to a Holy Cross caretaker, it seems that this Crosby fan, on hearing of his idol's death, reserved his own plot as close to Bing's as possible. Louella Parsons (1881–1972)—who is just across the driveway by a small tree—would have had a lot of fun with this one. Louella, by the way, had an interesting religious background: She was born Jewish, raised Episcopalian, and became a convert to Catholicism.

NOTE: *Hours are 7 to 6, daily.*

12. HILLSIDE MEMORIAL PARK
6001 Centinela Avenue

About a mile north of the Los Angeles International Airport, a big white-marble building atop a smooth green hillside instantly catches the eye of anyone driving along the San Diego Freeway. Below the building, a round monument with tall columns looks like a modern version of an ancient Greek temple and has water cascading down in front of it. What is all this anyway? The hill is called Mt. Scholum, the large white building is a mausoleum, and the little "temple" is the grave of the great entertainer, Al Jolson. The first actor ever to "talk" in a feature-length commercial motion picture, Jolson changed the course of film history with the words "You ain't heard nothin' yet," which he uttered in *The Jazz Singer* in 1927. Needless to say, he was right—because the success of the film meant that movies would never be silent again.

Al Jolson memorial, Hillside Memorial Park

A small statue of Jolson behind his tomb shows the entertainer kneeling with arms outstretched—just as he used to do when singing "Mammy."

A number of Jolson's cronies are also laid to rest in this vast Jewish cemetery. Up in the big white mausoleum, Jack Benny's large black-marble crypt is center stage in the alcove at the end of the Hall of Graciousness. Here, the perennially thirty-nine-year-old comedian is remembered as: "Beloved husband, father and grandfather . . . A Gentle Man . . . 1894–1974." Eddie Cantor and his wife Ida are to the left of Mr. Benny—and George Jessel, "The Toastmaster General of America," is outside in the mausoleum's central courtyard.

In that same courtyard is David ("The Fugitive") Janssen's wall crypt. Janssen, who succumbed to a heart attack in 1980, was barely fifty when he died. Back inside the mausoleum (on the second floor, directly above Mssrs. Benny and Jessel), another star who exited before his time: Ira Grossel—who died in 1961 of complications following surgery at the age of forty-two. Movie lovers will remember this handsome matinee idol better by his screen name . . . Jeff Chandler.

NOTE: *Hillside Memorial Park and Mortuary is open daily from 8 to 5, except Saturdays and Jewish religious holidays.*

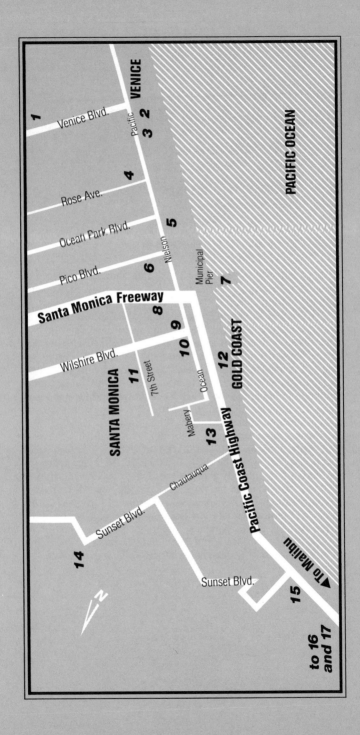

PACIFIC OCEAN

VENICE

Venice Blvd.

Pacific

Rose Ave.

Ocean Park Blvd.

Nielson

Pico Blvd.

Municipal
Pier

Santa Monica Freeway

Wilshire Blvd.

7th Street

Ocean

SANTA MONICA

GOLD COAST

Mabery

Pacific Coast Highway

Chautauqua

Sunset Blvd.

Sunset Blvd.

To Malibu

to 16
and 17

1
3 2
4
5
6
7
8
9
10
11
12
13
14
15

N

VENICE/ SANTA MONICA/ MALIBU

Hollywood by the Sea

*Gloria Swanson, with ukulele,
in her Mack Sennett Bathing Beauty days*

THERE are some people who look on all of L.A. as one big beach town. Although this is a vast oversimplification of the personality of America's second largest city, it cannot be denied that the proximity of the Pacific Ocean has much to do with the mystique and ultimate appeal of Los Angeles. And if we are to believe the history books, it was that same Pacific Ocean that attracted the first film crew to the area back in 1907. The crew was headed by director Francis Boggs who was working for the Chicago-based Selig Polyscope Company—and they are thought to have used the cliff-backed coast of La Jolla as a location for some especially dramatic ocean footage for an early version of *The Count of Monte Cristo*. Liking the territory, the Selig company eventually set up permanent quarters in downtown Los Angeles and later in Silverlake—but it was the ocean that brought them to L.A. in the first place.

That same ocean attracted other early filmmakers. Mack Sennett was one of them and he often used the beaches of Santa Monica and Venice as locations for his fabled Mack Sennett "Bathing Beauty" films. And then there was producer/director Thomas Ince, who thought he had found the perfect place for shooting Westerns on a large tract of land—which he called "Inceville"—where Sunset Boulevard meets the Pacific. Vitagraph was another important film company that had its first studio in Santa Monica. There was one serious problem with these seaside studios ... the weather. During certain parts of the year, the Southern California coast experiences foggy foggy mornings—which were especially bothersome to silent film companies that depended on the sun as their principal source of light. Eventually, all the movie companies moved inland.

But while the film factories headed east—their stars, directors, and producers often looked west ... back toward that big beautiful ocean. Instead of working by the sea, they would live alongside

Mack Sennett's Bathing Beauties, 1916

Statue of Myrna Loy outside Venice High School

it—at least in the summer and on weekends; and by the middle of the 1920s, many of Hollywood's leading lights had built "cottages" (some had as many as fifty rooms) along what soon came to be known as Santa Monica's "Gold Coast." Today, a number of these extraordinary homes are still standing and are among the many delights awaiting the movie lover who visits Santa Monica. Other treats in Santa Monica—as well as in the communities of Venice to the south and Malibu to the north—are Greta Garbo's first and longest Los Angeles residence, the site of one of Hollywood's most baffling unsolved murders, a funky amusement pier where the stars once played and where many famous films have been made, the ultimate movie-star colony, and an enormous state park in the Santa Monica mountains that was once a movie ranch where films like *How Green Was My Valley* and *M*A*S*H* were shot. This same park also has one of the most beautiful natural settings in all of Southern California.

NOTE: *Best places to walk: the Santa Monica Pier; the Gold Coast houses; downtown Venice; and Malibu Creek State Park. Proceed with caution along the Pacific Coast Highway. Look—only after you've arrived at your destination. This is especially true if you are the driver.*

1. VENICE HIGH SCHOOL
13000 Venice Boulevard

Standing in front of the Art Deco main building of Venice High School, a stylized sculpture depicts three dancing figures. One of the figures represents "the Physical," another "the Mental," and the third "the Spiritual." A then art instructor at the school named H. F. Winebrenner designed the statues in the 1920s, using students as his models. A football player was called on to pose for the Physical, a pretty girl with a high academic average modeled for the Mental, and another lovely young woman—with an especially lithe body—inspired the Spiritual. The whereabouts of the first two student models are anybody's guess. Miss Spiritual is another story. Her name was Myrna Williams and she was said to have been embarrassed about the statue and asked that her identity be kept secret. Somehow or other, the cat got out of the bag—especially once Miss Williams changed her last name and started making pictures at MGM. Today, movie lovers can catch Myrna Loy as the sophisticated Nora Charles on the reruns of her classic *The Thin Man* films on television and as a dancing teenager in front of her former alma mater in Venice, CA.

P.S.: Movie lovers can also catch Venice High's Art Deco façade in the opening sequence of *Grease*.

2. VENICE

It was an outlandish undertaking—even for Southern California. Convinced that the gentle climate and dramatic topography of Los Angeles would give rise to the ultimate flowering of American culture, a wealthy cigarette manufacturer and real-estate baron named Abbot Kinney decided to get the jump on the coming renaissance by building his own version of Venice, Italy, just south of Santa Monica. With plenty of cash to back up his dream, Kinney began hiring architects and engineers around the turn of the century to create a canal system as well as a master plan of buildings with extravagant Venetian colonnaded façades. On July 4, 1905, the fantasy city celebrated its grand opening.

It was fun for a while—what with gondolas and gondoliers plying the canals; exotic hotels, pavilions, and bath houses; and a 1600-foot pier for fishing and strolling. But the cultural renais-

Venice arcade today

Marlene and Claudette having fun on the Venice Pier at
Carole Lombard's 1935 bash

sance of Kinney's dreams never materialized—and Venice quickly
became little more than a glorified seaside amusement park.

Today, little is left of Kinney's Venice—just enough to make
seeing the city an intriguing archaeological experience. The best
examples of the city's neo-Italian-Renaissance architecture are the
arcaded buildings along Windward and Pacific Avenues, and
while most of the canals were declared health hazards and filled
in in the late 1920s, a few remain—along with their charming
arched bridges—at Carroll, Linnie, Sherman, and Howland.

In its early days, Venice—with its flamboyant architecture
and beautiful beach—quickly became a popular location for silent
movies. Two of the first producers to film here were Thomas Ince
and Mack Sennett. Sennett often used the beach for his famous
"Bathing Beauties"; he also shot his 1914 Keystone Production,
Kid Auto Races, in Venice; the film was Charlie Chaplin's second
movie—and the first in which he was seen wearing the moustache,
the baggy trousers, and carrying the cane that would eventually
become his trademarks.

Chaplin not only filmed in Venice he also relaxed here—
and is said to have stayed at the Waldorf Hotel, which is still
standing and is now an apartment building at the corner of
Westminster and Speedway. The grander St. Marks Hotel was
also popular with movie folk, and Rudolph Valentino and Douglas
Fairbanks both supposedly stayed there. Today, only a portion of
its colonnade remains at the corner of Windward and Ocean
Front Walk.

Known as a place for fun and play, Venice brought out stars
in search of good times and often turned them into children.
Marion Davies, one of Hollywood's wealthiest women, loved the
Pier, the hamburgers and hot dogs, the Ferris wheel, and once
rode the roller coaster until seven in the morning! Charlie Chaplin

was nuts over the bumper cars. In 1935, Carole Lombard, who like Miss Davies was always up for a good time, took over the entire Venice Pier and hosted one of Hollywood's most famous parties. Le tout Hollywood came to the party, rode all the rides, played all the arcade games, and let down all their hair. A famous photograph from this party shows Paramount Pretties Marlene Dietrich and Claudette Colbert zipping down a sliding board together.

In the mid-1950s, Dietrich returned to Venice to play the role of a sheriff's former mistress in Orson Welles' haunting film, *Touch of Evil.* By this time, Venice was practically at its lowest point—and Welles capitalized on its seedy state and crumbling arcaded buildings to portray the sleazy Tex/Mex border town in which his film took place. Another 1950s film which used Venice extensively was a very low-budget horror flick (occasionally on the late-late-late show) called *Bucket of Blood* which captures the town during its beatnik days of the late 1950s. It was during this era that a coffee house called the Gashouse drew the leading poets, comics, and musicians of the counterculture before less-enlightened locals managed to get the place shut down in 1960.

By the 1970s, however, Venice was on the upswing. Artists, especially, had discovered its great beach, its fantasy architecture, and, above all, its low rents—and this influx of new talent brought new life and a new look to the place. The most striking additions were the huge murals that began appearing on buildings all over town. In an odd way, Venice had come full circle: it was, at last, the prime site of a cultural renaissance in Los Angeles. Kinney's dream, at last, had come true. Of the recent films that have taken advantage of Venice's "new" dazzle, the 1983 remake of *Breathless,* with Richard Gere, beautifully shows off the city, its murals, and its restored buildings as they are today.

Janet Leigh in Venice in Touch of Evil

3. TONY BILL PRODUCTIONS
73 Market Street

One of Venice's most famous businessmen is former movie "juvenile" (he played Frank Sinatra's kid brother in the 1963 film version of Neil Simon's *Come Blow Your Horn*) Tony Bill. Bill went on to act in more films—but achieved his greatest fame through his activities on the other side of the cameras. In 1973, Bill co-produced *The Sting,* which was awarded the Academy Award for the best picture of the year and made him a producer to be reckoned with. Other Bill-produced films are *Hearts of the West, Harry and Walter Go to New York,* and *Steelyard Blues.*

Very much a symbol of the "New Hollywood," Bill operates out of a restored former rooming house in funky Venice. His latest business venture: a restaurant called 72 Market Street in which he's a partner with Dudley Moore. The restaurant is across the street from Bill's studio. Liza Minnelli is one of the investors in the project.

NOTE: *Phone for reservations: 392-8720.*

4. GOLD'S GYM
360 Hampton Drive

The original Gold's Gym was on Second Street in Santa Monica and it—along with Arnold Schwarzenegger—starred in the 1975 film *Pumping Iron.* Gold's was also the scene of a Mr. America contest in 1977 at which Mae West—eighty-five at the time—handed out the trophies. Indeed, Muscle Beach, Jane Fonda, and Gold's Gym have all been responsible for helping to make Santa Monica the unofficial "Fitness Capital of the U.S.A." Regulars at Gold's present location—it moved to Hampton Drive in 1981—include Lou ("The Incredible Hulk") Ferrigno, star woman bodybuilder Lisa Lyon, Morgan Fairchild, Bo Svenson,

The 1963 Academy Awards at the Santa Monica Civic Auditorium

Issac Hayes, and—because the weights are heavier than at her own "Workout" in Beverly Hills—Jane Fonda.

5. JANE FONDA HOUSE
152 Wadsworth Avenue

This block of restored Victorian houses between Barnard Way and Neilson Way would be worth seeing—even if Jane Fonda hadn't lived here in the 1970s with her husband, California State Assemblyman Tom Hayden. The ultra-unpretentious Fonda/Hayden house showed the world (and Hayden's liberal constituents) that Jane and Tom were just another California couple. Their once-a-year block-party beer-busts further added to the image. Today, the Haydens reside in a much posher Santa Monica neighborhood near Brentwood.

6. SANTA MONICA CIVIC AUDITORIUM
1855 Main Street

This is where the Academy Awards were presented and televised from 1960 to 1968. Built in 1958, the auditorium—with its huge stage, vast dressing room areas, and state-of-the-art electronic equipment—was the best place in town to accommodate an awards ceremony that had become one of the most widely watched television shows in the world. An extra added attraction of the Santa Monica Civic Auditorium was its sweeping driveway which made it ideal for focusing on star-car arrivals.

7. SANTA MONICA PIER
foot of Colorado Avenue

Jane Fonda and Michael Sarrazin marathon-danced their way to oblivion on it in *They Shoot Horses, Don't They?* Barbra

Robert Redford and the Santa Monica Carrousel in The Sting, *1973*

Streisand and Omar Sharif strolled along it (it was doubling as Brooklyn's Coney Island) in *Funny Girl.* Natalie Wood's crazy mother (Ruth Gordon) told fortunes here in *Inside Daisy Clover.* Paul Newman operated its carrousel (as well as an illegal gambling operation) in *The Sting.* These are but a few of the many screen appearances that the Santa Monica Pier has made in recent years. Besides movies, TV series constantly shoot at the Pier—their directors well aware that a little carnival/boardwalk ambience can do wonders to perk up an otherwise bland script.

One of Santa Monica's oldest and most famous attractions, the Pier has been around since the early part of the century. Also one of Santa Monica's most glorious survivors, the Pier has withstood both storms and developers—and recently was placed on the National Register of Historic Places. Its vintage merry-go round (built in 1922) is one of the best preserved all-wooden carrousels in the United States—and boasts fifty-six handsome hand-carved horses, each one unique. Today the Pier is more than a National Historic Landmark, it is a symbol of the innocent seashore resort that Santa Monica once was.

8. VITAGRAPH SITE
1438 Second Street

Next door to a porno movie theater, this little brick building is thought to be the oldest extant building in Santa Monica. Dating back to 1873, it started out as a saloon, later served as a city hall, Salvation Army office, political headquarters, and an art gallery. For movie lovers, its most interesting incarnation was around 1912 when the building was part of the offices of the Vitagraph film company, which also occupied a larger building (now gone) next door. Based in New York, Vitagraph came to Santa Monica as early as 1911 to do location shooting, and remained there until 1915 when it made East Hollywood its permanent base. In 1925, Vitagraph was absorbed by Warner Brothers.

Vitagraph Studios, 1914

General Telephone building,
Lawrence Welk Plaza

9. LAWRENCE WELK PLAZA
100 Wilshire Boulevard at Ocean Avenue

In the late 1940s, a bandleader with a funny accent was the most popular performer at the Aragon Ballroom on Santa Monica's Pacific Ocean Pier. The ballroom and the pier have long since been torn down—but the bandleader and his light, highly danceable "Champagne Music" went on to be piped into the households of millions of Americans every week. That thanks to television—which not only made Lawrence Welk one of the best-known bandleaders in America, but also one of the wealthiest in history. Symbolizing Welk's great fame and fortune is the downtown Santa Monica plaza that bears his name. Erected in 1969–1970 by Welk, Lawrence Welk Plaza contains the twenty-two-story General Telephone Building as well as a sixteen-story apartment house that's fittingly called "Champagne Towers." Another highrise office building was added in 1979 at Ocean and Arizona Avenues.

Besides the Lawrence Welk connection, television viewers may recall the General Telephone Building as a regular on the long-running series "Marcus Welby, M.D.," which was set in Santa Monica. Another familiar sight in the same series was Pacific Palisades Park, which is just across Ocean Avenue from Lawrence Welk Plaza and which was the photogenic Santa Monica locale where Dr. Welby had countless "meaningful" talks with the younger doctors working with him.

Miramar Hotel,
the "Garbo wing"

10. MIRAMAR-SHERATON HOTEL
101 Wilshire Boulevard

In the Spring of 1925, Louis B. Mayer went off to Europe to scout foreign talent for the newly formed Metro-Goldwyn-Mayer studio. In Berlin, Mayer's prime objective was to put director Mauritz Stiller under contract with MGM. Stiller, however, played hard to get, insisted that he would only come to America if Mayer also gave a contract to his protégée, a twenty-year-old Swedish actress named Greta Garbo. Mayer was not impressed with the pudgy Miss Garbo, but reluctantly met Stiller's terms and the Stiller/Garbo team arrived in California in September of the same year.

The studio rented a Santa Monica house with a pool for Stiller. Garbo was put up in a suite at Santa Monica's Miramar Hotel. Garbo's Santa Monica life was a simple one: She worked at the studio, took walks on the beach, often visited her friend Stiller where she enjoyed swimming in his pool. She lived at the Miramar longer than at practically any other address in Los Angeles . . . almost three years. A lot happened during those years. For one thing, the actress whom Mayer had not wanted to sign became the studio's greatest star. For another thing, in classic *A Star Is Born* fashion, Stiller's career instantly went downward and after bitter clashes with Mayer, he wound up never completing a film at MGM. His luck wasn't much better during the brief stint at Paramount that followed—and in 1927, Stiller returned to Europe a broken man. A Hollywood casualty, he died a year later. Garbo wept . . . and soon left the Miramar for her own house with a pool in Beverly Hills.

Today's Miramar is quite different from the hotel that Garbo knew. In her day, it consisted of an 1889 mansion (the former home of Santa Monica co-founder, Nevada Senator, and silver tycoon John P. Jones) and the six-story brick building erected in 1924 that housed her suite. In the late 1930s, the hotel lost the Jones mansion—and in 1959, it gained a modern ten-story tower. It also gained a new pool area which can be seen in the Bermuda sequence of *That Touch of Mink* (1962) with Cary Grant and Doris Day. The one part of the hotel that hasn't changed dramatically since Garbo's residence is the wing where she stayed.

11. ST. MONICA'S CHURCH
715 California Avenue

It swept the 1944 Academy Awards, winning Best Picture as well as Oscars for its star, Bing Crosby; its costar, Barry Fitzgerald; its writer and director, Leo McCarey; and one of its songs, "Swinging on a Star," by James Van Heusen and Johnny Burke. The film was *Going My Way* and although it was set in New York City, the two priests who are said to have inspired McCarey's screenplay were based in Santa Monica at this Mission Revival-style church on the corner of Seventh Street and California Avenue. The older priest (the Barry Fitzgerald character) was Monsignor Nicholas Conneally, who served as rector of St. Monica's from 1923 to 1949. The younger man (played by Bing Crosby) was Father John Siebert; he is now a Monsignor and is based at a parish in Fullerton, California.

12. THE GOLD COAST

Today, Malibu is the place that has Hollywood's star real estate as far as movie folk are concerned. But in the 1920s and 1930s, Santa Monica was where the stars all flocked and built lavish houses on the beach by the Pacific Ocean. Called the Gold Coast, the area along the Pacific Coast Highway directly below

William Randolph Hearst/Marion Davies Santa Monica beach house

Palisades Park and roughly between the Santa Monica Pier and Marguerita Street still has many of the original star homes of Santa Monica's most glamorous days.

Hard to miss is Cary Grant's former Gold Coast mansion. A half-timbered number with a bright orange tiled roof, it stands alone between two parking lots at 1038 Pacific Coast Highway (aka Ocean Front Road and Palisades Beach Road) with public parking lots on either side of it. For a while during the 1930s, Cary shared the place with fellow bachelor, Randolph Scott. The studios were reportedly less than thrilled with this living arrangement. Prior to Grant, the house belonged to Norma Talmadge and her husband Joe Schenck.

A good half mile further north (at approximately where the pedestrian walkway joins the Palisades Park with the street and beach below), number 707 Pacific Coast Highway is another handsome neo-Elizabethan house. It was here where MGM's second-in-command, production head Irving Thalberg, lived with his wife, MGM star Norma Shearer. The couple was married in 1927, built their beach house in 1931.

MGM's number-one man, Louis B. Mayer, had his Santa Monica palazzo not far from the Thalberg/Shearer property at 625 Pacific Coast Highway. Mayer employed his studio's top art director, Cedric Gibbons, to decorate the neoclassic Mediterranean villa. Equipped with a soundproof projection booth, Mayer's living room was frequently used to preview the latest MGM picture, the movie screen rising dramatically up from the living room floor. It is said that one of the first screenings of *Gone with the Wind* took place here. Some years later, another MGM name—actor Peter Lawford—owned the former Mayer villa and lived there with his then wife, Patricia Kennedy. JFK and RFK were frequent guests at the Lawfords and it is rumored that one

Louis B. Mayer's former beach house

Mae West's former Gold Coast house

or the other (or both) of these Kennedy gentlemen romanced Marilyn Monroe here in the early 1960s.

A few doors away, Harry Warner of Warner Brothers lived lavishly at numbers 605 and 607—which together formed one large residence. Before Warner, pioneer producer and a founder of Paramount Pictures, Jesse Lasky, built the original house at 607 as an addition to his large home (now gone) at 609.

Jesse Lasky's former partner, Samuel Goldwyn, built the mansion with the three garages at number 602. Later, the same house was occupied by producer/director Mervyn (*The Wizard of Oz*) LeRoy as well as by the Academy Award-winning writer and director of *Going My Way,* Leo McCarey.

Twentieth Century-Fox was represented on the Gold Coast at number 546—which was where the studio's long-time head, Darryl Zanuck, spent his beach time. Meanwhile, William Goetz—who was an important producer at Fox as well as Louis B. Mayer's son-in-law—was steps away from the Zanuck house at number 522. The Goetz house was designed by architect Wallace Neff, who also designed Douglas Fairbanks and Mary Pickford's Pickfair.

An even bigger name in architecture was responsible for designing Mae West's streamlined home at number 514. The architect: Richard Neutra, one of America's most important and innovative "modern" architects. Mae didn't even like the beach, indeed feared even the smallest amount of direct sunlight lest it flaw her alabaster skin. Still, she spent a fair amount of time at her seaside digs, since her companion of the last twenty-five years of her life, muscleman Paul Novak, preferred the beach to Miss West's opulent Hollywood apartment at Ravenswood. In town or by the sea, Mae knew what she wanted as far as decor went—and did up her Santa Monica residence with the same Louis XIV flash, the same gold, white, and cream colors of her apartment.

Next door to Mae's place, writer Anita (*Gentlemen Prefer Blondes*) Loos once lived in another attractive moderne manse—number 506—with her writer/producer husband John Emerson. A bit further down the beach, Harold Lloyd and his family had the Colonial "cottage" at number 443.

Last, but most assuredly not least, comes The Sand and Sea Club at number 415. It was formerly the servants quarters of the Gold Coast's grandest estate: the 118-room compound of Georgian buildings called "Ocean House" which all belonged to Marion Davies and William Randolph Hearst. Designed around 1926 by Julia Morgan, the Hearst/Davies headquarters consisted of a three-story main house, three guest houses, servants quarters, tennis courts, swimming pools (one spanned by a Venetian marble footbridge). Just as Hearst had done at his "ranch" at San Simeon, he imported whole rooms from fabulous European villas to be rebuilt at Ocean House. For parties—which sometimes had guest lists in the thousands!—Miss Davies would bring together the orchestras of several of L.A.'s top hotels, install carrousels, constantly create ingenious costume themes. Hollywood has never seen anything like the entertaining that went on here, before or since. When Hearst and Davies finally sold Ocean House (even Marion had come to call it a "white elephant" by that time) in the 1940s, the great estate went for a mere $600,000. Besides its initial cost in the millions of dollars, Marion said that she had spent another $7 million on the place during the fifteen or so years she had actively used it. After its sale, Ocean House became a beach club, later a hotel—until most of it was demolished in the mid-1950s. Today, all that is left of the grandest beach house ever built in California are the servants quarters. But even they provide a hint at what life was once like along Santa Monica's legendary Gold Coast.

NOTE: *There are several ways to see the Gold Coast. The most satisfying is to do it on foot, which allows movie lovers to look at many of the mansions from both the street and the beach. Naturally, the occupants should* never *be disturbed! Another way to see the same houses is from Palisades Park, which overlooks the Gold Coast from the cliffs above. From this vantage point, it's possible to get an even better idea of the scale, the layout, the green lawns, guest houses, and pools of some of these fabulous Santa Monica showplaces.*

13. SALKA VIERTEL HOUSE
165 Mabery Road

She collaborated on the screenplays of a number of Garbo's films, including *Queen Christina, Anna Karenina,* and *Conquest.* She also was one of Garbo's few close Hollywood friends—and the friendship lasted until her death in Switzerland in 1978. Her name was Salka Viertel and in the 1930s and 1940s, she and her husband, director Berthold Viertel, had this pretty little place on a beautiful street leading down to the Pacific in an area known as the Santa Monica Canyon. This part of Santa Monica—with its ocean views and lush vegetation—has long been a favorite of English and European expatriates, many of whom once gathered at the Viertel house on a regular basis. Besides Garbo, those who frequented the Viertels were Bertolt Brecht, Igor Stravinsky, Thomas Mann, Aldous Huxley, and Christopher Isherwood (who still lives in the neighborhood).

In his book, *Tales from the Hollywood Raj* (Viking Press, 1984), Sheridan Morley quotes from the diary of a British actress on holiday in Hollywood in the 1930s. Of her dinner party at the Viertel's, the actress had this to say: " 'Please do not dress up,' warned my hostess, 'and do not tell anyone you have been invited. Greta loathes meeting strangers and might not come.' . . . She appeared at the door, witch's hat tilted over her forehead, and because the famous dark glasses were missing I saw her eyes boring into mine. Salka rushed forward crying, 'Greta, darling.' But Greta darling turned on her flat heels and vanished into the darkness with her hostess in hot pursuit. Shamelessly we bent our ears to catch a few words of the low-voiced altercation in the garden. Presently footsteps were heard but Mrs. Viertel reappeared alone and, pointing an accusing finger at me, said, 'You stupid girl, it's all your fault. I told you to stay on the couch where Greta would not be able to see you.' "

Just another fun evening at Salka's.

14. WILL ROGERS STATE PARK
14253 Sunset Boulevard

The 187-acre Pacific Palisades estate of Will Rogers offers a glimpse of Hollywood at its most genteel. This is where the most civilized of picture people came on weekends to ride horses and to play polo on Rogers' 300 × 900-foot polo field. Old Hollywood's leading polo people were director Fred Niblo, Leslie Howard, Jack Warner, Spencer Tracy, Darryl Zanuck, Walter Wanger,

Will Rogers' ranch house

Robert Montgomery, Clarence Brown, Hal Roach, Walt Disney, Leo Carrillo, and, naturally, Will Rogers.

A former rodeo performer and later a Ziegfeld comedy star, Rogers came to Hollywood in 1919 to work for Samuel Goldwyn. At first, the "Cowboy Philosopher" had only moderate success in silent films—but once the great American humorist got on the radio and into the talkies, his career soared. Rogers, an important figure in early Beverly Hills, bought his Pacific Palisades "ranch" in 1922 as a country place. In 1928, he moved there permanently with his wife and three children. He died eight years later at the age of fifty-five in the same plane crash that killed his famous globe-circling aviator friend, Wiley Post. Upon the death of Rogers' wife in 1944, the property became a state park.

NOTE: *The Will Rogers State Park is open daily (except Thanksgiving, Christmas, and New Year's Day) from 8 to 5. It has hiking trails, picnic areas, and tours of Rogers' perfectly preserved thirty-one-room ranchhouse that is filled with mementos of his career. Besides the fact that this beautiful house and property are open to the public, another tribute to Will Rogers is the polo that is still played here on weekends. Sometimes, too, it's possible to catch a match that features the New Hollywood crowd (Sylvester Stallone, William Devane, Stefanie Powers) that's recently revived Hollywood's polo tradition. Admission to the park and the polo matches is free, although there is a parking fee as well as a charge for the house tour.*

15. THELMA TODD'S SIDEWALK CAFE SITE
17575 Pacific Coast Highway

Hollywood whodunit: About three miles north of Santa Monica's "Gold Coast," an attractive Spanish building with a tiled roof edges the east side of the Pacific Coast Highway. Back

Thelma Todd cafe site in the 1940s

in the mid-1930s, the building housed Thelma Todd's Beach Sidewalk Cafe, a racy roadhouse that was co-owned by a well-known movie comedienne named Thelma Todd. Thirty years old, Miss Todd had played wisecracking blonds opposite the Marx Brothers in *Monkey Business* (1931) and *Horse Feathers* (1932), had also appeared with Harry Langdon as well as Laurel and Hardy in several films, and had starred in a series of comedies that paired her with Zasu Pitts and later Patsy Kelly.

So much for the bio. On the night of December 14, 1935, Miss Todd had been guest of honor at a glamorous Hollywood party at the Trocadero nightclub. The party was hosted by comedian Stanley Lupino, father of actress Ida Lupino—who was also one of the guests. According to newspaper accounts at the time, Miss Todd was driven back to her home—it was located just above her restaurant—at around 4:20 a.m. on Sunday morning. The chauffeur supposedly dropped his passenger off in front of the restaurant and left her to negotiate the steps to her house on her own.

On Monday morning, "The Ice Cream Blonde" was discovered by her maid in her garage. She was still wearing her gown of Saturday evening, her diamonds, and her fur coat. She was seated at the driver's seat of her Lincoln Phaeton touring car—and she was dead. Although her face was streaked with blood, the coroner's report listed carbon monoxide poisoning as the cause of death. It was also decided that the bizarre demise of Thelma Todd was an accident.

To this day, Hollywood has thought otherwise. There were just too many unanswered questions, too many inconsistencies. For one thing, police ascertained that Miss Todd died at around 5:00 a.m. on Sunday morning. Yet, there were witnesses who claimed to have seen her driving her Lincoln on Sunday afternoon in the company of a "dark" gentleman companion. Another friend of Miss Todd's went on record as having spoken on the phone with her friend on that same Sunday afternoon; this same woman went on to say that she had invited Miss Todd to a party which she had agreed to attend.

What really happened? One theory pins the blame for Miss Todd's death on the Mafia who were said to have wanted to install an illicit gambling operation upstairs at Thelma's restaurant. When Miss Todd didn't play ball with the mob, they snuffed her out. A more widely believed explanation of the Todd case lists the prime suspect in this great unsolved mystery as Miss Todd's manager, business partner, and supposed lover. The man's name was Roland West and he had, among other things, made a living in Hollywood directing thrillers. Was Thelma Todd's murder his ultimate achievement? Whatever happened back in December of 1935, it would have made a marvelous movie.

P.S.: In recent years, the building that once housed Thelma Todd's Roadside Rest has been used as a center for the production of religious films.

*Aerial view of Malibu
in the 1930s*

16. MALIBU

In 1981, producer/director Blake Edwards took the ultimate
of satirical looks at the oddities and excesses of "New Hollywood"
in the film *S.O.B.* A sign of the times was that virtually none of
S.O.B. took place in Hollywood—or even in Beverly Hills.
Instead, almost all the action is centered in and around Malibu.
About ten miles north of Santa Monica along the Pacific Coast
Highway, this beach-edging township has some twenty miles of
coastline and somewhere between 12,000 and 15,000 property
owners. It also has far and away the greatest concentration of
movie celebrities of any area of greater Los Angeles—or of the
world, for that matter. Malibu residents include literally anybody
who is anybody in today's motion picture/television/recording
industries. Julie Andrews and Blake Edwards, Johnny Carson,
Farrah Fawcett, Ryan O'Neal, Larry Hagman, Goldie Hawn,
Dustin Hoffman, Jack Lemmon, Ali MacGraw, Shirley MacLaine,
Olivia Newton-John, Robert Redford, Linda Ronstadt, Steven
Spielberg, Barbra Streisand—all call Malibu home, for either all
or part of the year.

The cost of even the simplest house is rarely under $1
million and sometimes can be as much as $10 million. Many
people rent—and some pay between $10,000 and $15,000 a
month for the privilege of a Malibu maison. But nobody who
lives here complains—not even about the fact that Malibu has
no sewer system. Besides the beach and the rugged mountains

just behind it, the lures of Malibu are clean air, privacy, informality, and that heady feeling of knowing that you're living in the *only* place there is to be in Los Angeles.

For sightseers, Malibu can be an elusive place, since so many of its beaches and star compounds are private. If this star community has a center, it might be the area known as the Colony. At the junction of the Pacific Coast Highway and Webb Way (just before the Malibu Canyon Road), the Colony is an ultra-exclusive enclave of beach houses that is guarded by gates, barrier reefs, and a large security force. Movie lovers who venture into the small shopping center that is on the "public" side of the Colony gates may catch Dyan Cannon at the market, Goldie Hawn at the pharmacy, Burt Reynolds at the bank. The more intrepid might drive by the back sides of some of the Colony's houses along Malibu Road. The house with six—count 'em, folks, six!—garages was formerly Jack Warner's and recently belonged to L.A. lawyer Paul Ziffren. Bing Crosby once lived at number 1 Malibu Colony—as did Robert Redford. The Colony Crowd also includes Larry Hagman, Linda Ronstadt, Michael Landon.

Malibu is not just the Colony. It includes private and semiprivate (depending on the tides) clusters of beach properties both to the south (at La Costa and Carbon beaches) and to the north. These days, it seems, the further one ventures north, the choicer the address. Especially fashionable now are Paradise Cove, Point Dune, Broad Beach, Trancas Beach, Encinal Bluffs, Nicholas Cove. But the poshest Malibu pads of all are not by the beaches—but rather in the canyons. Recent Queen of the Canyons was B. Streisand, who—with former boyfriend Jon Peters—owned a sizable tract in Ramirez Canyon. Here, they had five houses and presided over a great estate that rivaled those built by some of Hollywood's silent superstars. Once the romance ended, however, each partner repaired to her/his houses and side of the property line.

Another famous canyon dweller is Jack Nicholson—who is said to own a good half of Decker Canyon off Yerba Buena Road almost at the Ventura County line. And then there's John Travolta who's gone so fashionably far north that his secluded ranch is on the outskirts of Santa Barbara! Still, he wasn't the first Hollywood celebrity to have that idea—his neighbors, the Ronald Reagans, have been there for years! It's a long way from Hollywood—but it's Hollywood all the same.

17. MALIBU CREEK STATE PARK
Las Virgenes Road

In 1940, director John Ford was all set to lens Richard Llewellyn's best-selling novel, *How Green Was My Valley,* for Twentieth Century-Fox. All Ford needed was a coal mining town in Wales. Needless to say, this was in the days when going on location overseas was practically unheard of—not to mention the

M*A*S*H set at Malibu Creek State Park

fact that World War II was in full swing in Europe. So, instead of going to Wales, Ford and Fox created a Welsh village in the Los Virgenes Canyon behind Malibu. The land used belonged at the time to a very exclusive mountaineering/country club called the Crags Mountain Club. In 1942, Fox again used the Canyon for *My Friend Flicka;* and by 1946, the studio had bought some 2300 acres of the property from the club and renamed it the Century Ranch.

The area making up the former Century Ranch is one of the most beautiful of Southern California and has been used over the last forty years by Fox as well as by other studios to depict the Old West, the jungles of Africa and Asia, foreign countries, alien planets. Some of the best-known Fox films that have been partially shot at the Century Ranch are *Viva Zapata* (1952), *The Rains of Ranchipur* (1955), *Love Is a Many-Splendored Thing* (1955), *Love Me Tender* (1959), *The Sand Pebbles* (1966), *Dr. Dolittle* (1967), *Planet of the Apes* (1968), *Beneath the Planet of the Apes* (1969), *Butch Cassidy and the Sundance Kid* (1969), *Tora! Tora! Tora!* (1970), *M*A*S*H* (1970), *Battle for the Planet of the Apes* (1973), *The Towering Inferno* (1974).

Non-Fox films done at the Ranch include: *Mr. Blandings Builds His Dream House* (RKO 1948), *Ma and Pa Kettle* (Universal-International 1949), numerous MGM *Tarzans*, *How the West Was Won* (MGM 1962), and *Finian's Rainbow* (Warner Seven Arts 1970). Television has also used the ranch extensively—with "Daniel Boone," "Custer," "Lancer," "Adventures in Paradise," and the long-long-running TV version of "M*A*S*H" among the many series that have shot sequences here.

Although the Century Ranch became a State Park in 1974

(Twentieth Century-Fox sold it to the State of California that year for $4.8 million), the land is still frequently used for filming. For movie lovers, the most interesting vestiges of the park's cinematic past are the house that portrayed Cary Grant's and Myrna Loy's ideal Connecticut country place in *Mr. Blandings Builds His Dream House* (it was built as a "real" house for a studio exec and still sits above the Camping Center near the Park's entrance), the Rock Pool—veteran of many a jungle and Western adventure, the Visitors Center—which has a display of "M*A*S*H" memorabilia as well as photos of famous films and television shows shot at the Century Ranch, the Reagan Picnic Area—named after its famous former owners, and "M*A*S*H's" Korean/Southern Californian hills.

NOTE: *Malibu Creek State Park is open daily from 8 to sunset. The area is vast: the Visitor Center with its "M*A*S*H" exhibit is almost a mile from the parking lot at the gatehouse; the Rock Pool is 1.1 miles from the same spot; the "M*A*S*H" hills, 2.5 miles; and the Reagan Picnic Area, 3.5 miles. To really enjoy Malibu Creek State Park, movie lovers should wear sturdy shoes, bring a picnic, and buy the map that is for sale at the main gate.*

When coming from Malibu, the easiest way to reach Malibu Creek State Park is to turn right off the Pacific Coast Highway at Malibu Canyon Road, head north for about five miles until the road merges with Las Virgenes Road. The Park entrance is another half-mile to the north. The ranch can also be reached from the San Fernando Valley by taking the Ventura Freeway to the Las Virgenes Road exit, then heading south along Las Virgenes.

Mr. Blandings' "dream house" at Malibu Creek State Park

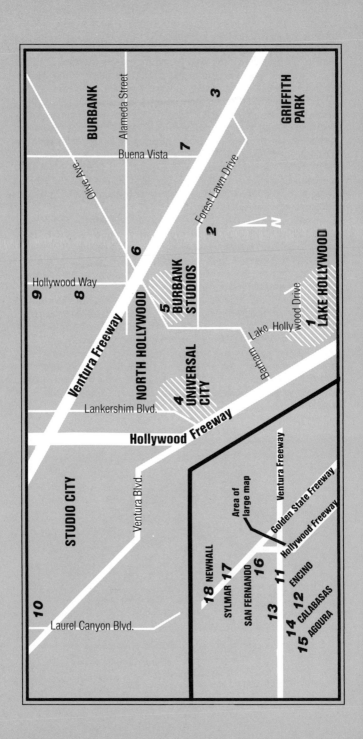

SAN FERNANDO VALLEY

The Big Spread

John Wayne, king of the Hollywood Wild West

THERE is Los Angeles ... and there is The Valley. The latter, roughly speaking, is everything on the other side of the Santa Monica mountains and Hollywood Hills—i.e., the seemingly endless sprawl of mostly middle-class communities characterized by tract houses, shopping centers, right-wing politics, "Valley Girls," and—surprise—movie studios! In fact, what with Disney, Columbia, Universal, Warner Brothers, CBS-MTM, and NBC Television all based in San Fernando Valley towns, the Valley is today responsible for more moviemaking and television production than any other area of Los Angeles.

The first moviemaker to see the potential of this vast and, at the time, sparsely populated stretch of countryside was Carl Laemmle, the founder of Universal. Laemmle came to California from New York in 1912 and first operated out of Hollywood. When success enabled him to build the studio of his dreams, he found the perfect location for it on the other side of the Hollywood Hills in the township of Lankershim. There, in 1914, he turned a 230-acre chicken ranch into the legendary Universal City. First National was another early film company to cross over the Hollywood Hills and into the Valley when it built a big studio in Burbank in 1918. Warner Brothers eventually bought out First National and the same Burbank lot has been Warner Brothers' headquarters ever since.

As Los Angeles prospered in the 1920s and its population and real-estate values soared, the Valley—which was developed several decades later than Los Angeles proper—became an extremely attractive "Hollywood" alternative for many studios. When Mack Sennett outgrew his Silverlake facilities in the late 1920s, for example, he didn't look for another lot in crowded Silverlake or Hollywood but instead headed for the wide open spaces of Studio City. A decade later, Walt Disney followed suit and moved from Silverlake to Burbank. At the same time, a number of Hollywood studios established and maintained annexes in the Valley; these were called "ranches" and, appropriately, were often used for the production of Western films. Not to be outdone, stars and moguls purchased Valley ranches, too, and horsey weekends in the country became the rage.

Today, not only the studios but some of the movie ranches in the San Fernando Valley are still going strong. Of particular interest to the movie lover is the fact that two of the greatest studios—Universal and Warner Brothers—are open to the public. In addition, NBC also offers a tour of its television complex. Besides studios, the Valley has other fascinating and sometimes off-beat connections to movie history. A few of them: the ranch that a great silent star willed to his community as a public park ... the housing development that once was Clark Gable's estate ... the battlefield of *The Birth of a Nation* ... and a cemetery where some of the most famous pets in Hollywood are lavishly laid to rest.

NOTE: *Both the Burbank Studios (home to Warner Brothers*

and also Columbia) Tour and the Universal Tour will take a good half day each. Before or after either of these tours would be a good time to cover items 1, 2, 6, 7, 8, and 9—all nearby. Items 10, 11, 12, 13, 14, and 15 are farther afield and should be seen separately—as should items 16, 17, and 18.

1. LAKE HOLLYWOOD

One of the biggest surprises in the Hollywood Hills, Lake Hollywood is the name of the reservoir formed by the Mulholland Dam which was built in 1925. The Dam is named—as is the Hollywood Hills' main East-West roadway—for William Mulholland, the head of the Los Angeles Water Department in the early part of the twentieth century and the man who engineered the aqueduct that brought water to Los Angeles and to the San Fernando Valley from some 233 miles away in the Owens Valley. The story of how certain unscrupulous speculators tricked the farmers of the Owens Valley into giving up their water rights so that real-estate fatcats in L.A. could get rich is one of the ugliest in the history of Los Angeles.

The 1974 Academy Award-winning film, *Chinatown,* takes on this very subject and fictionalizes the corrupt games that developers played with government officials in order to bring water to their real estate. Although fiction, it is interesting to note that in this grizzly Roman Polanski-directed film, the character of the Los Angeles water commissioner is named Hollis Mulwray—and you don't have to be Agatha Christie to figure what *Chinatown's* writer, Robert Towne, may have been getting at.

Chinatown even uses Lake Hollywood as a location. Early on in the picture, the aforementioned Hollis Mulwray is found dead along the shores of the lake the real William Mulholland

Lake Hollywood

D. W. Griffith directing real Civil War veterans in Birth of a Nation
battle scene, 1915

helped create. The same location also provides drama for another
1974 movie—*Earthquake.* In this Universal disaster epic, the
Mulholland Dam cracks open, spilling millions of gallons of water
down into a city that's already having a pretty rough go of things.

The irony of it all is that despite its history—both in real life
and in the movies—Lake Hollywood is an extremely beautiful
spot where locals can be found jogging around its fenced-in
shores. One of the easiest ways to reach the lake is to take Lake
Hollywood Drive off of Barham Boulevard on the north (Burbank)
side of the Hollywood Hills. Beyond the lake, the road leads to
some of the best views of the Hollywood sign.

2. FOREST LAWN
6300 Forest Lawn Drive, Burbank

Smaller and not nearly as impressive as its cousin in Glendale,
the Hollywood Hills branch of this famous Southern California
funeral institution celebrates America. Here, a 30-foot-high/165-
foot-long mosaic—"the largest historical mosaic in the world"—
is a composite of twenty-five famous paintings depicting major
events in early American history, from "George Washington
Crossing the Delaware" to "The Spirit of '76." Here, too, are
full-sized replicas of historic American places of worship: Boston's
Old North Church and Henry Wadsworth Longfellow's Church
of the Hills meeting house in New England.

For movie lovers, the hillside on which Forest Lawn has
been built has its own special place in history—not in the history
of America, but of American film. For it was here that in 1915,
D. W. Griffith shot most of the battle sequences for his own epic
look at the country, *The Birth of a Nation.* Veteran cameraman
Karl Brown, in his *Adventures with D. W. Griffith* (Farrar, Straus

& Giroux, 1973) was there for the filming and describes the location as "ideal . . . photographically. A sort of ridge of high ground curved around the rim of a gently descending slope of clear ground that ran down to where the dry-as-dust riverbed of the Los Angeles River lay baking in the sun. There were little clumps of trees clustered on both sides of this open area, with small hills rounding up here and there in the background to provide splendid location for artillerymen to rake the field with grape and canister, the two favorite close-range charges of the Civil War cannoneers.

"Not only the geography but the orientation of the field happened to be perfect. When shooting big stuff you must shoot either north or south, never east or west. On this location all the camera angles from the ridge would be shooting north, which meant cross light from the right during the morning, and from the left throughout the afternoon. A flat, dead-on light is no good because the shadows fall away back of the subject and there is no modeling, while a back light is murderous when there's any smoke in the air, because the smoke blinds everything and you can't see what's going on in the background."

Today, even when viewed from the road, the hillside looks just as Brown describes it.

NOTE: *Besides seeing where* The Birth of a Nation *was shot, a visit to Forest Lawn Hollywood Hills will also permit movie fans to see where Buster Keaton, Charles Laughton, Stan Laurel, Ernie Kovacs, Dan Duryea, and Freddie Prinze are laid to rest. Hours: 9 to 5, daily.*

3. LOS ANGELES EQUESTRIAN CENTER
480 Riverside Drive, Burbank

In the old days, the cream of Old Hollywood played polo at the Uplifters Club, Will Rogers' Ranch, and the Riviera Country Club. The polo set, headed by Will Rogers, included Darryl Zanuck, Walt Disney, Walter Wanger, Robert Montgomery, Gary Cooper, Hal Roach, Clarence Brown, Wallace Beery, and Leo Carrillo. Gable would have played, too, but his MGM contract forbade it. Spencer Tracy's did as well—but he often got around this by playing under the alias of Ivan Catchanozoff.

Today, practically fifty years later, New Hollywood has suddenly rediscovered polo—and is currently going at it with a vengeance. The place to catch polo now in L.A. is the 4000-seat "Equidome" at Griffith Park's Equestrian Center. The players to watch: Sylvester Stallone, Frank Stallone, Alex Cord, William Devane, producer Dan (*Footloose*) Melnick—not to mention top women riders Stephanie Powers and Barbie McQueen. Besides all the celebs on the field, many more can be seen in the box seats.

NOTE: *Matches are held Saturday evenings. For information, call: (818) 841-5981.*

The Universal Tour, 1975

4. UNIVERSAL STUDIOS
100 Universal City Plaza, Universal City

All over Southern California, huge billboards, TV and radio commercials, and newspaper and magazine ads proclaim the Universal Studios Tour. More than a tourist attraction, the Universal Tour has become a Hollywood institution—since for more than twenty years, it has been one of the few recognized places in town where the glamour and excitement of moviemaking have been packaged for public consumption. Whereas all (with the exception of one) of the other major studios do their best to keep the public on the other side of their walls and gates, Universal welcomes the world with open arms and cash registers. The tour—now drawing some 3 million visitors annually—makes the studio millions of dollars and now ranks with the Disney theme parks as among the most popular tourist attractions that people pay to see in the country, In fact, its tour is so lucrative that Universal is taking a cue from the Disney people and has tentative plans to recreate the whole thing in Orlando, Florida, in the near future.

Serious movie buffs may find the Universal Tour too commercial—but if one overlooks the fluff, it can be amusing and informative. Riding with 175 other people in a Super Tram, one not only gets a closeup look at the largest back lot left in Los Angeles, but is also treated to a whole series of crowd-pleasing "extras." During the two-hour ride, the tram is held captive inside a giant alien spaceship (inspired by the Universal TV series, "Battlestar Galactica"), attacked by "Jaws," flash-flooded, caught in an avalanche, stuck on a collapsing bridge—to name just a few of the movie-lot special effects programmed for the tour.

One of the most interesting segments of the tour is the stop at soundstages 30 and 32. Here, histories and explanations of numerous movie special effects—from matte painting to computer

Tourists watch a Harry Carey Western being shot at Universal in 1916

animation—are presented by tour guides as well as by Robert Wagner, who is present via the magic of mixed media.

After the tour is over, there's still more for the intrepid sightseer to experience at Universal—what with some five live-action shows being performed nonstop by actors, stunt people, trained animals, ghoulish monsters, and magicians. One of the newest of these shows—"The Adventures of Conan"—is billed as a "Sword and Sorcery Spectacular" and features Conan and his gal-pal Red Sonjia fighting off lasers, fireballs, evil sorcerers, and an 18-foot-tall fire-breathing dragon.

Today's wildly successful Universal Studios Tour began in 1963 when the studio management decided to boost business at the commissary by allowing a tour company to drive tourists around the lower back lot and then drop them off at the commissary for lunch. The following year, the tour debuted in earnest. However the tradition of allowing the public on the Universal lot actually goes back all the way to 1915. At that time, Universal's founder, Carl Laemmle, had just turned a 230-acre chicken ranch into his studio. Besides making movies, the enterprising Mr. Laemmle made even more money by letting the locals sit in bleachers he had set up around some of the outdoor stages. Here, for 25 cents a head, anyone could watch directors of the day putting actors through their paces.

Extremely popular back in those days were Universal's Westerns, which together with adventure reels comprised much of the studio's early product. The top stars in Universal's early years were Hoot Gibson, Mae Murray, Laura LaPlante, and Priscilla Dean. Directors included Erich von Stroheim, John Ford, and William Wyler (Laemmle's nephew). Universal was the studio where Irving Thalberg worked before moving over to MGM and where Columbia's Harry Cohn had his first job in the film business.

An early Universal standby was the "woman's picture."

Master of these early-thirties tearjerkers was director John Stahl. His most famous films—*Back Street* (1932), *Imitation of Life* (1934), and *Magnificent Obsession* (1935)—would all be remade at Universal by producer Ross Hunter in the fifties and sixties.

Universal's biggest contribution to the history of cinema, however, may well be its perfection of the Great American Horror Film. One of Universal's first big successes with this genre had Lon Chaney scaring the wits out of the world in *The Phantom of the Opera* (1925). Later, Bela *Dracula* Lugosi and Boris *Frankenstein* Karloff would join the studio's fright brigade.

In the mid-1930s, even Boris and Bela were unable to bail out the studio of some serious financial difficulties—and it would be a teenager named Deanna Durbin who saved Universal from bankruptcy with a string of light, low-budget musicals. More help came in the 1940s with the comedies of Bud Abbott and Lou Costello, the Arabian Nights romances of Jon Hall and Maria Montez, Basil Rathbone's *Sherlock Holmes* series, the *Ma and Pa Kettles,* and Donald O'Connor's numerous films that paired him with "Frances the Talking Mule."

By the end of the 1950s, however, Universal (now called Universal-International after a merger in 1946 with International Pictures) was again in financial trouble. It was saved this time by MCA—the talent agency that had become a very successful producer of television series. Needing more space for its television subsidiary, Revue Productions, MCA bought the Universal lot in 1959 and acquired the whole studio several years later.

Since then, Universal has been one of Hollywood's greatest success stories and that success is largely owing to its extensive involvement in television. In fact, so much went on at Universal in the 1960s and 1970s that this was the only studio in town that functioned like the traditional movie studio of Hollywood's grand days of the 1930s and 1940s. Until 1978, for example—long after all the other studios had dropped them—Universal still had a vital talent-development system that gave promising young actors and actresses the traditional seven-year contracts of Old Hollywood. Many of today's television stars grew up and out of the Universal contract system. Sharon Gless of "Switch," "Cagney and Lacy," and many a TV movie is a former Universal contract player—as are James Brolin, Katharine Ross, Gary Collins, Susan St. James, and Lee Majors.

Besides television, MCA-Universal has come on strong in the theatrical feature film department, too. Among the critical and/or commercial successes released through Universal over the last two decades are all of Alfred Hitchcock's later films (the *Psycho* house is one of the tour's top sights), *To Kill a Mockingbird, The Sting* (its Chicago street is another back-lot attraction), *Earthquake, Jaws, Animal House, On Golden Pond,* and *E.T.* Not to mention the studio's biggest success of all . . . its tour.

NOTE: *The Universal Studios Tour is given every day—except*

Psycho *house, Universal back lot*

Thanksgiving and Christmas—beginning at 10 weekdays and 9:30 weekends. In most instances, the last tram takes off at 3:30. Schedules may vary somewhat with the season. Presstime prices: $11.95, ages 12 and older; $8.95, ages 3 to 11; under 3, free; tickets for ages 55 and older discounted $2.50. Parking: $1.50 per car.

5. THE BURBANK STUDIOS
4000 Warner Boulevard, Burbank

If there's a best-kept secret in Hollywood, it may be the Burbank Studios' VIP tour—which, unlike other studios' VIP tours, is open to the public. The tour is expensive (currently $18), serious, limited to no more than twelve people, none of whom may be less than ten years old. For movie lovers, however, this tour is a must because it offers the rare opportunity to see the workings of one of Hollywood's most historic studios up close.

The history of The Burbank Studios began in 1918 when the lot was built by First National—an important early film company that featured the talents of Norma Talmadge, Constance Talmadge, Corinne Griffith, Anita Stewart, Hedda Hopper, Charles Chaplin, Buster Keaton, Pola Negri, Colleen Moore, Richard Barthelmess, Jackie Coogan, Barbara La Marr, Mary Astor, Nazimova, Ronald Colman, and Mickey McGuire (later Rooney).

In 1927, after Warner Brothers had revolutionized the motion picture industry with the sound success of *The Jazz Singer,* they took over First National and spent millions redoing the studio's Burbank lot for talkies. Thus, from the late 1920s up until the present, the history of the Burbank Studios is largely the history of Warner Brothers. (The studio was renamed the Burbank Studios in 1972 when Columbia Pictures abandoned its Hollywood studios—and came to an agreement with Warner Brothers to combine some assets and share production facilities in Burbank; although Warners and Columbia now share the same lot, the two studios remain separate entities.)

In the 1930s, Warner Brothers was known for gangster films, serious social dramas, Busby Berkeley's black-and-white musicals, and Paul Muni's biography (Emile Zola, Louis Pasteur) pictures. The studio was also known for being able to turn out pictures of great technical polish on extremely tight budgets. Queen of the lot was Bette Davis—who in 1936 became embroiled in a history-making legal battle with the studio when she refused to do roles the studio demanded she play. Although Miss Davis lost in court, she ultimately won the respect of the Brothers Warner and continued to be the studio's top star. Other big names at Warner Brothers in the 1930s were Humphrey Bogart, James Cagney, Edward G. Robinson, Errol Flynn, Joan Blondell, Ann Sheridan, Olivia De Havilland, Dick Powell, and Marion Davies (whose fourteen-room MGM "bungalow" was moved from Culver City to Burbank when she changed studios in the mid-thirties).

In the forties, Ida Lupino, Paul Henreid, Ronald Reagan, John Garfield, Peter Lorre, Sidney Greenstreet, and Alexis Smith all became firmly entrenched in the Warner Brothers pantheon. It was also at Warners that Joan Crawford made her post-MGM "comeback" pictures, the most notable of these being *Mildred Pierce,* for which she won an Oscar in 1945. The late forties and early fifties was the era of the Doris Day Technicolor musical at the studio, and the mid-fifties saw James Dean achieve screen immortality with just three films (*East of Eden, Rebel Without a Cause,* and *Giant*), all done at Warner Brothers.

The Burbank Studios Tour, 1982

One of the great pleasures of the Burbank Studios VIP Tour is the chance to see the lot on which so many memorable Warner Brothers pictures were filmed. "French Street," for example, will bring back memories of the Paris flashbacks in *Casablanca*. The tidy small-town-America block of houses from *King's Row* (1941) is another delight; it was later used for *The Music Man* as well as for the TV series "The Waltons." More déjà vu at "Brownstone Street"—setting for innumerable gangster films in the thirties and forties. On the same movie-set street, the façades of two theaters have also appeared many times on screen—from the ping-pong sequence in *The House of Wax*, to *Auntie Mame's* ill-fated road show, to the "Born in a Trunk" theater in the Judy Garland *A Star Is Born*. Speaking of *A Star Is Born*, practically all of the Warner lot was used to represent the Oliver Niles Studios in the 1954 film: The building that was Norman Maine's dressing room was recently producer/director William Friedkin's office; the payroll window where Esther Blodgett found her name changed to Vicki Lester is now the studio's credit union.

Besides seeing back lots, prop warehouses, scene and costume shops, the VIP Tour goes—whenever possible—onto "live" soundstages where films or TV sit-coms are being shot. If any "scoring" is being done at the time of the tour, the participants will be taken into a soundproof control room to witness how technicians match the music of a live orchestra (on the other side of the glassed-in room) to a film sequence that is projected over the heads of the musicians. It's a fascinating process—and one that outsiders are rarely permitted to see. Which is the whole point to this extremely interesting and worthwhile look into the innerworkings of Hollywood.

NOTE: *The Burbank Studios' VIP Tour is given at 10 and 2, Monday through Friday. In summer, two additional tours take off at 10:30 and 2:30. The current cost is $18 per person—and no children under ten years old are permitted. Reservations are necessary and should be made several weeks in advance—although last-minute openings occasionally occur. For those taking the tour in the morning, an added treat is the possibility of having lunch in the studio commissary, "The Blue Room." Reservations for lunch on the lot should be made when booking the tour. Call: (818) 954-1744.*

6. NBC TELEVISION STUDIOS
3000 West Alameda Avenue, Burbank

Welcome to "Beautiful Downtown Burbank!" Fans of Rowan and Martin's "Laugh-In" will remember that this expression put both the town of Burbank and its NBC TV studios on the map back in the late 1960s. In addition to the "Laugh-In" connection, audiences may also know of NBC's Burbank base through its long-time association with "The Tonight Show."

Designed to let the public experience its studios first-hand,

Postcard view of Warner Brothers in the 1930s

NBC offers a ninety-minute tour of its facilities. Billed as a "totally unstaged tour of a giant broadcasting complex," this walk around NBC covers dressing rooms, set construction and wardrobe departments, news rooms, plus visits to a number of studios—including the surprisingly tiny one used for "The Tonight Show."

NOTE: *The tour is offered daily, every half hour between 9 and 4, weekdays; 10 and 4, Saturdays; 10 and 2, Sundays. Cost: $4.50 for adults, $3.25 for children. No tours are given on Thanksgiving, Christmas, or New Year's Day. For tickets to television shows originating from the NBC Burbank Studios, the ticket counter at NBC is open from 8:30 to 5:30, Monday through Friday, and from 9:30 to 4, Saturday and Sunday. Tickets for "The Tonight Show" are available only on the day of the show and are distributed on a first-come first-served basis—so it is essential to be at the booth early. For further information, the number to call is (818) 840-3537.*

7. WALT DISNEY PRODUCTIONS
500 South Buena Vista, Burbank

Mickey and the gang moved from Walt's small headquarters on Hyperion Avenue in Silverlake to this big (51 acres) Burbank studio in 1940. Mickey, however, had nothing to do with the move. Blame it all on *Snow White*—for it was the tremendous success of this first-ever feature-length animated film that enabled the Disney Brothers (Walt was the artist, Roy the businessman) to greatly expand their operations.

The new Burbank studios were designed with artists in mind: Most rooms had windows that would admit only north light, and since drawing and sketching were such sedentary activities, there were ping-pong tables, horseshoes, and a volleyball court so that

Mickey Mouse stop sign at Disney Studio entrance

the Disney artists could exercise during breaks. According to Los Angeles artist and former Disney employee Tony Duquette, "All the best artists in town worked for Disney—especially during the Depression—because it was the one place where an artist could get paid for being an artist." It wasn't all idyllic, however, for in 1941, Disney animators went on strike, protesting the studio's authoritarian rule. A number of this group eventually resigned and went on to form a new company called United Productions of America.

Despite its labor problems at the beginning of the decade, Disney continued to flourish during the forties—with hits like *Dumbo, Bambi,* and *Song of the South.* Disney also became involved in nonanimated film projects and went on to produce such classic family fare as *Treasure Island, 20,000 Leagues Under the Sea, Old Yeller, Swiss Family Robinson, The Shaggy Dog* series, and *Mary Poppins.* When he died in 1966, Walt Disney had won more Academy Awards than any other individual in the history of the motion picture industry. His record number of twenty-seven Oscars still stands.

An important and historic studio, Walt Disney Productions is off-limits to tourists. In fact, nowhere on earth does Mickey Mouse look so fierce and unfriendly as at the gate of his Burbank studio where a stop sign depicts him as the toughest cop in town. But there's not much to see inside anyway: some soundstages, a small back lot, the original artists' buildings. The real Disney show—and a much friendlier Mickey Mouse—is down in Anaheim, some forty freeway minutes south of Burbank. There, the original Disneyland is Southern California's number-one attraction.

8. TBS-COLUMBIA RANCH
3701 West Oak Street, Burbank

For back-lot voyeurs, a walk around the high fence of this little-known movie ranch in the middle of a Burbank residential area will reveal such delights as a dilapidated train that's a veteran of numerous Western films, the tower of the Old North Church set from *1776,* and the unglamorous backs of all sorts of movie-set façades. Acquired by Harry Cohn's Columbia Studios in the late 1920s, the Columbia Ranch (as it was known up to the 1970s) was where the exterior sequences of many Columbia pictures—*Mr. Smith Goes to Washington, Mr. Deeds Goes to Town, You Can't Take It with You, The Three Stooges* series—were shot. It was here, too, where the plane-crash sequence of Frank Capra's *Lost Horizon* was lensed. Stanley Kramer's *High Noon* was also done here.

The ranch was especially important to Columbia in the 1950s when it came to be used heavily for television production. Columbia was the first of the major studios to meet the challenge of television head on. Whereas some studios tried to fight the new medium by not permitting their films to be sold to TV and, in some instances, not even allowing a television set to appear as a prop in their films—Columbia formed its Screen Gems division in 1949 with the expressed purpose of turning out product for the small screen. Some of the most famous TV series shot here were "Bewitched," "The Partridge Family," and "Leave It to Beaver." Today, the old Columbia Ranch is used by both Columbia and Warner Brothers as part of an arrangement in which they share studio facilities.

9. BURBANK-GLENDALE-PASADENA AIRPORT
2627 Hollywood Way, Burbank

Inaugurated in 1930, the Burbank Airport was L.A.'s major commercial air terminal up until 1947. It was then that most passenger carriers started using the larger Los Angeles Municipal Airport in Inglewood, which became today's Los Angeles International Airport.

But back to Burbank: First known as the United Air Terminal, this was the airport that all the chic and daring "prop-people" of the 1930s flew in and out of. Although highly fashionable in those days, plane travel—especially the transcontinental flights that most movie people made—was extremely rigorous. In 1932, for example, TWA's coast-to-coast routing went as follows: At 9:30 a.m., passengers would leave New York City aboard an eleven-passenger Ford Trimotor which stopped at Philadelphia, Harrisburg, Pittsburgh, Columbus, Indianapolis, before reaching Kansas City, where everyone spent the night. Next morning, the intrepid passengers reboarded their little plane (no in-flight meals, and blankets provided warmth) and continued on to Los Angeles via Amarillo, Albuquerque, and Winslow (Arizona), arriving at Burbank at 9:53 p.m. The trip wasn't cheap, either: A one-way ticket cost $288 in 1932—which in today's dollars would be in the neighborhood of $1850!

It was also in the 1930s that millionaire movie producer/aviator Howard Hughes used the Burbank Airport as a base for some of his considerable aeronautical experiments and exploits. Besides designing and redesigning aircraft at Burbank, Hughes set at least two world speed records flying out of the terminal. In 1936, he piloted a Northrup Gamma from Burbank to Newark, New Jersey, in a record nine hours and twenty-seven minutes. A year later, he again broke the transcontinental speed record—flying a plane of his own design called an "H1"—with a time of seven hours and twenty-eight minutes.

And then there was *Casablanca*. Movieland legends say that this classic film of intrigue and romance—set in North Africa but shot in Los Angeles at Warner Brothers' Burbank studios—used the Burbank Airport for that last tear-wrenching moment in which Humphrey Bogart doesn't fly away with Ingrid Bergman (but instead sends her off with Paul Henreid). Actually, according to Mr. Henreid himself, the foggy Moroccan tarmac was created on a Warner Brothers sound stage. Mr. Henreid and several historians do admit that the Burbank Airport may have been used for the long shot of the plane taking off—but no one knows for sure.

Casablanca or no, there's still something romantic about the Burbank Airport—with its glassed-in control tower and 1930s terminal building. They don't make airports like this any longer—just as they don't make films like *Casablanca.* "Here's looking at you, kid."

10. CBS-MTM STUDIO CENTER
4204 Radford Avenue, Studio City

His career had nowhere to go but down when Mack Sennett, "The King of Comedy," moved his studio from Silverlake to Studio City in the San Fernando Valley in 1927. And down it went: What with the triumph of the talkies as well as the rav-

*Outside Republic Studios
in the 1940s*

ages of the Great Depression, Sennett wound up selling his new studio in the early thirties and retiring from the industry a few years later.

Where Sennett failed, a man named Herbert J. Yates succeeded. It was in 1935 that Yates made the former Sennett studio the headquarters for his new Republic Pictures. A true motion picture factory, Republic turned out a constant stream of "B" pictures noted for their action, their surprisingly polished production values, and their predictable plots. Republic's trademark was the Western; and several of its stars of the 1930s and 1940s— Gene Autry, Roy Rogers, John Wayne—stand among Hollywood's legendary celluloid cowboys.

Another Republic property was the woman whose name is still one of filmdom's most unusual—Vera Hruba Ralston. A Czech skating star, Vera was Republic's answer to Twentieth Century-Fox's Sonja Henie. She was also Yates' girlfriend and he starred her in the studio's most lavish productions—such as *Lake Placid Serenade* (1944), *The Lady and the Monster* (1944) with Erich Von Stroheim, *Murder in the Music Hall* (1945), *The Fighting Kentuckian* (1949) with John Wayne. During her career, her name was changed several times—from Vera Hruba, to Vera Hruba Ralston, to Vera Ralston, and finally to Mrs. Herbert J. Yates in 1952.

After Republic went out of business in 1959, CBS took over the lot and used it for many TV series, including the long-long running "Gunsmoke" as well as "The Mary Tyler Moore Show." Today, as CBS-MTM (the MTM stands for Mary Tyler Moore productions), the lot is still used primarily for television—"Hill Street Blues," "St. Elsewhere," "Newhart."

NOTE: *CBS-MTM is closed to the public. A quick walk around the place offers a peek at its Western Street but the most interesting area to check out is the residential section of Studio City west of Radford Avenue. Here, edging tiny streets with names like Agnes, Gentry, and Ben, are lovely little homes and bungalows built to house studio personnel in the 1930s and 1940s. Another fascinating glimpse at how the real "Hollywood" once lived—and still does.*

11. CLARK GABLE ESTATES
4543 Tara Drive, Encino

In the 1930s, it was quite fashionable for picture people to have "ranches" in some of the small outlying communities of the San Fernando Valley. These ranged from vast tracts such as Jack and Harry Warner's race horse farm in Woodland Hills to Clark Gable's more modest 30-acre estate in Encino. More a Connecticut country place than a Western ranch, the "King of Hollywood's" Encino property was his L.A. home from the late 1930s up until his death in 1960.

In 1939, Gable brought his new bride and the love of his

Clark Gable and Carole Lombard's Encino ranch house

life, Carole Lombard, to live with him in Encino. They were Hollywood's ideal couple—adored by friends and gossip columnists alike. She had been married once before, he twice—but for the couple and for the world, this was the marriage that was going to last, the one made in heaven ... not Hollywood. And when Carole Lombard left Gable in January of 1942, it wasn't for another man—but for a cause: World War II ... a War Bond rally in her home state of Indiana. It was the last time they saw one another. On the flight home, Lombard was killed when her plane crashed near Las Vegas. Several months later, grief stricken as well as angry at the war that had taken his wife, Gable became one of Hollywood's first big leading men to enlist in the armed services. It is said that on his first home leave, his grief was still so painful that he couldn't face spending the night at the ranch—so he stayed in town.

After the war, Gable did return to Encino and went on to share his home there with two more wives, Lady Sylvia Ashley and Kay Williams Spreckles. The Gable-Ashley marriage (in 1949) lasted less than two years—but the Spreckles union (in 1955) endured for the rest of Gable's life. Felled by a heart attack a few months before the birth of his son in 1960, Gable never got to see his one and only child, John Clark. Mrs. Gable and son stayed on the Encino ranch until the early 1970s. Since then, the property has been subdivided into an expensive housing tract called Clark Gable Estates. The houses here—neo-Tudor, neo-Gothic, Plantation-moderne are the predominant architectural themes—are priced at as much as $1.5 million. New streets have been installed and given names such as Tara Drive and Ashley Oaks in honor of Gable's greatest film, *Gone with the Wind*. Tucked away behind a brick wall at 4543 Tara Drive, Gable's unpretentious home still stands in wonderful seclusion. Beyond Clark Gable Estates, there are more housing tracts, supermarkets, freeways—all a far cry from the peaceful little Encino of the 1930s where movie stars built ranches to get away from the hustle and bustle of Hollywood. Those days are gone ... with the wind.

12. MOTION PICTURE COUNTRY HOUSE AND HOSPITAL
23450 Calabasas Road, Woodland Hills

It's a pleasant place—47 green acres of gardens, plazas, low bungalow-style buildings, a chapel, and a hospital. Indeed, residents of the Motion Picture Country House have all they could ask for—except youth and, in many cases, good health. This has been the last stop in the careers of such Hollywood greats as Donald Crisp, Norma Shearer, Ellen Corby, Bruce Cabot, Herbert Marshall, Arthur O'Connell, Eddie ("Rochester") Anderson—all of whom lived and died here.

Residing at the Country House recently, the best known names have been Mary Astor, silent siren Viola Dana, Virginia Sale (*Oliver Twist, Topper*), screenwriter DeWitt Bodeen (*The Cat People*), and Mae Clark (*Frankenstein, The Front Page,* and *The Public Enemy,* in which Jimmy Cagney shoves a grapefruit in her face). Johnny Weissmuller was here too for a while—but had to be relocated when he started roaming the halls at all hours of the day and night, often letting loose with what was left of his "Tarzan" yell.

For those who are well and strong enough, activities abound at the Motion Picture Country House. One of the most popular is seeing movies at the Louis B. Mayer Memorial Theater—which shows two or three different films every week. There's also a Mr. and Mrs. L. B. Mayer Dining Room, a Cinema Beauty Salon, a John Ford Chapel, and a Samuel Goldwyn Plaza with shuffleboard and putting and croquet greens. Finally, there is show business— thanks to the many TV series such as "Quincy" and "Remington Steele" that not only use the institution as a location but often employ residents as extras. In the words of Mary Astor, "If you have to be institutionalized, this is the best."

13. SPCA PET MEMORIAL PARK
5068 North Old Scandia Lane, Calabasas

Mae West's monkey, Humphrey Bogart's cocker spaniel, Lionel Barrymore's dozen dogs and cats are all buried here—as are Tonto's horses, Good Scout and Smoke; Hopalong Cassidy's Topper; Valentino's dog, Kabar; and the "Our Gang" dog, Pete. Besides monkeys, dogs, horses, and cats, there are rabbits, birds, and at least one African lion among the 27,000 pets that have been interred here since the 1920s.

Burials are proper, often elaborate: Caskets with satin linings are available on the premises and many families make use of the "slumber room" for open-casket viewings of their dear departed doggies. The grave markers—all must be approved by the park— are often eye-grabbing and sometimes moving: "Who Is The Most Beautiful Girl? . . . Charlie Is." Some of the gravestones have likenesses of the animals embossed on the marble; others have Christian crosses or Jewish Stars of David; occasionally, there are inscriptions in Spanish. The grounds are well-tended and many of the graves are topped with fresh flowers.

NOTE: *The Park is open from 8 to 5, seven days a week. Not all of the celebrity animals' graves are marked—but the office staff is friendly and will direct visitors to those that are. To reach the Pet Memorial Park, take the Ventura Freeway West to the Calabasas Parkway exit.*

14. CALABASAS PARK GOLF CLUB
4515 Park Entrada, Calabasas

Built on land that once was part of the old Warner Brothers Ranch, this private golf and country club remembers its roots by naming holes on the golf course after some of the films that have been shot here: *Calamity Jane, Showboat, Stalag 17, High Noon, Carousel.* But moviemaking was only a sideline for the Warner Brothers at their ranch. The real purpose of the property was the raising of racehorses—a business that Harry and Jack Warner were passionately involved in along with Harry's son-in-law, Mervyn LeRoy of MGM. Thus when MGM needed a horsey locale for *National Velvet,* the Warner Ranch must have fit the bill perfectly. In fact, some of the barn buildings from the 1944 film can still be seen at the edge of the golf course.

Elizabeth Taylor in
National Velvet, *1944*

15. PARAMOUNT RANCH
2813 Cornell Road, Agoura

An unusual and cooperative venture between the Department of the Interior and the film industry, the Paramount Ranch is a working movie ranch administered by the National Park Service and open to the public. On any given weekday, visitors will not only be able to hike, picnic, and explore the rugged Wild-Western terrain of this 335-acre park, they may also catch a Hollywood film crew at work—either shooting in the wide open spaces of the ranch or in its Western Town. Recently restored by the park, the Western Town was designed and built with moviemaking, camera angles, and light in mind.

A bit of history: The Ranch belonged to Paramount from the late 1920s into the late 1940s. In those days, the studio used it for its own movies, also rented it out to other studios and to local ranchers. Among the early Paramount films shot here were the 1930 Western *The Sante Fe Trail,* Ernst Lubitsch's *Broken Lullaby* (1932) with Lionel Barrymore and Nancy Carroll, and *Thunder Below* (1932) with Tallulah Bankhead. The most lavish production of all, however, was Samuel Goldwyn's 1937 *Adventures of Marco Polo*—which used some 2000 horses, a number of elephants, and a huge fortress set. Gary Cooper was the star and Lana Turner had a bit part.

Paramount sold the ranch in 1946 but subsequent owners continued to rent out part of the original acreage for films and television shows. In the 1950s, when TV Westerns scored big with audiences, the ranch was frequently a location for "The Cisco Kid," "Bat Masterson," "Zane Grey Theater," and "Have Gun, Will Travel." More recently, the ranch doubled as the Spahn Movie Ranch—the place that the Manson Family called home—in the 1976 TV-movie version of the book, *Helter Skelter.* It's also been seen in numerous commercials plus episodes of "A-Team," "CHiPs," "B.J. and the Bear," and "The Fall Guy." The National Park Service acquired the property in 1981.

NOTE: *The Paramount Ranch is open from 8 to sunset, daily. Among the programs that the rangers and docents organize are exhibits on moviemaking as well as special movie history tours. For information as well as a brochure with map, call (818) 888-3770. To reach the Ranch, take the Ventura Freeway west and exit at Kanan; turn left at the exit, left again at Sideway Road, then bear right onto Cornell Road and continue about 2½ miles south.*

16. MISSION SAN FERNANDO
15151 San Fernando Mission Boulevard, San Fernando

The Mission San Fernando El Rey De España occupies a place of importance—both in the history of California and in the history of the American cinema. For California, the date of note

On location at the San Fernando Mission in 1919

was 1797, the year Padre Fermin Lasuen founded the mission, one of twenty-one Spanish outposts in California that brought the fruits and horrors of European civilization to this part of the New World.

For film buffs, the history-making year connected with the Mission was 1910. It was in that year that the visionary American director D. W. Griffith spent his first winter in California. Here, Griffith found not only good weather—but a whole new world as far as terrain, sights, and film locations were concerend. Taking advantage of this, Griffith carefully chose the perfect Southern California landscapes to match the films he was shooting. One of the locations Griffith discovered in 1910 was the town of San Fernando with its haunting old Spanish mission (in a state of semi-ruin at the time). For Griffith, this was the authentic Old West and he immediately used San Fernando and its mission in *Our Silent Paths,* a drama about the hardships endured by a miner and his daughter who have traveled cross-country aboard a prairie-schooner. Griffith is reported to have used the mission town of San Fernando in other early Westerns—including *Two Men of the Desert* and *Battle of Elderberry Gulch,* both 1913 films. A year later, the San Fernando Mission turned up in a movie directed by another American movie pioneer—Cecil B. DeMille's *Rose of the Rancho.*

Today, the Mission San Fernando El Rey de España looks quite a bit better than it did in Griffith's and DeMille's day— thanks to several major restorations (most of them after earthquakes). The most recent restoration—after the devastating 1971 San Sylmar earthquake—was the most complete and most historically accurate. Besides being a magnificent tourist attraction, the Mission is still being used by film companies when scripts call for a backdrop of Spain, Mexico, South America, or early

California. Television shows done at the mission have included segments of "The Love Boat," "Knight Rider," "Remington Steele," "The Incredible Hulk." TV movies: "The Greatest American Hero" (1981) and "Having It All" (1982).

NOTE: *The mission is open seven days a week from 9 to 5. To reach the site, take the Ventura Freeway west to the San Fernando exit; then head south along San Fernando Mission Boulevard.*

17. MERLE NORMAN TOWER OF BEAUTY
15180 Bledsoe Street, Sylmar

A most unusual museum built by the chairman of the board of the Merle Norman Cosmetics empire, this six-story gold-stucco monolith houses an eclectic collection of theater organs, mechanical music boxes, over a thousand automobile hood ornaments, and close to a hundred classic automobiles in mint condition. The star of the cars: a 1923 Avions Voisin with body by Rothschild and a silver hood ornament in the shape of a cobra. Its owner was one of the first of an eventual long line of movie-star car buffs, Rudolph Valentino. (The hood ornament, by the way, was a gift from Mary Pickford and Douglas Fairbanks in honor of Valentino's latest film at the time, *Cobra.*)

Also on view at the Merle Norman Tower of Beauty (sometimes referred to as "San Sylmar," à la William Randolph Hearst) is an American-built 1923 McFarlan Knickerbocker Cabriolet that was formerly owned by screen comic Roscoe "Fatty" Arbuckle. For those who prefer theater organs to fancy cars, a highlight of a visit to San Sylmar is seeing and hearing its "Mighty Wurlitzer"

Rudolph Valentino and his 1923 Avions Voisin automobile

with 2463 pipes. The organ was used by Carmine Coppola—Francis Ford Coppola's father—when he created the score for the reissued silent screen epic, *Napoleon.*

NOTE: *Visits to the Merle Norman "Classic Beauty Collection" must be booked in advance. Anyone wishing to make a reservation for a tour should call: (818) 367-2251; or write: Merle Norman Classic Beauty Collection Tours, 15180 Bledsoe Street, Sylmar, CA 91342.*

18. WILLIAM S. HART PARK
24151 Newhall Avenue, Newhall

"While I was making pictures, the people gave me their nickels, dimes, and quarters. When I am gone, I want them to have my home." Would that more movie stars shared the late William S. Hart's philosophy. One of the first great cowboys of the American cinema, Hart bequeathed his entire 250-acre ranch to the town of Newhall to be used as a public park upon his death. Hart died in 1946 and today his former ranch attracts locals who seem much more interested in picnicking or hiking than in the man who once lived here. But for anyone wishing to know about Hart and his career, they've come to the right place.

Hart—who had the soft-hard good looks of a Clint Eastwood—came to be a Western star somewhat circuitously. Born in the East, he learned about the West as a young boy through traveling there with his father—who was everything from an

William S. Hart hosts Barbara Stanwyck and Robert Taylor at his ranch in Newhall in the early 1940s

itinerant worker to an executive with a lumber mill, depending on the biography one reads. As a young man back East, Hart went into the theater and eventually became known for Shakespearian roles. His stage career was a long one and he was well into his forties when he again went West—this time to Hollywood—and started making western films with director Thomas Ince. Characterized by realistic plots and an unglamorous depiction of what the West was like, Hart's pictures did well at first but eventually were overshadowed by the more spectacular exploits of Tom Mix and Buck Jones.

Meanwhile, back at the ranch, today three of the original buildings on the Hart estate have been turned into museums. Near the park entrance, the old ranch house that was on the premises when Hart first leased them in 1918 for his William S. Hart Productions was formerly Hart's office and studio. It now contains photos of Hart and his friends (Calamity Jane, Maurice Chevalier, Charles Lindbergh, Pola Negri among them), Western gear from Hart's films, period furnishings, and other mementos of his career.

Up a hill from the ranch house, the bunkhouse is a little cottage that was originally built as a movie set and which Hart later used as a place to entertain the boys. Inside, there's a roulette table, small pool table, old-fashioned Victrola, Indian rugs and skins. At the top of the hill is Hart's permanent home—which he built after having made his final film, *Tumbleweeds,* in 1925. The handsome twenty-two-room Spanish mansion contains more old photographs, plus collections of guns, Western paintings, and native American art and artifacts. Hanging over "Big Bill's" bed is a painting of his best friend, his pinto pony "Fritz." (Fritz's elaborate grave is another attraction of the Park—as is the site where Hart's many dogs lie buried.) Married just once and for a mere matter of months, Hart lived on his ranch with his sister, Mary Ellen. She died in 1943, three years before her brother. At his death, Hart was eighty-one.

NOTE: *The William S. Hart Park is open every day from 10 to 7:30. Tours of the main house are given on the half-hour from 10 to 3, Wednesdays through Fridays and from 10 to 4 on weekends.*

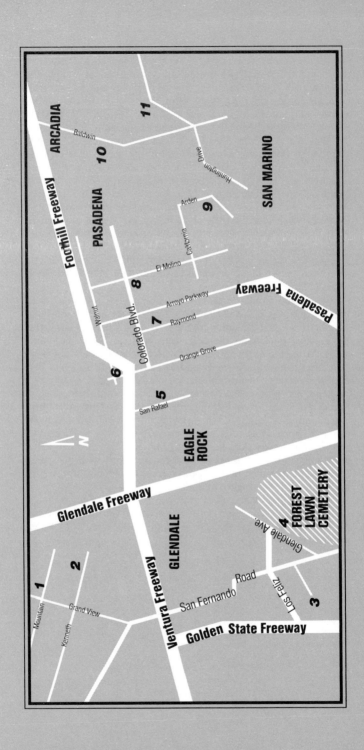

PASADENA/
GLENDALE

Another Country

Class act: Tom Mix on location in Pasadena in 1916

I T'S the first reel of *A Star Is Born*, the 1954 version. Norman Maine (James Mason) is the biggest movie star in America. He's rich, famous, powerful—and accustomed to getting anything he wants. He walks into the Cocoanut Grove looking for the young woman band singer (Judy Garland) who saved him from falling on his face in front of thousands of people at a benefit at the Shrine Auditorium earlier in the evening. The maître d' at the Grove, Bruno, tells Maine that the band left over an hour ago. Maine then checks out the available-women situation at the club. Bruno suggests several possibilities—but none is quite to the exacting Maine's liking. Except for the young girl in the green dress. When Maine expresses his interest to Bruno, the knowing maître d' shakes his head and says: "No, Mr. Maine . . . Pasadena. Leave it alone." Maine instantly understands, says no more. There are some things even a Norman Maine can't mess with—and Pasadena is one of them.

Only a matter of minutes from Hollywood, this ever-so-proper northern suburb of Los Angeles is worlds away in outlook, mores, lifestyle. Founded by Midwestern farmers in the 1870s, the city really took off several decades later when the railroads helped make it a fashionable winter resort for wealthy Easterners. Many of these winter visitors became so enamored of Pasadena's gentle climate, crisp air, lush gardens, and nearby snow-capped mountains that they built fabulous winter homes here. Eventually, many of these same Easterners gave up the East and became full-fledged, full-time Pasadenans. Whereas most of Los Angeles was settled by those seeking fortune and often fame, a large portion of Pasadena's population was made up of individuals and families who already had both.

Pasadena therefore has a long tradition of culture, class-consciousness, conservatism, indeed isolationism. Needless to say, when the movies came to Southern California, they didn't wind up in Pasadena. Pasadena, however, occasionally wound up in the movies—as many of its mansions provided early production companies with the grand (and often "East Coast") backgrounds they sometimes couldn't find in L.A. Today, despite tough laws that limit filmmaking, Pasadena's mansions still rank at the top of many location managers' lists as prime places for shooting. For the movie lover, therefore, a visit to Pasadena is a visit to one of L.A.'s most important back lots!

NOTE: *Also included in this chapter are the neighboring communities of Glendale and Arcadia. Just west of Pasadena, Glendale was and still is another popular location for films; it is also the home of the original Forest Lawn—the fantastic cemetery where perhaps the largest number of Hollywood's elite are buried. East of Pasadena, Arcadia boasts Hollywood's poshest and most historic racetrack as well as an extraordinary arboretum that's been seen in films since the 1930s. For sightseers, Pasadena and Arcadia can be covered in one jaunt; Glendale can be combined with Burbank or with the Los Feliz/Silverlake area of Hollywood.*

The Brand mansion

1. BRAND LIBRARY
1601 West Mountain Street, Glendale

A long spectacular driveway edged with palm trees leads to this marvelous white Middle Eastern palace at the foot of Glendale's Mount Verdugo. Built in 1904 by Leslie C. Brand, the controversial character who "developed" Glendale, the palace was inspired not by Brand's extensive Oriental travels but rather by a trip he had made to a world's fair in Chicago, where he had fallen in love with the East India Pavilion. Brand called his dream house El Miradero ("the lookout") and actually encouraged its use as a location for silent films since the excitement generated by these "shoots" helped publicize the town he had founded. One of the best-documented films shot here during the teens was a 1915 white-slave epic from Universal called *Under the Crescent* which effectively used El Miradero as the palace where the heroine is held captive by an evil prince.

Besides encouraging filmmaking, Brand staged other publicity stunts at El Miradero to promote the city of Glendale. Among the most outlandish of these were his "fly-in" parties to which all guests had to arrive in airplanes. Stars helped hype these events—especially when they piloted their own planes, as Mary Miles Minter and Ruth Roland were reported to have done in 1921. Cecil B. DeMille, however, flew the most glamorous airplane—a Junkers JL-6.

When Brand died in 1925, his will stipulated that El Miradero and its grounds be left to the city of Glendale upon the demise of his wife. Mrs. Brand died some twenty years later—and by 1956 the mansion had been converted into a library specializing in music and art. Today, film companies often come to El Miradero when in need of an exotic foreign locale. Needless to say, the old "Mission Impossible" TV series loved the place. Episodes of "The Six Million Dollar Man," "Fall Guy," as well as the movie version of Sidney Sheldon's *The Other Side of Midnight* are other productions that have taken advantage of this extraordinary Southern California site.

"Flamingo Road" house, Glendale

NOTE: *The Brand Library and Art Center are open from 12 noon to 9 on Tuesdays and Thursdays, and from 12 noon to 6 on Wednesdays, Fridays, and Saturdays. Closed on Sundays and Mondays.*

2. "GONE WITH THE WIND"?
727 Kenneth Road, Glendale

Although there seems to be little evidence to back it up, the legend persists that this impressive "antebellum" Glendale mansion was used as a location for *Gone with the Wind* for about two weeks in late 1938. If it wasn't, it certainly could have been with its huge pillars and sweeping driveway. While its *GWTW* connection is somewhat shaky, 727 Kenneth Road's more recent film career is better documented. Often called on to represent the Old South on television, it was used extensively in the series, "Flamingo Road," as the Florida estate seen at the opening of each episode.

3. SOUTHERN PACIFIC RAILROAD STATION
400 West Cerritos Avenue, Glendale

It was the "10:15 from Glendale" that Fred MacMurray boarded posing as Barbara Stanwyck's husband in the elaborate murder plot of Billy Wilder's *Double Indemnity* back in the early 1940s. Wilder shot the sequence—as he did much of the movie— on location. According to Wilder, he really wanted to use the Pasadena Train Station but couldn't get permission so he wound up at Glendale. He next decided to turn Glendale into Pasadena by changing the sign outside the station. That would have been fine—except that the name change caused such confusion among conductors that station officials made Wilder remove the Pasadena sign.

Besides its appearance in *Double Indemnity,* the highly photogenic Mission Revival-style Glendale station often turns up in television series, commercials, and print ads. The station was

Entrance to Forest Lawn, Glendale

built in the early twenties for the Southern Pacific Railroad—and today is part of the Amtrak network.

4. FOREST LAWN
1712 South Glendale Avenue, Glendale

The Disneyland of cemeteries, Forest Lawn in Glendale is one of Southern California's greatest attractions. Like many of the area's wonders, Forest Lawn was the creation of a man who dared to dream big. The man was Dr. Hubert Eaton and in 1917, he was the new manager of the very conventional and not very well tended Tropico Cemetery. Feeling that cemeteries should inspire the living, Eaton set out to create, in his own words, "a great park, devoid of misshapen monuments and other customary signs of earthly death, but filled with towering trees, sweeping lawns, splashing fountains, singing birds, beautiful statuary, cheerful flowers, noble memorial architecture with interiors full of light and color, and redolent of the world's best history and romances."

With the same spirit and energy of the great movie moguls—for whom all things were possible—Eaton acted on his dream, made it come true on a scale that must be seen to be believed. At Forest Lawn, there are no rows of ordinary tombstones. Instead, there are acres of gardens and courts, with names such as Slumberland, Lullabyland, Everlasting Love, Inspiration Slope, and Babyland, where flat stone markers scarcely alter the smooth contours of the green lawn. There is a swan lake. There are two mausoleums—one of which resembles a great sprawling Medieval abbey. There are churches that are full-sized reproductions of churches in England and Scotland. Not only used for funerals, these are sometimes the scenes of weddings. In 1940, for example, Ronald Reagan married Jane Wyman in Forest Lawn's Wee Kirk of the Heather.

At Forest Lawn, there is also . . . Art. Here, one can see not copies but "recreations" of some of the world's great masterpieces. The top artist whose works are "recreated" at Forest Lawn is Michelangelo. His colossal "David" stands in its own court—where a taped recording tells the story of David and Goliath for those who want to hear it. Meanwhile, there's more Michelangelo on view in the Memorial Court of the Great Mausoleum. Here, the star attraction is a gigantic stained-glass version of "The Last Supper," which is unveiled several times a day at regular intervals complete with special lighting effects, music, and "dramatic narration." In the same room with "The Last Supper" are reproductions in Carrera marble of Michelangelo's "Pieta," "Madonna of Bruges," "Medici Madonna and Child," and various other of his better known sculptures.

Movie lovers, however, should venture beyond the Court of Honor and over into the Sanctuary of Trust where they will find the wall crypts of Clark Gable and his former wife Carole Lombard lying beside one another. Not far away is the man who produced Gable's greatest film—*Gone with the Wind*—David O. Selznick. Unfortunately, the nearby Sanctuary of Benediction is cordoned off with a low locked gate. It is here where Sid Grauman, Marie Dressler, Alexander Pantages, Irving Thalberg, and Jean Harlow are buried.

Not off-limits to the public is the large memorial to another well-known Hollywood name that edges the driveway outside the main entrance to the Great Mausoleum. The name: Jean Hersholt—which is remembered every year at the Academy Awards when the Academy hands out its Jean Hersholt Humanitarian Award. Hersholt, born in Denmark, made a career doing character parts in silent films and also became known in Hollywood for his charitable activities. Another Hollywood figure known for good works, although she was considerably more controversial than Hersholt, was superstar evangelist Aimee Semple McPherson.

Tomb of Aimee Semple McPherson, Forest Lawn

Her large flat tomb (all monuments must be approved by the Forest Lawn management) lies in front of the Great Mausoleum down the hill and off to the left; it is guarded by kneeling angels.

From the Great Mausoleum, Cathedral Drive leads to Freedom Way and ultimately to the Court of Freedom and Freedom Mausoleum. Here, a 20 × 30-foot mosaic of John Trumbull's famous painting, "The Signing of the Declaration of Independence," sets the patriotic tone of this Forest Lawn enclave where Errol Flynn and baseball manager Casey Stengel are buried in the courtyard. Inside the Freedom Mausoleum—in the Sanctuary of Heritage—are the crypts of Alan Ladd, Nat King Cole, Gracie Allen, Jeanette MacDonald, Clara Bow and her husband, cowboy actor/Nevada Lieutenant Governor Rex Bell.

Back outside, secluded in a small walled garden just to the left of the entrance to the Freedom Mausoleum, is a marker that says Walter Elias Disney. Some Disney fans, however, don't believe that Disney's ashes are in this little garden and insist that their idol's body has been frozen and stored in a secret vault until the time when medical science can cure the cancer that killed him in 1966. Whether Disney is here or not (and it appears highly likely that he is at Forest Lawn), it seems fitting that he should be remembered in a place that has the same fantasy/reality quality of the great park that his own dreams created: Disneyland.

NOTE: *Forest Lawn is open daily from 9 to 5. The management does not provide information concerning where celebrities are buried. Visitors are requested to observe the same rules of decorum that they would when visiting any cemetery.*

5. "TOPPER" HOUSE
160 San Rafael, Pasadena

A Pasadena classic, this glorious Gothic behind the iron gates at 160 San Rafael Avenue achieved screen fame as the Connecticut estate of Cosmo Topper in the Hal Roach *Topper* series of the late 1930s/early 1940s. It was also home to Batman and Robin in the 1960s "Batman" TV series and more recently has been seen in director Ulu Grosbard's 1981 film about late 1940s Los Angeles, *True Confessions.*

6. THE FENYES MANSION
470 West Walnut Street, Pasadena

Typical of the many grand homes that edged Pasadena's Orange Grove Boulevard at the turn of the century, this magnificent columned mansion was built in 1905 by Los Angeles architect Robert D. Farquhar for Dr. Adalbert and Mrs. Eva Scott Fenyes. Besides being a leading social figure in Pasadena, Mrs. Fenyes was an accomplished artist and her home was a "salon" for painters, writers, and—which must have ruffled the feathers of her straight-laced Pasadena friends and neighbors—movie people!

Tom Mix in the 1916 film Western Life, *Feynes Mansion in the background*

D. W. Griffith was on the scene at the Fenyes Mansion as early as 1912 when he and a cast of costumed cavaliers used the place as the backdrop for a film called *The Queen's Necklace*. A few years later, Douglas Fairbanks' *Reggie Mixes In* was done here, as were films starring Harry Carey and Tom Mix. All the while, Mrs. Fenyes collected photos of the productions and made little notes on the backs of them. Typical of these is her synopsis of a "photoplay" done on her property in 1915: "An American girl who married a Turkish Prince. She was an actress and entered his harem after her marriage. Had many adventures and finally left him. Coming to America, she eventually joined the 'movies.' In a play, supposed to depict the principal events of her career, she and her company played several scenes in our grounds. This photo gives a scene supposed to take place in the harem. Her gown is a most gorgeous affair in brilliant strings of beads—mostly Emerald green." Besides showing Mrs. Fenyes' fascination with moviemaking, the note also gives an idea of the outlandish plots of many silent films.

Several generations later, Mrs. Fenyes' estate—now the headquarters of the Pasadena Historical Society—is still being used as a location for films. In *Being There,* for instance, it appears early on as the mansion where Peter Sellers is the caretaker. The estate has also appeared in the made-for-television films "The Immigrants," "A Testimony of Two Men," and—its grandest role—as the White House in "Franklin and Eleanor: The White House Years."

NOTE: *The house—with its priceless paintings, tapestries, antiques, and Oriental rugs—can be toured on Tuesdays, Thursdays, and on the last Sunday of the month, from 1 to 4. For information, phone: (818) 577-1660.*

Pasadena train station

7. PASADENA TRAIN STATION
222 South Raymond Avenue, Pasadena

It was the next-to-last stop on the West-bound run of the legendary "Super Chief"—and in the 1930s, it was the chic place to disembark when traveling from the East Coast to Los Angeles. Even after monumental Union Station was opened in downtown L.A. in 1939, the tiny Spanish Colonial Pasadena depot was still favored by moguls and movie stars—who would be met by drivers, limousines, and often the press, then whisked away to their homes in Beverly Hills. Today, Amtrak's version of "The Super Chief"—"The Southwest Chief"—still stops at Pasadena before heading into Union Station. You'll be hard-pressed to spot a movie star aboard, however.

8. PASADENA PLAYHOUSE
39 South El Molino Avenue, Pasadena

William Holden was "discovered" here. Tennessee Williams tried out plays here. And when Samuel Goldwyn thought a young Brit named David Niven needed a little more acting experience, he told him to head over to the Pasadena Playhouse. One of the

Pasadena Playhouse, 1935

oldest community theaters in the country, the Pasadena Playhouse was organized in 1918, inaugurated its attractive pueblo/Spanish quarters in 1925, and eventually grew to include five stages, a touring company, a radio and TV station, as well as one of the country's most important theater schools.

For Hollywood, the Pasadena Playhouse was an important source of talent, especially once talkies came in. Among the stars who went from the stages of the Pasadena Playhouse to the soundstages of Hollywood were Tyrone Power, Dana Andrews, Frances Farmer, James Arness, and the aforementioned William Holden. On the other hand, Eve Arden was discovered in a Playhouse production not by Hollywood but by Broadway! The year was 1933 and Eve was appearing in *Low and Behold!* (using her real name, Eunice Quedons) when she was scooped up by the Ziegfeld Follies. Eve's Hollywood career didn't begin in earnest until 1937. Raymond Burr is another star who made it to Hollywood via the Pasadena-New York-L.A. route.

In addition to the many performers who trace their theatrical beginnings to the Pasadena Playhouse, literally hundreds of established actors and actresses appeared there over the years. Indeed, for many years, the Pasadena Playhouse was one of the few centers of "live" theater in Los Angeles and therefore one of the few places where movie stars could prove that they were also serious actors. Despite its prestige, the Playhouse ran into severe financial difficulties in the sixties (some of them caused by the burgeoning small-theater scene in Los Angeles during the same decade) and was forced to close in 1970. The happy ending is that after being dark for some fourteen years, the landmark theater was extensively restored and refurbished for a grand 1985 reopening.

NOTE: *For information regarding what's on at the Pasadena Playhouse, phone: (213) 629-1394.*

9. "THE CARRINGTON MANSION AND ESTATE"
1145 Arden Road, Pasadena

"A peerless forty-eight-room Georgian mansion . . . built in 1915 . . . situated on a wooded 645-acre estate . . . unquestionably Denver's finest." So goes the description of Blake and Krystle Carrington's "Dynasty" digs in *Dynasty: The Authorized Biography of the Carringtons* (A Dolphin Book, 1984). Don't go looking for the Carrington Estate in Denver, however—and don't go looking for just one Carrington Estate . . . because there are two! One—used in those dramatic aerial shots—is the National Trust Property Fioli, located some 400 miles from L.A. in the San Francisco suburb of Woodside. The other Dynasty mansion—used mainly for closeups with actors—is, like so many great Hollywood movie mansions, in Pasadena! Surrounded by a stately iron fence and ornate gates, the Carrington main house can only be glimpsed from the street. But it's there all the same—a magnificent Palladian villa with formal gardens, tennis court, swimming pool, and lily

"Dynasty" mansion, Pasadena

pond (scene of a famous 1983 fight between Alexis and Krystal in which both ladies wound up making quite a splash).

Often used for filming, Arden Villa, as it is known to location managers, undergoes some major camouflaging when the "Dynasty" crew shoots here. This involves bringing in trees and shrubs to relandscape the property. It also calls for masking the house's stucco façade with giant panels that turn the place into the fabulous brick mansion that, according to the "authorized" biography of the Carringtons, "is more than just an imposing building and verdant gardens suitable for a dynasty . . . [but] is a home for a family—alternately shelter from the storm of outside events and the eye of the hurricane for family imbroglios."

10. LOS ANGELES STATE AND COUNTY ARBORETUM
301 North Baldwin Avenue, Arcadia

Remember "De plane . . . de plane!" that landed on the lake with the jungle and a whimsical Victorian house in the background? Welcome to "Fantasy Island!" Far from the South Pacific, the hit TV series' trademark locale was actually a public botanical park and gardens just east of Pasadena. One of L.A.'s most fantastic spots, the Los Angeles State and County Arboretum is a 127-acre preserve of exotic trees, plants, flowers, and birds. Among the latter, a huge population of peacocks roams freely, often begging for popcorn and other tidbits from the tourists.

The famous "Fantasy Island" house is not a movie set. It was built in 1881 by real-estate tycoon, E. J. Baldwin, as a guesthouse for his vast ranch that then encompassed the present-day arboretum property and much of the land surrounding it. The Baldwin ranch stayed in the Baldwin family until the mid-thirties—when it was purchased by a syndicate headed by Harry Chandler, publisher of the *Los Angeles Times.* It was also around that time that the movies discovered the property—with its lake and its jungly grounds—and Chandler's Rancho Santa Anita

Corporation was glad to rent it all out for location shooting. Among the films lensed here then were *Devil's Island* (1938), *The Man in the Iron Mask* (1939), Johnny Weissmuller *Tarzans,* and a couple of Dorothy Lamour South Seas spectaculars.

When the State and County bought the property in 1947 and turned it into the arboretum, the filming didn't stop. Offering the instant jungle, the arboretum was used for the *Jungle Jim* series, Gordon Scott *Tarzans,* and one of the classic jungle films of all times, *The African Queen.* Although most of the film was done on location in Africa and England, it is said that the famous leeches sequence had to be reshot once Humphrey Bogart was back in California. Needless to say, the Arboretum was a lot closer than Africa and just as realistic.

NOTE: *The Los Angeles State and County Arboretum is open every day except Christmas from 9 to 4:30.*

11. SANTA ANITA RACE TRACK
285 West Huntington Drive, Arcadia

It was a glamour track right from the day it opened—December 25, 1934. And much of the glamour came from its strong Hollywood ties. One of its founders was none other than producer Hal Roach who also served as its president for a time. Santa Anita—especially its ultra-posh/ultra-private Turf Club—lured the film world's most outstanding names and faces.

Some went to the races to be seen—feeling that horses and horseracing spelled class with a capital C. Others—like Bing Crosby, L. B. Mayer, Harry M. Warner, Raoul Walsh, Spencer Tracy, Howard Hawks, Barbara Stanwyck, Robert Taylor, George Raft, Zeppo Marx, Errol Flynn, Myron Selznick, Don Ameche, and William Goetz—went because they owned horses themselves. Finally, there were those who went because they were hooked. In fact, there was a time in Hollywood during the thirties and forties when the film colony was so obsessed with the ponies that the

"Fantasy Island" cottage—at the L.A. State and County Arboretum

A Day at the Races *(with Maureen O'Sullivan, Allan Jones, and several Marx Brothers) at the Santa Anita racetrack in 1937*

town's two trade papers, *The Hollywood Reporter* and *Daily Variety,* featured racing schedules as well as tips along with news of the motion picture industry.

Santa Anita wasn't the only track with Hollywood connections. Harry M. Warner of Warner Brothers was one of the men behind Hollywood Park in Inglewood and Bing Crosby was president and a principal owner of Del Mar near San Diego. It was during this race-crazed period in Hollywood's history that Groucho Marx is said to have gone to see an executive at MGM dressed as a jockey. Quipped Groucho when questioned about his attire: "This is the only way you can get to see a producer these days."

Picture people not only went to the races—they made movies about them. Among Hollywood's many racetrack epics, one of the funniest is the Marx Brothers' *A Day at the Races* (1937)—which was shot at Santa Anita. Santa Anita also turned up in David O. Selznick's not-so-funny *A Star Is Born* that same year—as well as in the Warner Brothers' 1954 remake. In both versions, Norman Maine has just returned from a sanitarium where he has stopped drinking. He goes to the track, has an altercation with his former press agent, and starts drinking again—the final fatal binge. (While on not-so-funny subjects, it must be noted that Santa Anita served as a detention center for Japanese Americans during World War II.)

Today, Santa Anita remains one of Southern California's premier racing centers—with its main thoroughbred season running from December through late April. The track's Turf Club is still posh, still exclusive, still a favorite hangout of the Hollywood elite—such as zillionaire TV-producer Aaron Spelling who, in the grand old movie-mogul tradition, breeds, raises, and races his own thoroughbreds.

INDEX

Page numbers in *italics* refer to illustrations.

A&M Records, 65–66, *66*
Abbey of Palms Mausoleum, 76
Abbott, Bud, 39, 275
ABC, 44
ABC Entertainment Center, 224
ABC Television Center, 120–21, *120*
Academy Awards, 6, 10, 15, 46, 98–99, 127, 146, 151, *250,* 251, 280, 299
Academy Awards Movie Theater, 15
Academy of Motion Picture Arts and Sciences, 10, 104, 146, 197–98, *197*
Acker, Jean, 12, 79
Ackerman, Forrest J., 116, 142
Acord, Art, 28
Adams, Nick, 53
Ade, King Sunny, 38
Adrian, 9, 33, *33*
"Adventures in Paradise," 264
"Adventures of Conan, The," 274
Adventures of Marco Polo, 287
AFRA (American Federation of Radio Artists), 49
African Queen, The, 305
Against All Odds, 44, 224
Agar, John, 222
Airport 1979, 147
Aldrich, Robert, 81
Alexander & Oviatt, 145
Alexander Hamilton, 96
Alexandria Hotel, 132, 139–40
Alex in Wonderland, 138
Ali, Mohammed, 23, 93
"Alice," 90
Allen, Gracie, 58, 300
  house of, 203, *203*
Allied Artists, 57, 119
"All in the Family," 90
All Night Long, 199
Allyson, June, 96
Alpert, Herb, 66
Altered States, 147
Altman, Robert, 28
Alto-Nido Apartments, 34, *35*
Aly Kahn, 205
Amalgamated Oil Company, 185
Ambassador Hotel, 85, 97–100, *98, 99*
Ameche, Don, 305
American Film Institute, 112, 189
American Gigolo, 188

American International, 66
American Legion, 27–28, *27*
American Mutoscope and Biograph Company (Biograph), 131
Anchors Aweigh, 29
Anderson, Eddie, 285
Anderson, Dame Judith, 33
Anderson, Margaret, 186
Andrews, Dana, 303
Andrews, Julie, 262
Angeli, Pier, 26
Angelino Heights, 126–27
Angelus Temple, 124–25, *125*
Anger, Kenneth, 204
Apartments (apartment houses)
  Alto-Nido, 34, *35*
  Bryson Apartment Hotel, 104–5, *104*
  Chateau Elysee, 58–60, *59*
  Colonial House, 174
  courtyard, 66–67
  El Royale, 89, *89*
  F. Scott Fitzgerald, 170–71, *170*
  Garden Court site, 7–8, *7*
  the Granville (formerly the Voltaire), 172, *172*
  Hillview Apartments, 20
  Le Trianon, 111–12, *111*
  Los Altos, 95–96, *95*
  Mayfair, 21
  Montecito, 26
  "Oleander Arms," 173, *173*
  Parva Sed-Apta, 35
  Patio del Moro, 175
  Ravenswood, 87–88, *88*
  Roman Gardens, 27
  Romany Villa, 175–76, *175*
  Sunset Tower, 165–66, *165*
  Talmadge, 101–2, *102*
  Villa Andalusia, 174
  Villa Celia, 176
  Villa d'Este, 171–72, *171*
  Villa Primavera, 174
Aquarius Theater, 50–51
Arbuckle, Roscoe (Fatty), 124, 154, 289
Arcadia, 295
Arden, Eve, 303
Armenian Americans, 76
Arnaz, Desi, 77, 190, 234
  house of, 205, *205*
Arnaz, Desi, Jr., 196

Arness, James, 303
Arthur, Jean, 110
Artists and Writers Building, 192
Artoo-Detoo, 6
Ashe, Arthur, 87
Ashley, Lady Sylvia, 284
"Aspen," 126
"Aspiration," 71
Astaire, Fred, 140
Astor, Mary, 56, 285
At Long Last Love, 147
"A-Team," 287
Auditorium Building site, 147–49, *148*
Auntie Mame, 278
Autry, Gene, 6, 27, 54, 55, 283

"Babylon" site, 117, *117*
"Baby Snooks," 44
Bacall, Lauren, 168, *187,* 188
   house of, 215–16
Back, Michael, 90
Back Street, 275
Bacon, James, 26
Baiano, Colly, *87*
Ball, Lucille, 77, 234
   house of, 205, *205*
Bank buildings
   Home Savings and Loan Association,
      48–49, *48*
   Israel Discount Bank, 193
   Los Angeles Federal Savings and
      Loan Building, 49
   Security Pacific, 13, *13*
Bankhead, Tallulah, 9, 99, 168, 287
Bara, Theda, 110, 140
   mansion of, 153–54, *154*
Bard, Lou, theater chain, 118
Barker, Bob, 26
Barris, Chuck, 192
Barrymore, John, 7, 17, 98, 99, 140,
      145, 164, 168
Barrymore, Lionel, 140, 285, 287
Barthelmess, Richard, 10, 31
"Bathing Beauties," 245, *245,* 248
"Batman," 60, 300
"Bat Masterson," 287
Battle for the Planet of the Apes, 264
Battle of Elderberry Gulch, 288
"Battlestar Galactica," 273
Beachwood Market, 57
Beatty, Warren, 194
Beauty Museum, Max Factor, 13–14
Becket, Welton, 45, 151
Becky Sharp, 72–73, 219, 234
Beelman, Claude, 101, 105
Beery, Wallace, 7, 10, 272
Begelman, David, 54, 93, 199
Being There, 301
Bel-Air, 213
Bel-Air Hotel, 213–14, *213*
Bell, Alfonso, 214
Bell, Rex, 300

Belushi, John, 168
Benchley, Robert, 18, 166, 169, 192
Beneath the Planet of the Apes, 264
Bennett, Constance, 25, 86, 162
Bennett, Joan, 86
Benny, Jack, 205, 241
Bergen, Candice, 203–4, 215
Bergen, Edgar, 6, 37
Berkeley, Busby, 12, 26, 277
Bernhardt, Sarah, 140
Bernheimer Residence, 23–25, *24*
Bernstein, Leonard, 33
Berry, Wallace, 140
Berwin, Gary, 39
Berwin Entertainment Complex, 38–39,
      38
Betsy, The, 147
"Beulah," 52
Beverly Boulevard
   7312 (El Coyote Restaurant), 91
   7421 (A. B. Heinsbergen & Company
      Building), 91
   7600 (Pan Pacific Auditorium), 90,
      90
   7800 (CBS Television City), 89–90
   8899 (International Creative
      Management), 199
   9039 (Chasen's), 198–99
"Beverly Hillbillies" house, 214, *214*
Beverly Hills, 31, 109, 185–209
Beverly Hills High School, 195–96
Beverly Hills Hotel, 186–88, *186, 187,*
      194
Beverly Theater, 193, *193*
Beverly Wilshire Hotel, 193–95, *194*
Beverly Wing, 194
"Bewitched," 281
Big Business, 227
Big Sleep, The, 215
Bill, Tony, Productions, 250
Biltmore Hotel, 146–47, *147*
Biograph, 131
Birth of a Nation, The, 9, 81, 117, 148–
      49, *148,* 271, *271*
Bison Studio, 124
Bitzer, Billy, 149
Bixby, Bill, 23
"B.J. and the Bear," 287
Black, Charles, 222
Black, Karen, 93
Black Cat, The, 115
Blackton, J. Stuart, 120
Blade Runner, 115, *115,* 141, 149, 152,
      152
Blondeau Tavern, 51
Blondell, Joan, 277
Blood Feud, 105
Bloom, Claire, 174
Blue Book Modeling Agency, 99
Blue Thunder, 149
Boardman, Eleanor, 206
"Bob Hope Chesterfield Specials, The,"
      44

"Bob Hope USO Club," 37
Bodeen, DeWitt, 285
Bogart, Humphrey, 50, 58, 140, 168, 277, 285
house of, 215–16
Boggs, Francis, 131, 245
"Bonanza," 60
Bonaventure Hotel, 149–50, *149*
Bondi, Beulah, 25, 32
Bookstores
Collectors Bookstore, 37
Larry Edmunds Bookshop, Inc., 18–19
Stanley Rose's, 18
Bow, Clara, 10, 48, 78, 96, 140, 168, 174, 300
Bowers, Donald, 146
Bowling centers, *54, 55*
Boyer, Charles, 190, 239
Brackett, Charles, 37
Bradbury, Lewis, 142
Bradbury, Ray, 192
Bradbury Building, 141–42, *142*
Brand, Leslie C., 296
Brand Library, 296–97, *296*
Brando, Marlon, 24
Brando, Marlon, Sr., 174
Brandt, Joe, 53
Breathless, 150, 249
Brecht, Bertolt, 259
Brentwood, 213
Brice, Fanny, 44, 195
Bride Wore Red, The, 9
Britton, Barbara, 26
Broadway. *See* South Broadway
Broken Lullaby, 287
Brolin, James, 275
Bronson Canyon, 60
Brooks, Mel, 220
Brough, Louise, 87, 196
Brown, Clarence, 260, 272
Brown, Horace, 178
Brown, Karl, 148, 271–72
Brown Derby
Vine Street, 46–47, *47*
Wilshire Boulevard, 100–1, *100*
Bruin Theater, 217
Bryant, Leland A., 111, 165
Bryson Apartment Hotel, 104–5, *104*
Buchanan, Jack, 11
Bucket of Blood, 249
Buck Rogers in the 25th Century, 149
Buddy Holly Story, The, 147
Budge, Don, 87
Bugs Bunny, 55
Bullocks Wilshire, 103–4, *104*
Bullwinkle, 168
Burbank-Glendale-Pasadena Airport, 281–82
Burbank Studios, 54, 55, 269, 276–78, *277*
Burke, Billie, 165
Burnett, Carol, 21, 38, 219

Burns, George, 58, 70
house of, 203, *203*
Burns, L. L., 80
"Burns and Allen Show, The," 52, 70
Burr, Raymond, 66, 303
Burton, Richard, 193
Busch, Mae, 20, 74
Bushman, Francis X., 33, 140
Buss, Jerry, 207
Butch Cassidy and the Sundance Kid, 264
Butterfield's, 164
Buttons, Red, 24
Byrnes, Ed "Kookie," 163

Cabot, Bruce, 16, 285
Caddo Pictures, 69
Cagney, James, 26, 195, 277
Calabasas Park Golf Club, 286
Calamity Jane, 291
California Historic Landmarks, 30
California State Bureau of Employment Security, 71
California Suite, 188
Cameo Theater, 139
Campbell, Alan, 178
Cannon, Dyan, 263
Cantor, Eddie, 241
Cantor, Ida, 241
Capitol Records Tower, 45, *45*
Capra, Frank, 53, 86
Captain Blood, 121
"Captains and Kings," 153
Carey, Harry, *274,* 301
"Carol Burnett Show, The," 89–90
Carrillo, Leo, 260, 272
"Carrington Mansion and Estate, The," 303–4, *304*
Carroll, Earl, 50–51
Carroll, Nancy, 287
Carroll Avenue, 109, 126–27, *126*
Carson, Johnny, 23, 163, 262
Carter, Howard, 17
Casablanca, 9, 50, 278, 282
Cassidy, Hopalong, 285
Cassidy, Shaun, 196
Castle Argyle, 58
Catholic Church, 87
Cavalcade, 226
CBC Film Sales Company, 53
CBS, 44, 51, 66
CBS-MTM Studio Center, 180, 282–83
CBS Playhouse Theater, 49
CBS Television City, 89–90
Cemeteries
Forest Lawn, 271–72, 298–300, *298, 299*
Hillside Memorial Park, 240–41, *241*
Hollywood Memorial Park, 65, 74–76, *75*
Holy Cross, 239–40, *240*
SPCA Pet Memorial Park, 285–86
Westwood Memorial Park, 216–17

Center Theater Group, 124
Century City, 213, 223–24, *223*
Century Ranch, 264–65
Chamberlain, Richard, 196
Champion (horse), 6
Champion, Marge, 38
Chandler, Dorothy, Pavilion, 151
Chandler, Harry, 56, 304–5
Chandler, Jeff, 241
Chandler, Norman, 38, 50
Chandler, Raymond, 26, 28, 104–5, 165
Chaney, Lon, 116, 275
Chaplin, Charlie, 10, 19, 39, 59, 65–67, 68, 86, 112–13, 124, 140, 176, 248–49
  houses of, 56, *56*, 206–7
Chaplin, Sid, 10
Chaplin Studios, 63–66, *66*
"Charlie Chan," 119
Charlie McCarthy, 6, 37
Chasen, Dave, 199
Chasen, Maude, 199
Chasen's, 198–99
Chateau Elysee, 58–60, *59*
Chateau Holiday Corporation, 111
Chateau Marmont, 166–68, *167*
Chemosphere, 181
Chester Place, *152*, 153
Chevalier, Maurice, 78, 291
Cheviott Hills, 213
Chilios, Bill, 46
Chinatown, 126, 147, 270–71
Chinese Theater, 5–7, *5*, 13, 17
"CHiPs," 287
Christie, Al, 51
Christie, Charles, 51
"Christie Comedies," 51
Churches
  Angelus Temple, 124–25, *125*
  Church of Scientology Celebrity Center International, 19
  Church of Scientology of California, 59–60
  Church of the Good Shepherd, 190–91, *190*
  First United Methodist Church of Hollywood, 25–26, *25*
  Metropolitan Community, 144
  St. Monica's Church, 255
Cinerama Dome Theater, 39, *39*
Ciro's, 163–64, *164*
"Cisco Kid, The," 119, 287
Citizen Kane, 18, 76, 234, 235
City Hall (Culver City), 236
City Hall (Los Angeles), *150*, 151
City Lights, 66, 138
Clansman, The. See *Birth of a Nation, The*
Clark, Mae, 285
Clayburgh, Jill, 167
Cleopatra, 9, 79, 224
Clifton's Cafeteria, 136, *137*
Clooney, Rosemary, 190

Close Encounters of the Third Kind, 9
Club(s)
  Calabasas Park Golf, 286
  Hillcrest Country, 226
  of the Hollywood Four Hundred, 24
  Hollywood Studio, 73–74, *74*
  Los Angeles Tennis, 85, 86–87, *87*
  Turf, 305, 306
Clune, William H., 81
Clune's Auditorium, 147–49, *148*
Coca-Cola Corporation, 54
Cocoanut Grove, 98–99, *99*
Cohn, Harry, 53–54, 75, 89, 274
Cohn, Jack, 53
Colbert, Claudette, 53, 78, *248*, 249
  house of, 214
Cole, Nat King, 45, 93, 162, 300
Collectors Bookstore, 37
Collins, Gary, 275
"Colombo," 133
Colonial House, 174
Colony, the (Malibu), 263
Columbia Pictures, 53–54, 93, 276–77
Columbia Ranch, 281
Columbia Square, 51–53, *51*
Columbia Studios, 281
Columbo, Ross, 11
Come Blow Your Horn, 250
Comedy Store, The, 163–64
Conneally, Monsignor Nicholas, 255
Conquest of the Planet of the Apes, 224
Coogan, Jackie, 66
Cooper, Gary, 30, 78, 86, 145, 190, 191, 272, 287
Coppola, Carmine, 290
Coppola, Francis Ford, 69–70, 219
Corby, Ellen, 285
Cord, Alex, 272
Cort, Bud, 167
"Cosmos," 119
Costello, Dolores, 20, 121
Costello, Lou, 39, 275
Count of Monte Cristo, The, 245
Country clubs
  Calabasas Park Golf Club, 286
  Hillcrest, 226
County Hospital, 236
Courtright, Hernando, 194–95
Courtright, Marcelle, 194
Courtship of Miles Standish, 118
Courtyard apartments, 66–67
Courtyard Complex, 122–23, *123*
Coward, Noel, 215
Crabbe, Buster, 38–39
Crain, Jeanne, 190
Crane, C. Howard, 134
Crane, Cheryl, 204
Crawford, Christina, 221
Crawford, Joan, 9, 15, 92–93, *93*, 161, 176, *212*, 236, 277
  house of, 220–21, *221*
Creature from the Black Lagoon, The, 9, 116
Crisp, Donald, 81, 285

Crosby, Bing, 16, 44, 78, 240, 255, 263, 305, 306
Crosby, Cathy Lee, 37
Crosby, Wilma W., 240
Cruickshank, Josephine, *87*
Cukor, George, 25, 198
Cultural Heritage Board, Los Angeles, 118, 127, 146
Culver, Harry H., 231
Culver City, 231–41
Culver City Hotel, 235–36, *235*
Culver Theater, 236
Cummings, Bob, *44*
Curlett, Aleck, 101
Curtis, Tony, 23
"Custer," 264

D.O.A., 141, 151
Daffy Duck, 55
Daisy, The, 192
Daisy Dell, 28–29
Dalton, David, 218
Damone, Vic, 26, 37
Dana, Viola, 285
"Daniel Boone," 264
Dark Passage, 215
Darmour, Larry, 76
Davenport, Dorothy, 234
Davies, Marion, 32, 45, 59, 75, 95, 98, 143, 178, 191, 248, 277
   houses of, 206, *255*, 258
Davis, Anne B., 74
Davis, Bette, 19, 32, 36, 92–93, *93*, 96, 174, 277
Davis, F. Pierpont, 27, 171
Davis, Joan, 239
Davis, Sammy, Jr., 177, 215
Davis, Walter S., 27, 171
Daw, Marjorie, 74
Day, Doris, 255, 277
Day at the Races, A, 306, *306*
Day of the Locust, The, 32–33, 35, 50, 115, 125
Dean, James, 26, 52–53, 113–14, *114*, 174, 217–19, 277
Dean, Priscilla, 274
"Death Valley Days," 81
De Carlo, Yvonne, 51
De Havilland, Olivia, 277
De La Motte, Marguerite, 8
DeLongpre Park, 71, *71*
Del Rio, Dolores, 110, 141, 195
Deluxe Laboratories, 110
DeMille, Cecil B., 3–4, 6, 9, 11, 17, 19, 29–30, 49, 65, 75, 78, 79, *108*, 109, 172, 234, 288, 296
   mansion of, 112–13, *108, 112*
DeMille, Constance Adam, 75
DeMille, Mrs. C. B., 73
DeMille barn, 29–30, *30*
DeMille Drive, 112–13, *112*
De Niro, Robert, 167
Designing Woman, 187, 188
Desilu, 79, 234

Devane, William, 260, 272
Devil's Island, 305
De Witt, Eleanor, 33
Dietrich, Marlene, 78, 86, 168, 175–76, *248*, 249
   house of, *204*, 205
Diller, Barry, 196
DiMaggio, Joe, 14, 160, 202, 216
Dinner, Michael, 112
Dino's Lodge, 163
Disney, Roy, 279
Disney, Walt, 39, 72, 81, 109, 122, 260, 269, 272, 279, 300
Disney, Walt, Productions, 279–80, *280*
Disney Studios, 109, 122–24, *123*
Dr. Doolittle, 264
Dr. Detroit, 105
Dog's Life, A, 66
Doheny, Edward L., Jr., 188–89
Doheny, Edward L., Sr., 188
Donald Duck, 6
Don Juan, 54
Dora (Formosa waitress), 68
Dorothy Chandler Pavilion, 151
Dorsey, Tommy, 50
Double Indemnity, 55, *55*, 167, 297
Dougherty, Jim, 61
Douglas, Buddy, 187
Douglas, Kirk, 30, 194
Dove, Billie, 110
Dracula, 116
"Dragnet," 151
Dressler, Marie, 299
Dreyfuss, Richard, 181, 196
Driver, The, 152
Duke, Doris, 209
Dunaway, Faye, 125
Dunne, Irene, 187, 195
Dupont, Gretl, *87*
Duquette, Beegle, 178
Duquette, Tony, 178, 203, 280
Durante, Jimmy, 6, 190, 191, 239
Durbin, Deanna, 275
Duryea, Dan, 272
"Dynasty," 67, 89, 147, 303

Earl Carroll Theater, 50–51
Earthquake, 49, 127, 271
East of Eden (film), 277
"East of Eden" (television show), 126
"East Side Kids, The," 119
Eaton, Hubert, 298
"Ebony and Ivory," 66
Echo Park, 109, 125–26
Eck, Johnny, 116
Eddy, Nelson, 75
Eden, Barbara, 74
Edendale, 109
"Edgar Bergen and Charlie McCarthy," 52
Edwards, Blake, 234, *234*, 262
Egyptian Theater, 13, 16–17, *16*
El Capitan (now Paramount Theater), 11

El Capitan (now the Palace), 44
El Coyote Restaurant, 91
El Miradero, 296
El Royale Apartments, 89, *89*
Embassy Club, 15
Emerson, John, 258
Emmy Awards, 39
Ennis-Brown house, 114–15, *115*
Entwistle, Peg, 57, 74
Ephron, Nora, 196
Escape Artist, 70
Essanay, 118, 231
E.T., 235
Evans, Linda, 38
"Every Breath You Take," 66
"Every Day Was the Fourth of July,"
    127
"Exposition Internationale des Arts
    Décoratifs et Industriels
    Modernes," 145

F.I.S.T., 50
Fabray, Nanette, 38
Factor, Max, 13–14
Factory, The, 177
Fairbanks, Douglas, 6, 10, 16, 17, 19,
    64, 67, 68, 107, 133–34, 146, 248,
    289, 301
  house of (Pickfair), 185, 207, *208,*
    257
  reflecting pool and tomb of, 75, *76*
Fairbanks, Douglas, Jr., 220–21
Fairbanks, Douglas, Productions, 81
Fairchild, Morgan, 250
"Falcon Crest," 105, 147, 219, 220
Falcon Lair, 208–9, *209*
Falcon Takes Over, The, 165
"Fall Guy, The," 287, 296
"Family Feud," 121
Famous Monsters of Filmland, 116
Famous Players, 78, 81
Fantasies Come True, 179
"Fantasy Island," 304–5, *305*
Farewell, My Lovely, 165
Farmer, Frances, 36, 78, 303
Farquhar, Robert D., 300
Farrell, Charles, 87
Farrell, Henry, 19
Farrell, Mike, 38
Father of the Bride, The, 190
Faulkner, William, 18, 33
Fawcett, Farrah, 262
Faye, Alice, 50, 105
Fazenda, Louise, 124
Feature Players Company, 49
Felix, Maria, 141
Fenyes, Adalbert, 300
Fenyes, Eva Scott, 300
Fenyes Mansion, 300–1, *301*
Ferguson, Helen, 110
Ferrer, José, 190
Ferrigno, Lou, 250
Fields, W. C., 113

Film Strip U.S.A., 239
Finch, Peter, 75, 96, 190, 191
Finian's Rainbow, 264
First National, 55, 269, 276
First United Methodist Church of
    Hollywood, 25–26, *25*
Fisher, Carrie, 196
Fisher, Eddie, 202
Fitzgerald, Barry, 255
Fitzgerald, F. Scott, 18, 166, 168, 169
  apartment of, 170–71, *170*
"Flamingo Road," 297, *297*
Flanner, Janet, 122–23
Fleming, Peggy, 110
Fleming, Rhonda, 196
Fleming, Victor, 76
Floradora Girl, The, 45
Florentine Gardens, 61
Flynn, Errol, 36, 86–87, *87,* 164, 168,
    277, 300, 305
  house of, 180–81, *180*
Folger, Abigale, 208
Fonda, Jane, 199, 251
Fonda, Jane, Workout, 199
Ford, Harrison, 115, *115*
Ford, John, 263, 274
Forest Lawn, 271–72, 298–300, *298,
    299*
Formosa Cafe, 68
Foul Play, 147, 155
Fountain Avenue, 159, 160
  8229 (Patio del Moro Apartments),
    175
  8313 (Loretta Young villa), 176
  8320–8328 (Villa Celia), 176, *176*
Fox, William, 110, 225
Fox Film Corporation, 225
Fox Studios, 110
Fox Village Theater, *216,* 217
Frankenstein, 116
Franklin, Bonnie, 196
"Franklin and Eleanor: The White
    House Years," 301
Franklin Avenue, 112
  5930 (Chateau Elysee), 58–60, *59*
  5959 (Villa Carlotta), 59
  6200 (Hollywood Tower), 58
  6650 (Montecito Apartments), 26
  6817 (First United Methodist Church
    of Hollywood), 25–26, *25*
  7001 (Magic Castle), 23, *23*
  7047 (Highland Gardens Hotel), 22–
    23
  7425 (Anita Stewart house), 21
  chateau apartment houses on, 43,
    58–60, *59*
Frawley, William, 89
Freaks, 116
Freed, Arthur, 237
Fremont Place, 93
Friedkin, William, 278
Frykowski, Voytek, 208
Funny Girl, 120, 252

Gable, Clark, 28, 46, 53, 58, 86, 145, 230, 299
  home of, 283–84, 284
Gable, Clark, Estates, 283–84
Gable, John Clark, 284
Gable and Lombard, 152
Gabor, Zsa Zsa, 176
Garbo, Greta, 10, 167, 192, 254–55, 258, 259
  house of, 206
Garden Court Apartments site, 7–8, 7
Garden of Allah, 168–69, 168
Garden of Allah, The, 233
Gardner, Ava, 19
Gardner, Beatrice (Bappy), 19
Garfield, John, 277
Garland, Judy, 9, 89, 155, 160, 173, 191, 195, 215, 278, 295
Garner, James, 24, 38
Garr, Teri, 70
Gaynor, Janet, 10, 23, 29, 74, 86, 110, 172
  home of, 33, 33
General Telephone Building, 253, 253
Gentlemen Prefer Blondes, 144
Gere, Richard, 167, 249
Getty, J. Paul, 94
Ghostbusters, 66
Giant, 53, 277
Gibbons, Cedric, 60, 104, 146, 256
Gibson, Hoot, 274
Gilbert, John, 7, 10, 110, 206
Girl from Yesterday, The, 81
Gish, Lillian, 7, 31, 117
Glendale, 295, 296
Gless, Sharon, 275
Globe Theater, 136
Glorious Betsy, The, 20, 121
Glover, Tom, Sr., 24
Goddard, Paulette, 165
Godfather II, 153
Goetz, William, 162, 257, 305
Going Bye-Bye!, 236
Going My Way, 255
Gold Coast, 255–58
Gold Diggers of 1933, The, 121
Golden West Broadcasters, 54
Gold Rush, The, 66
Gold's Gym, 250–51
Goldwyn, Samuel, 3–4, 29, 60, 67, 78, 238, 257, 260, 287, 302
Goldwyn, Samuel, Company, 68
Goldwyn, Samuel, Jr., 68
Goldwyn, Samuel, Studios, 67, 68
Gone with the Wind, 162, 191, 230, 233, 234, 235, 284, 297, 297
Gonzales, Pancho, 87
Goodman, Ezra, 215
Good Neighbor Sam, 141
Gordon, Ruth, 252
Gould, Elliott, 28
Gower Gulch, 52, 52
Gower Gulch Shopping Plaza, 52

Gower Plaza Hotel, 52–53
Grable, Betty, 6, 50, 110
Graham, Sheila, 168, 170–71
Grammy Awards, 155
Grant, Cary, 23, 58, 84, 255, 256, 265
Granville, the, 172
Grauman, Sid, 5, 6, 10, 16–17, 140, 299
Grauman's Chinese Theater, 5–7, 5, 13, 17
Grauman's Egyptian Theater, 13, 16–17, 16
Grease, 121, 247
Great Dictator, The, 66
"Greatest American Hero, The," 289
Greatest Show on Earth, The, 79
Green, Burton E., 185
"Green Acres," 206, 207
Greenstreet, Sidney, 277
Grey, Joel, 196
Greystone Park and Mansion, 188–89
Griffith, Corinne, 121
Griffith, D. W., 9, 36–37, 68, 81, 117, 131, 140, 148, 271, 271, 288. 301
Griffith Park, 60
Griffith Park Observatory, 113–14, 114
Grosbard, Ulu, 300
Gulf & Western, 79
"Gunsmoke," 60, 283

Hagen, Jean, 174
Hagman, Larry, 262, 263
Haines, William, 161–62
Hair, 51
Haley, Jack, 190, 239
Hall, Hon, 275
Hall, Jon, 116
Hal Roach Studios, site of, 232
Hamilton, George, 207
Hammett, 70
Hampton, Hope, 110
Hampton, Jesse D., 67, 118
Hancock Park, 85, 87–88
"Happy Days," 77, 85–86, 86
Harding, Ann, house of, 181, 181
Hardy, Oliver, 109, 127, 127, 227, 232, 233, 236, 261
Harlow, Jean, 33, 69, 70, 86, 166–67, 299
Harmetz, Aljean, 236
Harper's Bazaar, 123
Harris, Barbara, 58
Harris, Mildred, 140
Harris, Phil, 50
Harris, Richard, 105
Hart, Mary Ellen, 291
Hart, William S., 80, 95–96, 120, 140, 234, 290–91, 290
Hart, William S., Park, 290–91
Hartford, Huntington, 49
Harvey, Arthur E., 58
Harvey, Rev. Xen, 219
Hats Off, 127

Hauser, Gaylord, 192
"Have Gun, Will Travel," 287
Haver, June, 196
Haver, Phyllis, 124
Haver, Ronald, 92, *92*
"Having It All," 289
Hawks, Howard, 305
Hawn, Goldie, 262, 263
Hayakawa, Sessue, 234
Hayden, Tom, 251
Hayek, Julie, 37
Hayes, Helen, 49
Hayes, Isaac, 251
Hayworth, Rita, 53–54, 205
Head, Edith, 198
Hearst, William Randolph, 32, 58–59, 74, 95, 98, 143, 191, 206
    Santa Monica beach house of, *255, 258*
Heart of a Racing Tout, The, 131
"Heart of Screenland" fountain, *231*
Hedren, Tippi, 105
Heinsbergen, A. B., & Company Building, 91
Heinsbergen, Anthony B., 91
Hello Dolly!, 213, 224–25, *224*
Hells Angels, 69, 70
Helter Skelter, 287
Hemingway, Margaux, 177
Hemingway, Mariel, 177
Hendison, Paul, 44
Hendrix, Jimi, 23
Henie, Sonja, 6
Henreid, Paul, 277, 282
Hepburn, Katharine, 174, 195
Herald Examiner Building, 143, *143*
Herrick, Margaret, Library, 198
Herrmann, Bernard, 18
Hersholt, Jean, 299
Higgins, Colin, 219
High Anxiety, 220
"High Chapparal," 60
Highland Avenue. *See* North Highland Avenue
Highland Gardens Hotel, 22–23
High Tower, 28
Hillcrest Country Club, 226
"Hill Street Blues," 283
Hillview Apartments, 20
Hilton, Conrad Nicholson, 190, 191
Hilton, James, 32
Historic Hollywood Trust, 30
Hitchcock, Alfred, 9, 190, 191, 275
Hoffman, Dustin, 167–68, 262
Holden, William, 34, 94, 170, 302
"Hold that Ghost," 138
Hollygrove, 73
Hollywood, 76, 196
    arrival of first movie folk in, 3–4, 24
    origin of name, 3
    preservationist movement in, 4, 7–8, 30, 33, 39, 44, 97, 100

Hollywood Athletic Club, 38–39, *38*
Hollywood Boulevard, 4–5, *4*
    5400 (Hollywood Professional School), 110–11
    5951 (Florentine Gardens), 61
    6233 (Pantages Theater), 43, 45–46, *46*
    6433 (Pacific Hollywood Theater), 20–21, *21*
    6531–6535 (Hillview Apartments), 20
    6541 (Janes house), 19–20, *20*
    6658 (Larry Edmunds Bookshop, Inc.), 18–19
    6667 (Musso & Frank Grill), 17–18, *18*
    6712 (Egyptian Theater), 13, 16–17, *16*
    6763 (Montmartre Cafe site), 15–16, *15*
    6764 (Hollywood Theater), 16, *17*
    6767 (Hollywood Wax Museum), 14–15
    6777 (Security Pacific Bank Building), 13, *13*
    6834–6838 (Paramount Theater), 11
    7000 (Hollywood Roosevelt Hotel), 10–11, *10*
    7021 (Garden Court Apartments site), 7–8, *7*
    7051 (Hollywood Museum), 9–10
    Highland Avenue and (Hollywood Hotel site), 11–12, *12*
    Vine Street and, *42,* 43, *44*
    Walk of Fame, 8–9, *8*
Hollywood Bowl, 28–29, *28*
Hollywood Cafe Legends, 80
Hollywood Center Studios (formerly Hollywood General Studios), 69–71, *70*
Hollywood Chamber of Commerce, 8–9, 30, 49, 57–58
Hollywood General Studios, 22, 70, *70*
Hollywood Heights, 28
Hollywood Heritage, 30
Hollywood High School, 37–38
"Hollywood Hotel," 12
Hollywood Hotel (film), 12
Hollywood Hotel site, 11–12, *12*
Hollywood Knickerbocker Hotel, 35–37, *36*
Hollywoodland, 56–58
Hollywoodland Realty Company, 57
Hollywood Memorial Park Cemetery, 54, 65, 74–76, *75*
Hollywood Museum, *2,* 9–10
"Hollywood Palace," 44
Hollywood Palladium, 50
Hollywood Playhouse, 43–44
Hollywood Professional School, 110–11
Hollywood Roosevelt Hotel, 10–11, *10*
Hollywood sign, 56–58, *57,* 75
Hollywood Studio Club, 73–74, *74*

Hollywood Television Center, 72–73, *72*
"Hollywood Television Theater," 119
Hollywood Theater, 16, *17*
Hollywood Tower, 58
Hollywood USO, 37
Hollywood Wax Museum, 14–15
Hollywood Wilcox Hotel, 19
Holmby Hills, 213
Holmes, Burton, 33
Holy Cross Cemetery, 239
Home Savings and Loan Association, 48–49, *48*
"Hooray for Hollywood," 12
Hoover, Herman, 163, 164
Hopalong Cassidy, 81
Hope, Bob, 37, 78, 195
Hopkins, Miriam, 78
Hopper, Hedda, 198
Hotel(s), 131–32
 Adams, 235
 Alexandria, 132, 139–40
 Ambassador, 97–100, *98, 99*
 Beverly Hills, 186–88, *186, 187,* 194
 Beverly Wilshire, 193–95, *194*
 Biltmore, 146–47, *147*
 Chateau Marmont, 166–68, *167*
 Culver City, 235–36, *235*
 Garden of Allah, 168–69, *168*
 Gower Plaza, 52–53
 Highland Gardens, 22–23
 Hollywood Hotel site, 11–12, *12*
 Hollywood Knickerbocker, 35–37, *36*
 Hollywood Roosevelt, 10–11, *10*
 Hollywood Wilcox, 19
 Miramar-Sheraton, 254–55, *254*
 Park Plaza, 105
 Plaza, 47–48
 Washington, 236
 Westin Bonaventure, 149–50, *149*
Houdini, Harry, 23, 36, 180
House of Wax, 15
"House of Wax, The," 278
House on Haunted Hill, The, 115
Houses. *See under individual names of owners, movies, or television shows associated with them*
Howard, Leslie, 259
How Green Was My Valley, 263–64
How the West Was Won, 264
Hudson Street, 19
Hughes, Howard, 46, 70, 77, 99, 165, 167, 213, 282
 former headquarters of, 68–69, *69*
Human Wreckage, 234
Hunt, Marsha, *44*
Hunter, Ross, 275
Huntington Hartford Theater, 49
Hustler, The, 152
Huston, John, 198
Hutton, Betty, 78
Huxley, Aldous, 259

Hyams, Leila, 162
Hyde, Johnny, 195

"I Love Lucy," *70,* 71, 162
Imitation of Life, 275
"Immigrants, The," 127, 301
Imperial Garden Sukyaki, 166
In a Lonely Place, 174
Ince, Thomas, 19, 58–59, 79, 231–32, 234, 238, 245, 248
Ince, Mrs. Thomas, 58, 59
"Incredible Hulk, The," 289
Incredible Shrinking Man, The, 9
Inside Daisy Clover, 252
Intermezzo, 233
International Creative Management, 199
Intolerance, 117
Invasion of the Body Snatchers, The, 57, 60, 119
Ireland, John, 174
Irene (MGM costume designer), 36
Isherwood, Christopher, 259
Island Records, 38
It Cafe, The, 48
It Conquered the Earth, 60
It Happened One Night, 53
It's a Mad Mad Mad Mad World, 39
Iturbi, José, 29, 190

Jack Dempsey Story, The, 105
Jackson, Michael, 127, 137, 155
James, Harry, 50
Janes house, 19–20, *20*
Janssen, David, 241
Jasper Studios, 70
Jay Ward Productions, 168
Jazz Singer, The, 54, 121
"Jerry Lewis Show, The," 44
Jessel, George, 241
Jet Pilot, 235
Jillian, Ann, 37
Jolson, Al, 195, 240–41, *241*
Jones, Buck, 110
Jones, Carolyn, 15
Jones, Grace, 38
Jones, John P., 255
Jones, Spike, 239
Joplin, Janis, 22–23
Julia, Raul, 70
Jungle Jim series, 305
Jurado, Katy, 174

KABC, 121
Kalem Motion Picture Company, 231
Kalmus, Herbert, 72
Kalmus, Natalie, 72
Kaplan, Gabe, 163
Karloff, Boris, 115, 167, 275
Kashfi, Anna, 174
Kaufman, George S., 166, 169
KCET Studios, 118–19

Keaton, Buster, 124, 272
Keaton, Diane, 167
Kellerman, Sally, 38
Kelley, Kitty, 190–91
Kelly, Gene, 29, 90
Kelly, Patsy, 261
Ken Murray's Blackouts, 44
Kennedy, John F., 89, 187, 256–57
Kennedy, Joseph P., 58, 77, 234
Kennedy, Patricia, 256
Kennedy, Robert F., 100, 256–57
Kent, Craufurd, *87*
Key Largo, 215
Keystone Comedy Company, 124
Keystone Kops, 124
Keystone Productions, 248
KFAC Radio, 26
KFSG, 125
Kid, The, 66
Kid Auto Races, 248
King, Billie Jean, 87
King Kong, 16, 76, 116, 147, 155, 234
King of Kings, 6, 234
King's Row, 278
Kinney, Abbot, 247
Kirby, George, 37
Klemperer, Werner, 166
KMPC, 55
"Knight Rider," 289
KNX Columbia Square, 51–53, *51*
Koala Blue, 179
"Kojak," 105
Korda, Alexander, 70
Kovacs, Ernie, 272
Kramer, Jack, 87
Kramer, Stanley, 81
Krol, Natalie, 239
KTLA, 54–55, *54*
Kwan, Nancy, 74

Ladd, Alan, 78, 300
"Lady in Black," 75
Lady in the Lake, The, 104–5
Laemmle, Carl, 3, 19, 269, 274
L.A. Heartbreakers, 169
Laird International Studios, 233–35,
    234
Lake, Veronica, 78
Lake Hollywood, 270–71, *270*
Lalique, René, 145–46
La Marr, Barbara, 17, 31, 32, 75
Lamarr, Hedy, 91–92
Lambert, Phyllis, 147
Lamour, Dorothy, 78
Lamparski, Richard, 144
Lamparski's Hidden Hollywood, 144
Lancaster, Burt, 30
"Lancer," 264
Landis, Carole, 165
Landis, John, 137
Landmark Motel, 22–23
Landon, Michael, 263
Landsburgh, G. Albert, 135, 137, 155

Lane, Rollin S., 23
Lang, Fritz, 116
Langdon, Harry, 261
Lankershim, 269
Lansburgh, G. Albert, 11, 96
Lantz, Walter, Productions, 73
Lanza, Mario, 239
LaPlante, Laura, 274
La Rocque, Rod, 10
Larry Edmunds Bookshop, Inc., 18
Lasky, Jesse, 3–4, 17, 29–30, 49, 76,
    78, 257
"Last Supper, The" (da Vinci), 15
Last Tycoon, The, 147, 170, 171
"Laugh-In," 278
Laughton, Charles, 272
Laurel, Stan, 109, 121, 127, *127,* 227,
    232, 233, 236, 261, 272
Laurel Avenue, 179
Laurel Canyon, 160
Laurel Canyon Boulevard, 179–80
Lautner, John, 181
"Laverne and Shirley," 77
Lawford, Peter, 177, 215, 256
Lawrence, Gertrude, 11
Lawrence Welk Plaza, 253, *253*
"Lawrence Welk Show, The," 50
Lazar, Irving, 215
"Leave It to Beaver," 281
Le Dome, 161–62, *161*
Lee, Dixie, 16, 240
Lee, Ruta, 38
Lee, S. Charles, 14, 135–36, 138, 217
Leigh, Janet, *249*
Leigh, Vivien, 70, *230*
Lemmon, Jack, 262
Leo the Lion, 237
LeRoy, Mervyn, *87,* 237, 257, 286
Le Trianon, 111–12, *111*
Letterman, David, 163
Lewis, Jerry, 163
Liberty, 235
Library
    Brand, 296–97, *296*
    Louis B. Mayer, 112
    Margaret Herrick, 198
Library of Congress, 18
Lidke, Dennis, 44
Lights of New York, The, 54
Lillie, Bea, 11
Lindbergh, Charles, 291
Linkletter, Jack, 196
Lipstick, 177
Little Lord Fauntleroy, 233
Liu's Chinese restaurant, 193
Llewellyn, Richard, 263
Lloyd, Harold, 6, 10, 70, 76, 86, *130,*
    197, 232, 258
    house of, 206, *207*
Lockhart, Gene, 25
Loew, Marcus, 10
Lombard, Carole, 46, 58, 86, 110, 174,
    248, 249, 284, 299

Lone Wolf, The, 76
Long Goodbye, The, 28
Loos, Anita, 144, 258
Loper, Don, Salon, 161, 162
Lord, Jack, 172
Loren, Sophia, 195
Lorre, Peter, 75, 277
Los Altos Apartments, 95
Los Angeles, 3, 4, 5, 128–55
Los Angeles Civic Light Opera, 119
Los Angeles Conservancy, 133
Los Angeles County Museum of Art,
    92, *92*
Los Angeles County Music Center, 148
Los Angeles Federal Savings and Loan
    Building, 49
Los Angeles Job Corps, 74
Los Angeles Music Center, 124, 151
Los Angeles Orphans Home Society, 73
Los Angeles Philharmonic Orchestra,
    147–48, 151
Los Angeles State and County
    Arboretum, 304–5
Los Angeles Tennis Club, 85, 86–87,
    87
Los Angeles Theater, 135
Los Angeles Times, 104
Los Feliz Theater, 116–17
Los Feliz, 109
Los Feliz Boulevard, 112
Los Virgenes Canyon, 264
"Lou Grant," 105
Louis B. Mayer Library, 112
Louis B. Mayer Memorial Theater, 285
Louis B. Mayer Pictures, 21
Love, Bessie, 121
Love at First Bite, 9
"Love Boat, The," 67, 289
Loved One, The, 188, 190
Love Is a Many-Splendored Thing, 264
Love Me Tender, 264
"Love That Bob," 70
Loy, Myrna, *246,* 247, 265
Lubin Manufacturing Company, 118
Lubitsch, Ernst, 79, 287
"Lucky Strike Hit Parade, The," 52
Luft, Sid, 215
Lugosi, Bela, 39, 115, 116, 239, 275
Lupino, Ida, 277
Lupino, Stanley, 261
"Lux Radio Theater," 49
Lyon, Lisa, 250
Lytton Industries, 191

Ma and Pa Kettle, 264
MacArthur, Douglas, Park, 105
"MacArthur Park," 105
McCadden Place, 17
McCarey, Leo, 255, 257
McCarthy, Kevin, 57, 60
McCrea, Joel, 38
MacDonald, Jeanette, 300

MacDonald, Marie ("The Body"), 51
McDonald's, 50
MacGraw, Ali, 6, 220, 262
McKenney, Eileen, 35
MacLaine, Shirley, 262
MacMurray, Fred, 30, 55, 78, 104, 167,
    297
McPherson, Aimee Semple, 124–25,
    125, 299–300, *299*
McQueen, Barbie, 272
McQueen, Steve, 194
Magic Castle, 23, *23*
Magnificent Obsession, 275
Majestic Productions, 76
Majors, Lee, 275
"Male Model U.S.A.," 150
Malibu, 255, 262–65, *262*
Malibu Creek State Park, 263–65, *264,*
    265
Malone, Dorothy, 74
Man in the Iron Mask, The, 305
Mann, Thomas, 259
Mann's Bruin Theater, 217
Mann's Chinese Theater (formerly
    Grauman's Chinese Theater),
    5–7, *5*
Manson Family, 91, 100, 208, 239, 287
Man Who Loved Women, The, 224
March, Fredric, 25, 29
Mark of Zorro, The, 81
Mark Taper Forum Theater, 124
Marshall, Herbert, 285
Marshall, John, High School, 121–22,
    122
Martin, Dean, 163, 215
Martin, Steve, 23
Marx, Groucho, 46, 306
Marx, Harpo, 6
Marx, Zeppo, 305
Marx Brothers, 261, 306
"Mary Tyler Moore Show, The," 283
M*A*S*H (movie), 264, *264*
"M*A*S*H" (television series), 264,
    265
Mason, James, 99, 155, 191, 295
Masonic Hall, 11
Masonic Temple, 36–37
Max Factor Building and Beauty
    Museum, 13–14
Mayan Theater, 143–44, *144*
May Company Department Store, 91–
    92
Mayer, Louis B., 7, 10, 21, 140, 146,
    161, 164, 197, 206, 238, 254, 305
    beach house of, 256, *256*
Mayer, Louis B., Library, 112
Mayer, Louis B., Memorial Theater,
    285
Mayfair Apartments, 21
Mayfair Supermarket, 122–24
Mayo, Luther T., 95
MCA (Music Corporation of America),
    191, 275

"Me and Mom," 150
Meet Me in St. Louis, 238
Melnick, Dan, 272
Melnitz Hall Theater, 219
Melrose Avenue, 159, 160
    5335 (Western Costume Company),
        80–81
    7366 (Koala Blue), 179
    7408 (Fantasies Come True), 179
    8687 (Pacific Design Center), 177
Mengers, Sue, 199
Menjou, Adolphe, 28, 75, 121, 145
Mercer, Johnny, 12, 45
Meredith, Burgess, 32–33
Merkel, Una, 96
Merle Norman Tower of Beauty, 289–
        90
"Merv Griffin Show, The," 44
Metropolis, 116
Metropolitan Community Church, 144
Meyer and Holler, 13, 16–17, 38
MGM (Metro-Goldwyn-Mayer), 45,
        238, 254
MGM Studios, 105, 231, 236–39, *239*
MGM/UA, 238
Michael's restaurant, 116
"Mickey McGuire," 76
Mickey Mouse, 109, 123, 280, *280*
Midler, Bette, 22
Mildred Pierce, 151, 277
Mile, Miracle, 91
Milland, Ray, 78
Milland, Vicki, 215
Million Dollar Theater, 133, 140–41,
        141
Mimieux, Yvette, 38
Mineo, Sal, 114, *114*
Minnelli, Liza, 203–4, 250
Minnelli, Vincente, 160, 203
Minter, Mary Miles, 102–3, 296
Miramar-Sheraton Hotel, 254–55
Miranda, Carmen, 9, 190
"Mission Impossible," 219, 296
Mission San Fernando, 287–89, *288*
*Mr. Blandings Builds His Dream
        House,* 264, 265, *265*
Mitchell, Lisa, 73
Mix, Tom, 110, 140, 197, 225, *294,*
        301, *301*
Modern Problems, 127
Modern Times, 66
Mommie Dearest, 221
Monogram Pictures, *118,* 119
Monroe, Marilyn, *2,* 9, 14, 61, 67, 73,
        74, 99, 144, 160, 167, 172, 187,
        195, 257
    houses of, 202, *202,* 223
    tomb of, 216
Montand, Yves, 187
Monterey Pop, 22
Monterey Rock Festival (1967), 22
Montez, Maria, 275
Montgomery, Robert, 260, 272

Montmartre Cafe site, 15–16, *15*
Monument to the Stars, 196–97, *196*
Moore, Colleen, 110
Moore, Dudley, 250
Moorehead, Agnes, 178
Moreno, Antonio, 121
Moreno, Rita, 74
Morgan, Julia, 74, 143, 258
Morgan, Michèle, 176
Morgan and Walls, 138
"Mork and Mindy," 77
Morley, Sheridan, 259
Morosco, Oliver, 136
Morris, William, Agency, 195
Morris, William, Office, 87
Moss, Jerry, 66
Motion Picture Country House and
        Hospital, 285
Motion Picture Tournament (1938), *87*
Moulin Rouge, 51
Mount St. Mary's College, 153, 219–20,
        220
Movie houses, 132
    Beverly Theater, 193, *193*
    Chinese Theater, 5–7, *5*
    Culver Theater, 236
    Fox Village Theater, *216,* 217
    Hollywood Theater, 16, *17*
    Mann's Bruin Theater, 217
    Mayan Theater, 143–44, *144*
    Melnitz Hall Theater, 219
    Million Dollar Theater, 133, 140–41,
        141
    Nuart Theater, 223
    Pacific Hollywood Theater, 20–21,
        21
    Paramount Theater, 11
Movie studios. *See* Studios
MTM (Mary Tyler Moore
        productions), 283
Mulholland, William, 270
Mulholland Dam, 270, *270,* 271
Mulholland House, 180–81, *180*
Munchkins, 67
Muni, Paul, 277
Murder My Sweet, 165
Murray, Ken, 44
Murray, Mae, 7, 274
Museums
    Hollywood Museum, 9–10
    Hollywood Studio Museum, 29–30,
        30
    Hollywood Wax Museum, 14–15
    Los Angeles County Art Museum,
        92, *92*
    Merle Norman Tower of Beauty,
        289–90
Music Box, The, 109, 127
Music Center complex, 45
Music Man, The, 278
Musso & Frank Grill, 17–18, *18*
Mutiny on the Bounty, 238
My Best Girl, 134

Myers, Carmel, 74
My Friend Flicka, 264
My Sister Eileen, 35

Nagle, Conrad, 20, 28, 197
Napoleon, 290
National Film Corporation, 76
National Legion of Decency, 87
National Park Service, 287
National Register of Historic Places, 126, 133, 252
National Trust Property Fioli, 303
National Velvet, 286
Nazimova, Alla, 121, 168
NBC Radio, 49
NBC Television studios, 278–79
Nederlander theater organization, 46
Neff, Wallace, 257
Negri, Pola, 10, 99, 172, 291
Nelson, David, 22, 38
Nelson, Harriet, 22, *22*
Nelson, Ozzie, 22, *22,* 87
Nelson, Ricky, 22, 38, 181
Nestor Film Company, 51
Nestor Film Corporation, 3
Neutra, Richard, 257
"Newhart," 90, 283
Newhart, Bob, 190
Newman, Paul, 177, 252
Newton-John, Olivia, 90, 159, 179, 262
New York, New York, 105, 138, 147
New York Motion Picture Company, 124
New York Philharmonic Orchestra, 54
Niblo, Fred, 197, 259
Nicholson, Jack, 126, 192, 263
Nickelodeon, 127
Night of the Bloodbeast, 60
Nightspots
    Ciro's, 163–64, *164*
    Cocoanut Grove, 98–99, *98*
    The Comedy Store, 163–64
    The Daisy, 192
    Earl Cornell Theater, 50
    The Factory, 177
    Florentine Gardens, 61
    Hollywood Palladium, 50
    The It Cafe, 48
    Montmartre Cafe, 15–16, *15*
    The Roxy, 161
    Studio One, 177
    Trocadero Cafe, 162, *162*
Niven, David, 215, 302
Nixon, Richard, 189
Normand, Mabel, 102–3, 109, 120, 124
North, Sheree, 51
North Highland Avenue
    1521 (Hollywood High School), 37–38
    1666–1668 (Max Factor Building and Beauty Museum), 13–14, *14*
    2000 (Roman Gardens), 27

2035 (American Legion), 27–28, *27*
2300 (Hollywood Studio Museum), 29–30, *30*
2301 (Hollywood Bowl), 28–29, *28*
North Ivar Avenue
    1641 (Hollywood USO), 37
    1714 (Hollywood Knickerbocker Hotel), 35–37, *36*
    1817 (Parva Sed-Apta Apartments), 35
    1851 (Alto-Nido Apartments), 34, *35*
North Roxbury Drive
    1000 (Lucille Ball's house), 205, *205*
    1002 (Jack Benny's house), 205
    822 (Marlene Dietrich's house), *204,* 205
    918 (Jimmy Stewart's house), 205
North Vine Street
    1411 (McDonald's), 50
    1500 (Home Savings and Loan Association), 48–49, *48*
    1615 (Huntington Hartford Theater), 49
    1628 (Brown Derby), 46–47, *47*
    1637 (Plaza Hotel), 47–48
    1735 (The Palace), 43–44
    1750 (Capitol Records Tower), 45, *45*
Nothing Sacred, 233
Novak, Jane, 95–96
Novak, Kim, 9, 54, 74
Novak, Paul, 257
Novarro, Ramon, house, 60–61, *61*
Now Voyager, 32
Nuart Theater, 223

Oblath family, 80
Oblath's restaurant, 80
Ocean Front Road. *See* Pacific Coast Highway
Ocean House, 191, 258
O'Connell, Arthur, 285
O'Connor, Donald, 110, 221, 275
Oh, God, Book II, 152
"Oleander Arms" apartments, 173, *173*
Olivier, Laurence, 70
Olmedo, Alex, 87
O'Neal, Ryan, 110, 161
One Foot in Heaven, 25
One from the Heart, 70
Oneida, 58–59
Orpheum Theater, 135
Orpheum vaudeville circuit, 137
O'Sullivan, Maureen, 190
Other Side of Midnight, The, 147, 296
"Our Gang," 285
"Our Miss Brooks," 52
Our Silent Paths, 288
Outlaw, The, 69
Oviatt, James, 145–46
Oviatt Building, 145–46
"Ozzie and Harriet Show, The," 22, 70

Pacific Avenue, 248
Pacific Coast Highway, 255–58, 260, 262, 263
Pacific Design Center, 177
Pacific Electric Railroad, 150
Pacific Hollywood Theater, 20–21, *21*
Pacific Southwest Championship, 86
Pacific Studio and Laboratory, 76
Pacific Theaters, 46
Pacino, Al, 176
Page, Geraldine, 125
Palace, The, 43–44
Palace Theater, 137
Palisades Beach Road. *See* Pacific Coast Highway
Palladium, 50
Pan Pacific Auditorium, 85, 90, *90*
Pantages, Alexander, 46, 138, 145, 299
Pantages, Lloyd, 165
Pantages Downtown Building, 145
Pantages Theater, 43, 45–46, *46*, 138, 145
Paramount Gate, 77–78, *78*
Paramount Pictures Corporation, 49, 79, 254
Paramount Ranch, 287
Paramount Studios, 30, 65, 75, 76, 77–79, *78*, 85, 87–88
Paramount Theater (El Capitan), 11
Parent, Steven, 208
Parker, Dorothy, 166, 169, 178–79
Parker, Frank, 87
Park Plaza Hotel, 105
Parks
    DeLongpre, 71, *71*
    Douglas MacArthur, 105
    Echo, 125–26
    Greystone Park and Mansion, 188–89
    William S. Hart Park, 290–91
    Malibu Creek State Park, 263–65, *264, 265*
    Will Rogers Memorial Park, 188
    Will Rogers State Park, 259–60, *259*
Parsons, Louella, 12, 16, 59, 143, 161, 198, 240
    house of, 203
"Partridge Family, The," 281
Parva Sed-Apta Apartments, 35
Pasadena, 295
Pasadena Playhouse, 302–3
Pasadena Train Station, 302, *302*
Pathé, 234
Pathé West Coast Studio, 124
Patio del Moro Apartments, 175
Peck, Gregory, *187*, 188, 194, 198
Peck, Lydell, 23
"Peggy Fleming in Russia," 110
Pellissier Building, 97, *97*
Perfect Day, A, 232, 233
"Perry Mason," 66
Peters, Jon, 263
Pet Memorial Park, SPCA, 285–86

Phantom of the opera, 116
Phillips, Eleanore, 15–16
Pickfair, 185, 207, *208,* 257
Pickford, Mary, 6. 9, 10, 17, 49, *64, 67,* 68, 73, 75, 93, 111, 112, 133–34, 146, 178, 197, 198, 289
Pickford-Fairbanks Studios, *64, 67,* 68
Pike, James J., 38
Pitts, Zasu, 74, 165, 239, 261
Planet of the Apes, 264
Players Club, 166
Plaza Hotel, 47–48
Polanski, Roman, 208, 270
Polanski, Sharon Tate, 239
Polo Lounge, 187, 188
Pons, Lily, 58
Porky Pig, 55
Portman, John, 149
Post, Wiley, 260
Poverty Row, 52, 53
Powell, Dick, 12, 36, 165, 277
Powell, Eleanor, 75
Powell, Michael, 70
Powell, William, 86, 96, 174
Power, Tyrone, 75, 303
Powers, Stephanie, 38, 260, 272
Presley, Elvis, 36, 68, 90, 189, 193
Pressman, Joel, 214
Prevost, Marie, 124
Price, Vincent, 15
Prinze, Freddie, 272
Prisoner of Zenda, The, 233
Producers Studios, 81, 93
Pryor, Richard, 163
Psycho, 275, *276*
Public Enemy, 121
Pumping Iron, 250

"Queen for a Day," 51
Queen's Necklace, The, 301
"Quincy," 285
Quinn, Anthony, 113
Quinn, Katherine DeMille, 113
Quon, Lem, 68

Radio City, 49
Raft, George, 89, 305
Raiders of the Lost Ark, 39
Rainbow, The, 160
Raines, Claude, 116
Raines, Ella, 105
Rains of Rainchipur, The, 264
Raintree County, 238
Raleigh Studios, 81, 93
Ralston, Vera Hruba, 283
Rambova, Natacha, 31, *34,* 99
Ramona, 81
Rand, Ayn, 74
Rappe, Virginia, 154
Rathbone, Basil, 275
Ratkovitch, Wayne, 97, 146
"Rat Pack," 215
Ravenswood, 87–88, *88*

Rawls, Lou, 93
Ray, Charles, 118
Raye, Martha, 37
Reagan, Ronald, 12, 15, 26, 27, 81, 198, 232, 277, 298
Reap the Wild Wind, 11
Rebecca, 233
Rebel Without a Cause, 94, 113–14, *114,* 121, 277
Red Cars, 150
Redford, Robert, *251,* 262, 263
Reed, Donna, 74
Reeves, George, 66
Reggie Mixes In, 301
Reid, Wallace, 121, 234
Reiner, Rob, 196
"Remington Steele," 285, 289
Republic Studios, 180, *282,* 283
Restaurants
  Brown Derby, 46–47, *47,* 100–1, *100*
  Butterfield's, 164
  Chasen's, 198–99
  Clifton's Cafeteria, 136, *137*
  El Coyote, 91
  Formosa Cafe, 68
  Imperial Garden Sukyaki, 166
  Le Dome, 161
  Musso & Frank Grill, 17–18, *18*
  Players Club, 166
  Polo Lounge, 187, 188
  The Rainbow, 160
  Rex II Ristorante, 146
  Romanoff's, 192–3
  72 Market Street, 250
  77 Sunset Strip, 162
  Thelma Todd's Sidewalk Cafe site, 260–61, *260*
  Villa Capri, 26
  Yamashiro, 23–25, *24*
Revue Productions, 275
Rex II Ristorante, 146
Reynolds, Burt, 263
"Rich Man, Poor Man," 147
Rickman, Tom, 112
Rin-Tin-Tin, 121
Ritter, John, 38, 163
RKO Pantages, 46
RKO Studios, 76–77, *77,* 234
Roach, Hal, 70, 76, 227, 260, 272, 300, 305
Robards, Jason, 38
Robe, The, 226
Robertson, Cliff, 93
Robin Hood, 16
Robinson, Edward G., 277
Robinson-Shaw, Jill, 215
"Rockford Files, The," 151
Rodeo Drive, 192. *See also* North Rodeo Drive
Rodeo Land and Water Company, 185, 186
Rogers, Beverly, 198
Rogers, Buddy, 15, 111, 134, 178, 198

Rogers, Charles (Buddy), 207
Rogers, Ginger, 58
Rogers, Roy, 6, 283
Rogers, Will, 10, *184,* 187, 188, 192, 197, 260, 272
  estate of, 259–60, *259*
Roland, Gilbert, *87*
Roland, Ruth, 296
Romance of Tarzan, The, 76
Roman Gardens, 27
Romanoff, Mike, 192, 215
Romanoff's, 192–3
Romany Villa, 175–76, *175*
Romero, Caesar, 174
Ronstadt, Linda, 262, 263
Rooney, Mickey, 8, 76, 87, 110
Roosevelt Hotel, 10–11, *10*
Rose, Helen, 190
Rose, The, 22
Rose of the Rancho, 288
Ross, Harold, 199
Ross, Katharine, 275
Rosson, Hal, 167
Roxbury Drive. *See* North Roxbury Drive
Roxy, The, 161
Royal Scandal, 9
Russell, Rosalind, 32, 190, 191, 239, *240*

S.O.B., 262
Sacks, Herman, 103
Sagan, Carl, 119
"Saint, The," 52
St. Cyr, Lili, 61, 163
"St. Elsewhere," 283
Saint Laurent, Yves, 195
St. Marks Hotel, 248
St. Monica's Church, 255
St. James, Susan, 275
St. John, Jill, 110
Sale, Virginia, 285
"Salem's Lot," 127
Samson and Delilah, 79
Sand and Sea Club, The, 258
Sand Pebbles, The, 264
San Fernando Mission, 287–89, *288*
San Fernando Valley, 269–91
San Simeon, 143
Santa Anita Race Track, 305–6, *306*
Santa Fe Trail, The, 287
Santa Monica, 245, 250–55
Santa Monica Boulevard
  6000 (Hollywood Memorial Park Cemetery), 65, 74–76, *75*
  6725 (California State Bureau of Employment Security), 71
  7156 (Formosa Cafe), 68
  11272 (Nuart Theater), 223
Santa Monica Civic Auditorium, *250, 251*
Santa Monica Pier, 251–52
Save the Tiger, 144

Sayonara, 24
Scarface, 69, 176
Scharfe, Elizabeth, 47
Scharfe, Walter, 47
Schary, Dore, 215
Schary, Jill, 215
Schenck, Joseph, 10, 31, 101, 110, 154,
    165, 192, 225, 256
Schildkraut, Joseph, 32
Schlesinger, John, 35
Schockley, William, 38
Schoelkoff, Caroline Hunt, 214
Schools
    Beverly Hills High School, 195–96
    Hollywood High School, 37–38
    Janes House, 19
    John Marshall, 121–22, *122*
    Venice High School, 246–47, *246*
    Westlake School for Girls, 215
Schulberg, Budd, 174
Schwab's, 169–71, *169*
Schwarzenegger, Arnold, 250
Scott, Gordon, 305
Scott, Martha, 25
Scott, Randolph, 256
Scott, Ridley, 152–53
Screen Gems, 281
Screenwriters, 57
"Scroll of Fame," 14
"Scruples," 147, 150, 153
Sebring, Jay, 208
Security Pacific Bank Building, 13, *13*
See-Threepio, 6
Selig, William, 131, 198
Selig Company, 124
Selig Polyscope Company, 131, 245
Selznick, David O., 25, 162, 222, 233,
    299, 306
Selznick, Myron, 305
Selznick International Studios, 233, *233*
Sennett, Mack, 56, 119–20, 124, 180,
    198, 245, 248, 269, 282–83
72 Market Street, 250
"77 Sunset Strip" (restaurant), 163
"77 Sunset Strip" (television series),
    163
Seven Year Itch, 2, 9, 14
Shampoo, 188
Sharif, Omar, 252
Shearer, Norma, 256, 285
Sheik, The, 98
Shelby, Charlotte, 102, 103
Shelley, Mary, 116
Sheridan, Ann, 277
Sherman, Harry (Pop), 81
Sherwood, Ben, 122
Sherwood, Lois, 122
Shields, Brooke, 37
Shields, Frank, *87*
Shore, Dinah, 87
Showboat, 238
Shrine Auditorium, *154,* 155

Siebert, Father John, 255
Siegal, Bugsey, 165
Sigma Nu, 217–19, *218*
Sign of the Cross, The, 79
Silent Man, The, 140
"Silly Symphonies" cartoons, 72
Silverlake, 109
Simmons, Jean, 105
Sinatra, Frank, 29, 36, 50, 198, 215,
    226, 250
"Six Million Dollar Man, The," 296
Skatetown, U.S.A., 50
Skelton, Red, 66
Skolsky, Sidney, 170
Skouras, Spyros, 172
Smeraldi, Giovanni, 146
Smith, Al, 100
Smith, Albert E., 120, 121
Smith, Alexis, 38, 176, 277
Smith, Stan, 87
Snively, Emmaline, 99
Snow White and the Seven Dwarfs,
    122, 123, 279
Somborn, Herbert K., 47, 100
"Sonny and Cher," 90
Sothern, Ann, 172
South Broadway
    304 (Bradbury Building), 141–42,
        142
    307 (Million Dollar Theater), 133,
        140–41, *141*
    518 (Roxie Theater), 139
    528 (Cameo Theater), 139
    534 (Arcade Theater), 138
    615 (Los Angeles Theater), *132,* 135,
        137–38, *139*
    630 (Palace Theater), 137
    648 (Clifton's Cafeteria), 136, *137*
    744 (Globe Theater), 136
    802 (Tower Theater), 135–36, *136*
    842 (Orpheum Theater), 135
    933 (United Artists Theater), 133–34,
        134
    1111 (Herald Examiner Building),
        143, *143*
    theater district, 132–33
Southern Pacific Railroad Station, 297–
    98
SPCA Pet Memorial Park, 285–86
Spelling, Aaron, 67
Spiegelgass, Leonard, 88
Spielberg, Steven, 235, 262
Spinal Tap, 150
Splash, 147
"Spirit of Transportation," 103
"Splendor in the Grass," 127
Spreckles, Kay Williams, 284
Squaw Man, The, 4, 5, 29, 49, 78
Stahl, John, 275
Stallone, Frank, 272
Stallone, Sylvester, 260, 272
Stanwyck, Barbara, 55, *290,* 297, 305

Star Is Born, A, 29, 92, 92, 98–99, 147, 155, 162, 173, 178, 188, 191, 233, 278, 295, 306
Star Wars, 6
Steele, Alfred, 221
Stein, Jules, 191
Stengel, Casey, 300
Sterling, Tish, 196
Stern, Jacob, 29
Stevens, Connie, 110
Stevens, Craig, 176
Stevenson, Christine Witherill, 29
Stewart, Anita, 21, 121
Stewart, Jimmy, 194, 195, 198, 205
Stiller, Mauritz, 254
Sting, The, 250, 251, 252, 275
Stoker, Bram, 116
Stompanato, Johnny, 204
Stravinsky, Igor, 259
"Streetcar Named Desire, A," 153
Streisand, Barbra, 120, 199, 251–52, 262, 263
Stripes, 105
Struthers, Sally, 74
Studio City, 124, 269
Studio One, 177
Studios
  Burbank, 276–78, 277
  CBS-MTM Studio Center, 282–83
  Chaplin, 65–66, 66
  Walt Disney Productions, 279–80, 280
  Hal Roach, site of, 232
  Hollywood Center, 69–71, 70
  Jay Ward Productions, 168
  KCET, 118–19
  Laird International, 233–35, 234
  NBC Television, 278–79
  Paramount, 65, 76, 77–79, 78, 85, 87–88
  Pickford-Fairbanks, 64, 67, 68
  Raleigh, 81
  Republic, 282, 283
  RKO Studios, 76–77, 77, 234
  TBS-Columbia Ranch, 280–81
  Twentieth Century-Fox, 224–26, 224, 225
  Universal, 273–76, 273, 274, 276
  Vitagraph, 252, 252
  Warner (Burbank), 276–78, 279
  Warner (Hollywood), 67–68
Sturges, Preston, 79, 165, 166
Subway Terminal Building, 150
Sullivan, Louis, 149
Summer, Donna, 105
Summers, Gene, 147
Sunset Boulevard, 33, 34, 78, 78, 170
  mansion used in, 94–95, 95
Sunset Boulevard (Sunset Strip), 43, 159, 160, 160
  4401 (KCET Studios), 118
  5858 (KTLA), 54–55, 54

6121 (KNX Columbia Square), 51–53, 51
6215 (Hollywood Palladium), 50
6230 (Aquarius Theater), 50–51
6290 (Los Angeles Federal Savings and Loan Building), 49
6360 (Cinerama Dome Theater), 39, 39
6525 (Berwing Entertainment Complex), 38–39, 38
7014 (Collectors Bookstore), 37
8024 (Schwab's site), 169–70, 169
8150 (Garden of Allah site), 168–69, 168
8218 (Jay Ward Productions), 168
8221 (Chateau Marmont), 166–68, 167
8225 (Imperial Garden Sukyaki), 166
8358 (Sunset Tower), 165–66
8426 (Butterfield's), 164
8433 (The Comedy Store), 163–64
8524 ("77 Sunset Strip"), 163
8610 (Trocadero steps), 162
8720 (Le Dome), 161
9009 (The Roxy), 161
9015 (The Rainbow), 160
9461 (Beverly Hills Hotel), 186–88, 186, 187
14253 (Will Rogers State Park), 259–60, 259
  at Cañon Drive (Will Rogers Memorial Park), 188
  Gower Gulch, 52, 52
Sunset-Gower Studios, 53–54
Sunset Park, 188
Sunset Tower building, 165–66, 165
"Superman," 66, 151
Svenson, Bo, 250
Swanson, Gloria, 10, 17, 33, 34, 36, 58, 77, 80, 100, 124, 234, 244
Sylmar, San, 289–90

Tallchief, Maria, 196
Talmadge, Constance, 10, 76
Talmadge, Norma, 5–6, 10, 31, 76, 101–2, 154, 177–78, 256
Talmadge, The, 101–2, 102
Taper, Mark, Forum Theater, 124
Tarzan films, 305
Tarzan of the Apes, 76
Tate, Sharon, 74, 91, 100, 239
  house of, 208
"Taxi," 77
Taylor, Elizabeth, 9, 190–91, 193–95, 194, 198–99, 286
  house of, 202
Taylor, Robert, 26, 290, 305
Taylor, William Desmond, 102–3
TBS-Columbia Ranch, 280–81
Tech-Art Studios, 81
Technicolor, Inc., 72–73, 72

Television studios. *See* Studios
Temple, Shirley, 215
  back-lot cottage of, 225, *225*
  house of, 222, *222*
Ten Commandments, The, 9, 17
Terminal Man, 115
"Testimony of Two Men, A," 153, 301
Thalberg, Irving, 237, 256, 274, 299
Thalberg, Irving, Building, 105, 238
That Hamilton Woman, 70
That Touch of Mink, 255
Theater district, 132–33
Theater Jewelry Center, 144–45
Theaters, 132–41. *See also* Movie
  houses
  Aquarius Theater, 50–51
  Arcade, 138
  Cinerama Dome Theater, 39, *39*
  Globe, 136
  Huntington Hartford Theater, 49
  Los Angeles, *132,* 135, 137–38, *139*
  Los Felix, 116–17
  Orpheum, 135
  Palace, 43–44, 137
  Pantages Theater, 43, 45–46, *46*
  Pasadena Playhouse, 302–3
  Roxie, 139
  Tower, 135–36, *135*
  United Artists, 133–34, *134*
  Vagabond, 105
  Vista, 118
  Wiltern, 96–97, *97*
They Shoot Horses, Don't They?, 251
"This Is Your Life," 11, 44
Thomas, Danny, 33
Thomas, Marlo, 196
"Thorn Birds, The," 126
Three Musketeers, The, 81
"Thriller," 127, 137
Thunder Below, 287
Time After Time, 9
Toberman, C. R., 5
Todd, Mike, 202
Todd, Thelma, Sidewalk Cafe site, 260–
  61, *260*
To Have and Have Not, 215
Tomlin, Lily, 109, 113
"Tonight Show, The," 278, 279
Tony Duquette Studio, 177–78
Top Hat, 234
Top Hat Malt Shop, 38
Topper, 103, 300
"Topside," 33
Tora! Tora! Tora!, 264
Tosh, Peter, 38
To Kill a Mockingbird, 275
Touch of Evil, 249, *249*
Tours
  of Broadway, 133
  of Burbank Studios, 269–70, 276,
    277, 278
  of Carroll Avenue, 127

  of Culver City, 232
  of Ennis-Brown house, 115
  of Fenyes Mansion, 301
  of William S. Hart Park, 291
  of KCET, 109, 119
  of Merle Norman Tower of Beauty,
    290
  of movie-star residences, 201
  of NBC Television studios (Burbank),
    279
  of Whitley Heights, 33–34
  of Paramount Ranch, 287
  of Tony Duquette Studio, 178
  of Universal Studios, 270, 273–74,
    273
Towering Inferno, The, 264
Tower Theater, 135–36, *135*
Towne, Robert, 219, 270
Tracy, Spencer, 195, 259, 272, 305
Trapped in the Snow Country, 121
Travolta, John, 263
Treacher, Arthur, 172
Triangle Pictures, 238
Triangle Scene Shop, 119–20, *119*
Trigger, 6
Trocadero Cafe, *158,* 162, *162*
Trousdale Estates, 189
True Confessions, 152, 300
Truffaut, François, 18–19
Tryon, Tom, 61
Tuchman, Mitch, 88
Turf Club, 305, 306
Turner, Florence, 120
Turner, Lana, 38, 170, 204–5, 287
Turning Point, The, 155, 224
Turpin, Ben, 124
Twentieth Century Films, 110
Twentieth Century-Fox, 80, 110, 224,
  263–65
Twentieth Century-Fox Studios, 213,
  224–26, *224, 225*
"$25,000 Pyramid, The," 90
Two Men of the Desert, 288
Typhoon, The, 234

UA Hollywood Egyptian Theater, 13,
  16–17, *16*
UCLA (University of California at Los
  Angeles), 217–19
Under the Crescent, 296
Under the Yum Yum Tree, 171
Union Station, 151–53, *152*
Union Station, 152
United Artists, 28, 68, 133–34, 238
United Artists Theater, 133–34, *134*
United Productions of America, 280
Universal, 3, 90
Universal City, 269
Universal-International, 275
Universal Studios, 269–70, 273–76,
  273, 274, 276

Universal Tour, 270
University of California at Los Angeles (UCLA), 73

Vagabond Theatre, 105
Valentino, Rudolph, 12, 27, 15, 39, 49, 67, 71, *71*, 78, 79, 139–40, 190, 191, 197, 248, 285, 289, *289*
grave of, 75
house of (Falcon Lair), 208–9, *209*
Whitley Heights house of, 31, *34*
Valentino Stables, 208
Vallee, Rudy, 36, 87, 181, *181*
Valley of the Dolls, 188
Vampire Bat, The, 76
Van Pallandt, Nina, 28
Van Patten, Joyce, 175
Van Patten, Vincent, 87
Velez, Lupe, 85–86, 163, 204
Venice, 245–50
arcades of, *247,* 248
Venice High School, 246–47, *246*
Vertigo, 9
Vidor, King, 146, 206
Viertel, Berthold, 258–59
Viertel, Salka, 258–59
Vignola, Robert, villa of, 32, *32*
Villa Andalusia, 174
Villa Capri, 26
Villa Carlotta, 59
Villa Celia, 176, *176*
Villa d'Este, 27, 171–72, *171*
Villa Nova restaurant, 160
Villa Primavera, 174
"Villa Valentino," 27
Villa Vallambrosa, 33, *33*
Vincent, Jan-Michael, 220
Vine Street. *See also* North Vine Street
Hollywood Boulevard and, *42,* 43, *44*
Vine Street Theater, 49
"Visions," 119
Vista Theater, 118
Vitagraph, 120–21, *120*
Vitagraph Studios, 21, 252, *252*
Viva Zapata, 264
Voltaire, 172, *172*
von Sternberg, Josef, 79, 175
von Sternberg, Riza, 175–76
von Stroheim, Erich, 78, 80–81, 274

"W. C. Fields and Me," 138
Wagner, Jane, 113
Waldorf Hotel, 248
Walk of Fame, 8–9, *8*
Wallace, Beryl, 51
Walsh, Raoul, 305
"Waltons, The," 278
Wanger, Walter, 187, 259, 272
Ward, Burt, 196
Warner, Harry M., 187, 257, 286, 305, 306
Warner, Jack, 146, 162, 259, 263, 286

Warner, W. B., 68
Warner Brothers, 12, 25, 50, 54, *54,* 67, 96, 110, 121, 145, 252, 269, 281
Warner Brothers Ranch, 286
Warner Brothers studios, 269–70
Burbank, 276–78, *279*
Hollywood, 67–68
Warner Brothers Theater, 20–21, *21*
War of the Colossal Beast, 113
War of the Worlds, The, 25, 116, 151
Washington, Boulevard, West
9336 (Laird International Studios), 233–35, *234*
9820 (Culver Theater), 236
10202 West (MGM Studios), 236–39, *239*
at National Boulevard (Hal Roach Studio site), 232
Wax Museum, Hollywood, 14–15
Wayne, John, 6, 39, 48, 165, 235, *268,* 283
Way We Were, The, 152, 188
Wedding March, 80–81
Wedgewood Place, 31
We Fall Down, 235
Weissmuller, Johnny, 38–39, 86, 163, 285, 305
Welch, Raquel, 44
Welk, Lawrence, 50, 253
Welles, Orson, 23, 249
West, Mae, 78, *84,* 86, 163, 195, 250, 285
Gold Coast house of, 257, *257*
home of, 87–88, *88*
West, Nathanael, 35, 115, 125
West, Roland, 261
Western Costume Company, 80–81
West Hollywood, 27, 159–81
Westin Bonaventure Hotel, 149–50, *149*
Westlake School for Girls, 215
West Los Angeles, 110
Weston, Eugene, Jr., 28
Weston, Jack, 174
Westside, the, 213–27
Westways, 73
Westwood, 213
Westwood Memorial Park, 216–17
Westwood Village, 213, 217
Whatever Happened to Baby Jane?, 19, 81, 92–93
Whatever Happened to Baby Jane? house, 92–93, *93*
What Every Woman Knows, 49
What Makes Sammy Run?, 174
What Price Hollywood?, 25, 234
When Worlds Collide, 113
Whistler, The, 76
White, Pearl, 110
White, Preston S., 95
Whiting, Richard, 12

Whitley, H. J., 31
Whitley Heights, 30–34, *31–34*
Whitley Heights Civic Association, 33–34
Whitley Heights Heritage Tours, 34
Whitney, Cornelius Vanderbilt ("Sonny"), 72–73
Whitney, Jock, 162
Whitney, John Hay, 72–73, 192, 233
Wilcox, Harvey, 3
Wilcox, Mrs. Harvey, 3
Wilde, Cornel, 30
Wilder, Billy, 34, 55, 79, 94, 167, 170, 192, 297
Wilerson, W. R., 162, 163
Willat, Irwin C., Productions, 190
Williams, Esther, 105
Williams, Paul R., 191
Williams, Robin, 163
Williams, Tennessee, 302
Willis and Ingles, 118
Will Rogers Memorial Park, 188
Will Rogers State Park, 259–60, *259*
Wilshire, H. Gaylord, 85
Wilshire and Berendo Company, 101
Wilshire Boulevard, 85
    101 (Miramar-Sheraton Hotel), 254–55, *254*
    2071 (Bryson Apartment Hotel), 104–5, *104*
    2509 (Vagabond Theatre), 105
    3050 (Wilshire Bullocks), 103–4, *104*
    3278 (Talmadge), 101–2, *102*
    3377 (Brown Derby), 100–1, *100*
    3400 (Ambassador Hotel), 97–100, *98, 99*
    3780 (Wiltern Theater), 96–97, *97*
    4121 (Los Altos Apartments), 95–96, *95*
    5905 (Los Angeles County Museum of Art), 92, *92*
    6067 (May Company Department Store), 91–92
    8949 (Academy of Motion Picture Arts and Sciences), 197–98, *197*

    9500 (Beverly Wilshire Hotel), 193–95, *194*
    at Ocean Avenue (Lawrence Welk Plaza), 253, *253*
Wilshire District, 82–105
Wiltern Theater, 96–97, *97*
"Winds of War, The," 147, 220
Windsor, Marie, 38
Windward Avenue, 248
Winebrenner, H. F., 246
Witch's House, 189–90, *189*
Wizard of Oz, 9
Wizard of Oz, The, 67, 235–37
Wolfe, Tom, 168
Wood, Natalie, 110, 252
    grave of, 217
Woollcott, Alexander, 169
Works Project Administration, 43–44
Wright, Frank Lloyd, 29, 60, 109, 115, 214
Wright, Teresa, 174
Wyler, William, 274
Wyman, George, 142
Wyman, Jane, 190, 220, 298
Wynter, Dana, 57, 60

Xanadu, 90

Y.W.C.A., 73–74
Yamashiro (formerly Bernheimer Residence), 23–25, *24*
Yates, Herbert J., 283
Young, Clara Kimball, 121
Young, Loretta, 176, 187
Young Doctors in Love, 105

"Zane Grey Theater," 287
Zanuck, Darryl F., 164, 187, 192, 225, 257, 259, 272
    grave of, 216–17
Ziffren, Paul, 263
Zoetrope Studios, 70
Zukor, Adolph, 78, 81
Zwebell, Arthur, 67, 174–75
Zwebell, Nina, 67, 174–75

PHOTO CREDITS

Page 2, courtesy of the Hollywood Museum; 4 and 5, Larry Ashmead collection; 7, Mark Wanamaker/Bison Archives; 8, Roy Barnitt; 10, Mark Wanamaker/Bison Archives; 12, 13, and 14, Richard Alleman; 15, Mark Wanamaker/Bison Archives; 16, J. Evan Miller; 17, Jim Heimann collection; 18 and 20, Mark Wanamaker/Bison Archives; 21, Larry Ashmead collection; 22, Johnson Research Associates collection; 23, Richard Alleman; 24, Larry Ashmead collection; 25 and 27, Richard Alleman; 28, L. A. Morse; 30, 31, and 32, Richard Alleman; 33 and 34, Whitley Heights Archives; 35 and 36, L. A. Morse; 38, Mark Wanamaker/Bison Archives; 39, Richard Alleman; 42 and 44, Mark Wanamaker/Bison Archives; 45, courtesy of Capitol Records; 46 and 47, Mark Wanamaker/Bison Archives; 48, L. A. Morse; 51, Richard Alleman; 52, Mark Wanamaker/Bison Archives; 54, Jim Heimann collection; 57 and 59, L. A. Morse; 61, Richard Alleman; 64, 66, and 67, Mark Wanamaker/Bison Archives; 69, L. A. Morse; 70, Mark Wanamaker/Bison Archives; 71, 72, 74, and 75, Richard Alleman; 77, Jim Heimann collection; 78, Mark Wanamaker/ Bison Archives; 84, Jerry Ohlinger collection; 86, L. A. Morse; 87, courtesy of Los Angeles Tennis Club; 88 and 89, L. A. Morse; 90, Richard Alleman; 92, courtesy of Los Angeles County Museum of Art; 93, L. A. Morse; 94, Larry Edmunds collection; 95, courtesy of Evelyn Letecia; 97, Bruce Boehner; 98, L. A. Morse; 99, Mark Wanamaker/Bison Archives; 100, L. A. Morse; 102, Richard Alleman; 104(a), courtesy of Bullocks Wilshire; 104(b), Richard Alleman; 108, Mark Wanamaker/Bison Archives; 111, Richard Alleman; 112, Mark Wanamaker/Bison Archives; 113, Richard Alleman; 114(a), Mark Wanamaker/Bison Archives; 114(b), Julius Schulman; 115, Collectors Book Store collection; 117 and 118, Mark Wanamaker/Bison Archives; 119, Richard Alleman; 120, Mark Wana-maker/Bison Archives; 122 and 123(a), Richard Alleman; 123(b), Mark Wanamaker/Bison Archives; 125 and 126, Richard Alleman; 127, Mark Wanamaker/Bison Archives; 130, Jerry Ohlinger collection; 132, Bruce Boehner; 134, 135, and 137, J. Evan Miller; 139, Terry Helgesen; 141, Mark Wanamaker/Bison Archives; 142, Julius Schulman; 143, Bruce Boehner; 144, L. A. Morse; 147, courtesy of The Biltmore; 148, Mark Wanamaker/Bison Archives; 149 and 150, Richard Alleman; 152(a), © copyright The Blade Runner Partnership (originally appeared in the *Blade Runner* souvenir magazine, Ira Friedman Productions Inc., New York); 152(b) and 154, Richard Alleman; 155, Collectors Book Store collection; 158, Mark Wanamaker/Bison Archives; 160, Richard Alleman; 161 and 162, Mark Wanamaker/Bison Archives; 164, John Vernon Russel; 165 and 167, Richard Alleman; 168, Jim Heimann collection; 169, Mark Wanamaker/Bison Archives; 170, Richard Alleman; 171, L. A. Morse; 172, 173, 175, and 176, Richard Alleman; 180, Mark Wanamaker/Bison Archives; 181, Johnson Research Associates collection; 184, Mark Wana-maker/Bison Archives; 186, Jim Heimann collection; 187, Collectors Book

Store collection; 189 and 190, Richard Alleman; 193, Mark Wanamaker/ Bison Archives; 194, 196, and 197, Beverly Hills Chamber of Commerce; 198, Richard Alleman; 201, Mark Wanamaker/Bison Archives; 202, Johnson Research Associates collection; 203, Larry Ashmead collection; 204, Jim Heimann collection; 205, Larry Ashmead collection; 207, Richard Alleman; 208, Mark Wanamaker/Bison Archives; 209, Larry Ashmead collection; 212, Jerry Ohlinger collection; 213, Tim Street-Porter; 214, Mark Decker; 216, 218, and 220, Richard Alleman; 221, Johnson Research Associates collection; 222, Jim Heimann collection; 223, courtesy of Century City Chamber of Commerce; 224, Richard Alleman; 225, Mark Wanamaker/Bison Archives; 230, Jerry Ohlinger collection; 231 and 232, Richard Alleman; 233, Mark Wanamaker/Bison Archives; 234 and 235, Richard Alleman; 237, courtesy of MGM/UA; 239, Mark Wanamaker/Bison Archives; 240 and 241, Richard Alleman; 244 and 245, Mark Wanamaker/Bison Archives; 246, 247, and 248, Richard Alleman; 249, Larry Edmunds collection; 250, Mark Wanamaker/ Bison Archives; 251, Collections Book Store collection; 252, Mark Wanamaker/Bison Archives; 253, Bruce Boehner; 254, Richard Alleman; 255, Jim Heimann collection; 256 and 257, Richard Alleman; 259, Larry Ashmead collection; 260, Mark Wanamaker/Bison Archives; 262, Jim Heimann collection; 264, Ed Wanner; 265, Richard Alleman; 268, Jerry Ohlinger collection; 270, Larry Ashmead collection; 271, 273, and 274, Mark Wanamaker/Bison Archives; 276, Mark Wanamaker/Bison Archives, Universal Studios; 277, courtesy of Burbank Studios; 279, Jim Heimann collection; 280, Mark Decker; 282, Mark Wanamaker/Bison Archives; 284, Larry Ashmead collection; 286, Jerry Ohlinger collection; 288, 289, and 290, Mark Wanamaker/Bison Archives; 294, Pasadena Historical Society; 296 and 297, Richard Alleman; 298 and 299, Mark Decker; 301, Pasadena Historical Society; 302(a), Richard Alleman; 302(b), Mark Wanamaker/Bison Archives; 304, Mark Decker; 305, courtesy of the Greater Los Angeles Convention and Visitors Bureau; 306, Gunnard Nelson collection.